❖ COOKING ❖
GREAT MEALS
EVERY DAY

·COOKING·
GREAT MEALS
EVERY DAY

*Techniques, Recipes
and Variations*

R I C H A R D   S A X

in collaboration with
DAVID RICKETTS

Random House 🏠 *New York*

*Portions of some of the recipes in this book have appeared, in somewhat different form, in various
publications:*
The recipe on page 84 (Rice Salad) is reprinted with permission from the December
1976 *House Beautiful*, Copyright, The Hearst Corporation. All rights reserved.
The recipe on page 90 (Zucchini Gratin) is reprinted with permission from the April
1981 issue of *Cuisine* Magazine.
The recipe on page 63 (Pasta with Uncooked Tomatoes) is loosely based on recipes
from *Pasta* (Lyceum Books) by Vincenzo Buonassisi. Printed with permission.
The recipe on page 154 (Navarin of Lobster in Pernod Cream Sauce) by André Soltner
is reprinted with permission from the January–February 1979 issue of *The Pleasures of
Cooking*, a publication of Cuisinart Cooking Club, Inc.
The recipes appearing on pages 6, 60, 63, 102, 112, 122, 124, 127, 131, 134, 135, 144,
146, 186 and 253 are reprinted with permission from the September 1978, April 1979,
July 1979, August 1979, September 1979, and September 1980 issues of *Food & Wine*
Magazine. © 1978, 1979, 1980 by The International Review of Food & Wine
Associates.
The recipes and notes on pages 175–179 are copyright by Barbara Tropp.
The quote from Prince Talleyrand on page 254 is reprinted with permission from
Coffee (Penguin Books, Ltd.), © 1977 by Claudia Roden.

Library of Congress Cataloging in Publication Data
Sax, Richard.
Cooking great meals every day.
Includes index.
1. Cookery.   I. Ricketts, David.   II. Title.
TX715.S275   641.5   82–40325
ISBN 0–394–51601–X   AACR2

THIS BOOK IS DEDICATED TO MY GRANDMOTHER.

—R.S.

PREFACE

T he foreword to a book need not agree with its introduction. If I were telling someone beforehand that the writer involved in introducing himself was an idealistic and passionate enthusiast, I might be thought prejudiced, but at least the reader would be warned of my warning. In the same way, my preface might disagree with the writer's book itself, as I happen to do, with complete admiration.

I disagree on two counts. One is that *Cooking Great Meals Every Day* is obviously prejudiced about the pure joys of cooking with both idealism and enthusiasm, and is too generous. It gives so many exciting and logical examples of how to make what Richard Sax wants us to that we risk surfeit in reading it, overwhelmed at times by its suggested possibilities. We need to lie back and digest what has been offered us, before we go forth and try to do likewise.

The other count against this book, which of course can be voiced in a preface but not in the sorcerer's introduction, is that I do not believe a normal human being can eat a "great" meal every day. I believe that everything we put down our gullets should be good, and made of honorable ingredients. It should, in other words, be worthy of its purpose, to nourish us as best possible. But a Great Meal is not an everyday thing. It happens unexpectedly, and the more we understand why it is great and not simply good, the better off we are for the rest of our conscious lives. But it simply cannot and dare not happen on schedule.

It should be like a game, one of the exercises people perform at interviews or in front of cameras or around a campfire, to remember the greatest meal of one's life, or the three or ten. It could be evocative, nostalgic, perhaps even profitable, if all the electronics were in sync, just as it could be plain fun, on a summer night . . .

Yes . . . the first Great Meal in my life! I was about eight, with my father and my little sister, driving in our Model T from the desert foothills of Southern California where a greatuncle had a fruit ranch named Valyermo. Irish Mary, called that to make things clearer between various other females there called Mary, baked a big peach pie for the trip down past Los Angeles to our little town of Whittier, and beside it in the wooden lug-box she put a pint Mason jar of thick cream, with three old chipped soup plates and three spoons and a knife, and we started off, one Sunday afternoon.

The long ride across the desert was not too hot for late August, and Father only had to change two tires before we got to Palmdale. Once down into the winding mountain roads, live-oaks cooled the air, and we stopped at a camp where there were some tables, and ate the whole peach pie, still warm from Irish Mary's oven and then the desert air. We poured cream from the jar onto the pieces Father cut for us, and thick sweet juices ran into delicious puddles. Then we put the empty things back in the box, to wash in Whittier where there was more water, and headed south. Father and I sang "Clementine" and "Sweet Violets" while the little sister slept. We were full of love and warmth and a Great Meal, and no human beings can ever hope for more. Even once is a miracle! And once can be enough, of course, but why?

In the case of this book, even if my own feeling that not all meals either can or should be memorable and world-shaking, there is ample proof that no meal ever need be anything but good . . . very good indeed. It is puzzling to me that otherwise sensitive people develop a real docility about the obvious necessity of eating, at least once a day, in order to stay alive. Often they lose their primal enjoyment of flavors and odors and textures to the point of complete unawareness. And if ever they question this progressive numbing-off, they shrug helplessly in the face of mediocrity everywhere. Bit by bit, hour by hour, they say, we are being forced to accept the not-so-good as the best, since there is little that is even good to compare it with. For instance, they say listlessly, tomatoes no longer taste or smell or even look like tomatoes. Deep-freezing and mass-production, they say in a familiar dirge, convenience foods and artificial picking/shipping/storing/ripening . . . waily-waily.

And what about housing, to provide for the second of our three basic needs? Where is the warmth and security and privacy that all creatures, even us humans, must have in order to live and die with decency? And as for love, or sex, or whatever it may be called, where is its once jubilant force in our lives, its purity and fulfillment? Ah, waily-o!

And that is why there are books like this one of Richard Sax's, to refute at least a few of the dulled resigned plaints of the citizenry. It is skillful, because he has gone to good teachers and learned well; it is calculated, because he knows instinctively as well as by training what helplessness reigns in our kitchens as well as in our hearts. It is, above all, filled with the kind of ardor that all good priests and healers must feel, to tell us how best to survive.

I honestly do not believe that Mr. Sax, in turn, believes that every meal we eat can be "great." I do know, though, that his methods for showing us how to make good things out of ingredients that we take for granted are fine indeed. They are subtle, plain, sometimes lengthy to follow, but oftener as easy as sticking a TV dinner in the oven and making some instant-brew to wash it down our desensitized and sluggish maws. He brings us, to make life better, his own fervent purity of taste, so that we cannot question his firm ignoring of synthetic kitchen-aids, nor his confident assumption that fresh honest decent food is available to all of us, if we will bother to find it.

Rarely does he mention anything that even a crossroads market cannot add to a neighbor's garden or barnyard produce, and to one's own awakening curiosity about making some dish long forgotten, or something undreamed of as yet. There may be one mention of caviar, one use of fresh salmon, in this teasing collection of recipes, but mostly it is about seasonal or all-year foods that are procurable at fair prices almost everywhere in our vast country. When there are no fresh herbs, he uses dried. When there is no good chicken stock to hand, he suggests a commendable tinned kind. And when there is no good meat, he goes without, in a nimble about-face that is skillful and entertaining, as well as fine to savor.

Like any good manual, *Cooking Great Meals* is simple, without long sections on canapés and pickling and so on. If I could make only one change, I would add another little companion to it, the kind that might be bound within or alongside, of all his "basics," his concise instructions about soups, the cooking of meats and fish and eggs . . . They were well worth the price of admission to any show on earth, and what better one than to eat with amusement and satisfaction?

I am preoccupied, as I think about this book and about living well, which I plan to continue to do with increased enjoyment, now that I have stated that not all meals either can or should be *great*. One of the recipes nags most forcefully at me, from all the other tantalizers: the *Ribollita*. When shall I try this cousin of Tuscany's bread soup? Who will be here when I serve it forth? What wine will I open for it? And would it be better to wait for a nippy day, perhaps in late October?

I pretend to think of other matters, other more immediate meals. But the recipe nags at me, and I find, almost without wanting to, that I have every ingredient needed for it this very minute, except for the little white beans that make it so creamy and rich. I can get them at the country store and cook them myself, instead of using them from a can as Richard Sax suggests. (His is a practical and good shortcut, but we are partly Italian in Sonoma Valley and can buy every size and color of dried beans from big gunny sacks . . .) So . . . why not tomorrow, or next week? Here are all the vegetables, the herbs, the good olive oil. I am hungry!

I'll need at least five guests, and we can sit in the cooling August twilight . . . perhaps the new people planting a vineyard on the next ranch, and the ex-belly-dancer studying to be a CPA and her cabinet-maker husband, and the Buddhist calligrapher? We'll try three wines, and end with a good gutty Barbera from down the road for the crusty casserole. Why wait until autumn? I must put *Cooking Great Meals Every Day* aside, and make some telephone calls . . .

Brillat-Savarin often said that with a good recipe, miracles might happen. Fresh peach pie in a dusty grove of live-oak trees . . . baked *ribollita* on a summer balcony . . . Suddenly a Great Meal again?

M.F.K. Fisher
Glen Ellen, California

July 30, 1982

T
hanks are in order to many people who helped with this book: to the chefs, who generously shared their recipes. To Susan and Robert Lescher, and Jason Epstein, for their confidence. To Gail Winston, who helped focus early hazy material. To Anne Freedgood, for guidance, and coming up with the right title at last. To Nancy Inglis, Diane Hodges, Margery Tippie, and Cord Hamilton, for help with the manuscript. And to Helen Witty and all the friends (M.V., R.B., P.S., J.K., J.L., C.S., T.Z., and T.R.) who gave advice and critical suggestions throughout.

CONTENTS

INTRODUCTION

I've never taken for granted my good fortune in earning my living at something I love as much as food. Recently, however, a friend presented an arresting challenge: is food really *serious?* Do I feel that I am contributing something worthwhile in a larger sense?

I didn't even have to think before answering. Without ever having articulated them before, I realized that the deeper reasons for my involvement with food had long been clear in my mind.

Today we live in the most "advanced" society ever known, yet millions of people need alcohol or Valium just to get by. Given the state of the world and a bewildering economy, I've found that cooking and eating well are prime ways of getting in touch with the wonderful adventure that life should be.

Good food is one of the most immediate forms of pleasure available to us. No less than sex or art, food offers total involvement in the realms of appetite, sensual pleasure, and the imagination. And eating well is one of the few pleasures that simultaneously provide stimulation and satisfaction.

The best part is that good food can easily be enjoyed every day. Rather than wait for a "blowout" dinner party every three weeks and then eat junk in between, you can concentrate on dishes that are healthy and delicious but require little time, effort, or expense.

Having worked in several locales and learned from many gifted cooks, I have gathered together here a personal, eclectic choice of recipes and techniques that I use all the time. Many, including some of my favorites, are prepared in minutes. Others, like the hearty soups, allow me to cook once, then reheat small amounts for several days. In any case, by encouraging you to understand cooking procedures, this book can help you express your own tastes in cooking rather than simply follow recipes blindly.

Some people consider fine food, theater, and music expendable—enjoyable but frivolous. But shouldn't life hold more than mere survival? What about quality? What about excitement? When I teach people to bring an adventurous spirit to their cooking, I know that I am bringing joy to their lives in a way that they can appreciate immediately and viscerally.

And for that, I have not a moment's regret.

—RICHARD SAX

New York City, March 1982

❖COOKING❖
GREAT MEALS
EVERY DAY

❖1❖

SOUPS

BROTHS: A BASIC REPERTOIRE

CHICKEN BROTH
MIXED MEAT AND POULTRY BROTH
MIXED VEGETABLE BROTH
FISH BROTH
A FEW SIMPLY GARNISHED SOUPS

SOUP-STEWS FOR A HEARTY MEAL

HOT AND SOUR SOUP WITH CABBAGE, PORK, AND MUSHROOMS
JEWISH SWEET AND SOUR CABBAGE SOUP
ALSATIAN CREAM OF CHICKEN SOUP WITH RIESLING
MUSHROOM BARLEY SOUP
CHRIS STYLER'S MINESTRONE
RIBOLLITA (TUSCAN VEGETABLE BREAD SOUP BAKED WITH CHEESE)
CHILI-BEAN SOUP WITH CHEDDAR CHEESE AND SOUR CREAM

HEARTY SOUPS MADE FROM LEFTOVERS

BASIC METHOD FOR SOUPS MADE FROM LEFTOVER MEATS
SCOTCH BROTH
HEARTY CORN CHOWDER
HEARTY BEEF SOUP WITH HUNGARIAN PAPRIKA AND SOUR CREAM
FLEMISH BEER SOUP

PURÉE SOUPS

BASIC PROCEDURE FOR VEGETABLE PURÉE SOUPS
CARROT SOUP WITH ORANGE
   CREAM OF FRESH ASPARAGUS SOUP
   CREAM OF FRESH PEA SOUP
   CREAM OF BROCCOLI SOUP
CELERY ROOT, ONION, AND POTATO SOUP
   CREAM OF JERUSALEM ARTICHOKE SOUP
PUMPKIN SOUP WITH APPLES

FRUIT SOUPS

CREAM OF CANTALOUPE SOUP
CHILLED PLUM SOUP

A GAMUT OF FISH SOUPS

SCALLOPS *À LA NAGE*
MIXED SEAFOOD *À LA NAGE* WITH FENNEL AND HERBS
NEW ENGLAND CLAM CHOWDER
FISH CHOWDER WITH CREAM AND TOMATOES
BOULLINADA (CATALÁN FISH STEW WITH RED PEPPERS AND GARLIC)
FRESH SALMON SOUP WITH SPINACH NOODLES
HERBED SEAFOOD BISQUE

W hy are so many cooks discouraged from making soups at home?
For one thing, we're used to thinking that soups require long hours
of simmering—hours that many of us cannot afford. We are also put off
by recipes that blithely call for ten cups of veal stock, or suggest substituting oversalted or canned facsimiles.

A bowl of good homemade soup, however, does not require hours at
the stove, nor does it need to rely on inappropriate shortcuts. Throughout the world's cuisines, soups have always represented a form of al-
chemy: the almost magical transformation of a few inexpensive
ingredients, including leftovers, into a rich homemade meal. The thrifty
French housewife has been doing this for centuries, prompting the
gastronome Edouard Nignon to dub the humble potage "the way to
national glory."

Conceive of a hearty soup as a meal in itself, rather than a prelude.
Simply add bread, perhaps a salad or vegetable, and you've got a satisfying, no-nonsense meal. Many of the soups in this chapter can be prepared quickly; those that require a bit more time for simmering need not
be closely watched. In any event, your effort will be repaid over several
days: simply reheat small amounts as you need them, adding, if you like,
such extras as a sprinkling of fresh herbs, some chopped vegetables, or
leftover bits and pieces.

Thus, by cooking a good soup once, you can eat well again and again
—without ever resorting to opening a can on a tired evening.

Making any soup is *a building process* involving a few fundamental
components. Familiarize yourself with the techniques in this section,
and you'll be improvising on your own in no time, using scraps in the
fridge for delicious meals.

1. *Aromatics* are a variety of vegetables and seasonings providing the
   flavor foundation for the soup. Some, such as onions, carrots, and
   celery, are cooked in fat at the beginning of the process. A bouquet garni, a basic herb bundle, lends flavor throughout the
   cooking time, and is then discarded at the end. Other aromatics,
   such as mushrooms and freshly ground pepper, are added later
   to preserve their fresh flavor and texture.
2. *Liquid* is added to the aromatics to carry and unite all the soup's
   elements.

3. *Main ingredients* define the soup's character—anything from a vegetable, meat, poultry, or herbs to in some cases the broth itself.

Once all the elements are present, different cooking treatments will result in a variety of soups: broths; long- and short-simmered soups; purées, smooth or coarse; soup-stews thickened with purées of half the ingredients; and so on.

BROTHS: A BASIC REPERTOIRE

While the home cook often has neither the time to prepare a variety of classic stocks nor the space to store them, a basic homemade broth (for which there is no real substitute, though some canned broths will do in a pinch) is less trouble than you think. And a good broth can itself serve as a soup, garnished as outlined on page 12. Making such a broth can be a simple matter if you collect bones and trimmings in the freezer and simmer a large potful every few weeks.

Freeze the broths in small, tightly sealed containers, labeled with the name of the broth and the date. Or freeze in ice cube trays, later gathering the cubes into plastic bags and storing in the freezer. Use them in small amounts to lend flavor to sautés and stews, or as the base for a wide variety of fresh seasonal soups.

CHICKEN BROTH

If you use the optional whole chicken in this recipe, you'll have the added bonus of moist, tender chicken to be served hot or cold. See Chicken Curry (page 199) and Chicken Pot Pie (page 204) for other uses. Kept refrigerated, this broth will last nearly two weeks if brought to the boil and then cooled every three days. Use within three or four months if frozen; boil before using.

Makes about 3 quarts reduced broth

5 pounds chicken parts: backs,
  necks, carcasses, feet (skin
  removed), and giblets (no livers)
Cold water as needed
1 stewing chicken, trussed
  (optional)
2 large onions, coarsely chopped
2 ribs celery, with leaves, cut up
3 carrots, trimmed, peeled, coarsely
  chopped

2 cloves garlic, halved or sliced
1 small bunch parsley stems
Large pinch dried thyme
1 bay leaf
1 teaspoon salt
5 whole peppercorns, white or
  black

1. Place chicken parts in large stockpot; cover with cold water. Bring to boil. Immediately drain in large colander; rinse well in cold water; drain. Rinse pot. (This process removes excess scum-foaming albumen from the chicken, resulting in a clearer stock.)

2. Return chicken to pot. Add optional trussed whole chicken, onion, celery, carrot, and garlic. Cover with cold water by at least 2 inches. Cover pot; bring to boil. Lower heat; skim. Add parsley, thyme, bay leaf, and salt. Simmer, uncovered.

3. When thigh meat of trussed chicken is tender, after about 1 hour, remove; reserve for other uses.

4. Continue to simmer 4 to 6 hours, skimming occasionally. Add hot water as needed if liquid level drops below solids. Add peppercorns for the last 15 minutes.

5. When flavor is fully developed, remove and discard chicken parts. Strain broth into large bowl through colander lined with three layers of dampened cheesecloth. Gently press down on solids to extract liquids; discard solids. Return broth to rinsed pot. Reduce by one-third to one-half over high heat or until flavor is very concentrated. Skim.

6. Cool broth in bowl to room temperature on wire rack. If you have time, refrigerate stock overnight. Remove fat from surface with spoon. Pour broth into appropriate storage containers, label, and date; refrigerate. Or freeze defatted broth in ice cube trays; unmold and store in plastic bags in freezer.

MIXED MEAT AND POULTRY BROTH

Using the above method, you can combine meat and poultry ingredients for a rich, golden, gelatinous broth that can be used in nearly any soup, or in fact as a soup itself, and in any meat or poultry dish calling for stock.

Makes about 2½ quarts

3 pounds beef and veal bones, cracked into 2-inch pieces

1½ to 2 pounds chicken backs, necks, carcasses, and giblets (no livers)

1 meaty veal knuckle

2 medium onions, with skins, quartered

2 carrots, trimmed, peeled, cut into chunks

2 Tablespoons vegetable oil

1 small rib celery

4 parsley sprigs

1 bay leaf

½ teaspoon dried thyme

1 leek, trimmed, halved, rinsed

2 cloves

1 piece pork rind (about 5-inch square), rolled scroll-fashion, tied, blanched for 5 minutes, drained

1 pound lean beef (such as shin), cut into 1-inch cubes

Cold water as needed

1 whole head garlic, outer papery skin removed

1 ripe tomato, cored, cut into chunks

½ cup chopped mushroom stems (optional)

1 teaspoon salt

6 black peppercorns

1. Preheat oven to 450°.

2. Place beef and veal bones, chicken parts except giblets, veal knuckle, onion, reserving 1 onion quarter, and carrot in large roasting pan. Drizzle vegetable oil over all; mix together. Roast, uncovered, stirring occasionally, until bones and vegetables are dark brown, about 45 minutes.

3. Meanwhile, tie celery rib, parsley sprigs, bay leaf, and thyme between leek halves; reserve bouquet garni.

4. Stick 2 cloves in the reserved onion quarter. Add the contents of the roasting pan, the chicken giblets, the pork rind, and lean beef to the stockpot. Cover with cold water by 2 inches, about 3½ quarts or more if needed. Pour off fat from roasting pan. Deglaze pan with water; add

to stockpot. Bring to simmer over medium-low heat; this should take 30 minutes or longer. When liquid reaches simmer, skim and discard collected foam from surface. Add 1 cup cold water. Allow foam to collect again; skim. Add reserved bouquet garni, garlic, tomato, mushroom stems, and salt.

5. Simmer broth, partially covered, until rich stock develops, 6 to 8 hours or longer. Adjust heat as necessary to maintain steady simmer. Skim as necessary. Add peppercorns during the last 15 minutes of simmering.

6. Strain broth into large bowl through colander lined with three layers of dampened cheesecloth. Gently press down on solids to extract liquids; discard solids. Cool stock to room temperature on wire rack. Refrigerate, covered, overnight.

7. Remove solidified fat from surface of broth with large spoon. Remove last traces of fat with paper towels squeezed out in hot water. Refrigerate broth, tightly covered, up to 3 days, or up to 2 weeks if boiled every 2 or 3 days. Or freeze broth in ice cube trays; store cubes in freezer bags, up to 2 months. Reheat to boiling before using.

MIXED VEGETABLE BROTH

Recipes for a good, flavorful, meatless broth are difficult to come by, although nearly every old French cookbook details a *bouillon maigre* for fast days.

Cooking Tip: Save vegetable cooking liquids to replace part or all of the water called for below.

Makes about 1½ quarts

2 Tablespoons unsalted butter
1 Tablespoon olive oil
3 medium onions, sliced
2 large leeks, white part only,
cleaned, sliced
2 or 3 thin carrots, trimmed,
peeled, sliced
2 or 3 ribs celery, with leaves,
trimmed, sliced
1 teaspoon salt
Piece fresh ginger, size of quarter,
peeled
1 small turnip, peeled, diced
1 medium-large boiling potato,
peeled, diced

1 whole head garlic, outer papery
skin removed
3 to 4 ounces mushrooms, chopped
coarsely
2 tomato skins
2 sprigs fresh thyme, or ½
teaspoon dried
6 parsley stems
1 bay leaf
1 whole clove
Cold water as needed
1 to 1 ½ cups shredded lettuce
4 peppercorns, white or black

1. Heat butter and oil in large saucepan. When foam subsides, add onion, leek, carrot, celery, salt, and ginger; toss to coat with oil. Cook, covered, over medium-low heat, tossing occasionally, until vegetables are slightly wilted and begin to exude their juices, 7 to 8 minutes.

2. Uncover pan; raise heat slightly. Sauté vegetables, tossing often to prevent sticking, until edges of vegetables begin to caramelize slightly, about 10 minutes. (This lends flavor to the broth.)

3. Add turnip, potato, garlic, mushrooms, tomato skins, thyme, parsley stems, bay leaf, clove, and enough cold water to cover all ingredients generously. Bring to boil; skim. Simmer, partially covered, 30 minutes.

4. Add shredded lettuce. Simmer, partially covered, until everything is tender, about 45 minutes longer. If necessary, add water to keep vegetables covered.

5. Strain broth through sieve lined with a double thickness of dampened cheesecloth, gently pressing down on solids with the back of a wooden spoon to extract all the juices. Discard solids. Chill; remove fat.

FISH BROTH

Fish broth is the easiest of all broths to prepare, since the essences are drawn from the bones in less than half an hour. Ask your fish merchant to save you the frames, head, and tail whenever you buy fish.
Makes 1½ to 2 quarts

2 Tablespoons unsalted butter

3 medium onions, halved, sliced

1 teaspoon salt

1 or 2 ribs celery, trimmed, sliced

1 carrot, trimmed, sliced

½ cup chopped mushroom stems (optional)

5 parsley stems

3 to 3 ½ pounds fish frames, heads, tails from non-oily fish

such as cod, flounder, halibut, or bass, rinsed in cold water, cut to fit pot

1 to 2 sprigs fresh thyme, or ¼ teaspoon dried

1 small bay leaf

1 bottle dry white wine (about 3 ¼ cups)

Cold water as needed

3 or 4 white peppercorns

1. Heat butter in large noncorrosive pot. When foam subsides, add onion and salt. Toss to coat. Cook, covered, over medium heat, stirring occasionally, until wilted, 5 to 10 minutes.
2. Add celery, carrot, and mushroom stems. Toss to coat. Sweat, covered, 3 to 4 minutes more. Add parsley stems, fish frames, heads and tails. Toss to coat; cook, uncovered, 2 to 3 minutes.
3. Add thyme and bay leaf; pack ingredients compactly in pot. Add wine and enough water to cover all ingredients. Cover, bring to boil. Skim foam. Lower heat; simmer, partially covered, 25 to 30 minutes. Add peppercorns for last 5 minutes.
4. Strain broth through colander lined with double thickness of dampened cheesecloth. Press down on ingredients to extract all liquid, but don't push solids through; discard solids. Add salt if needed. For stronger flavored stock, omit salt, return broth to rinsed pot; reduce by about one-third. Correct seasoning.

❖ A Few Simply Garnished Soups ❖

Any broth—poultry, meat, vegetable, or fish—quickly sprinkled with one of the following garnishes can serve as a fine soup on its own. Or use garnishes to bring new life to any of the soups in this chapter, as the leftovers appear for the second or third time.

Fresh Herbs: Sprinkle chopped parsley, chives, dill, tarragon, thyme, basil, or mint, or a mixture, over each cup of soup.

Homemade Croutons (page 139): Sprinkle over soup to add textural contrast.

Watercress-Lemon: Blanch coarsely chopped watercress leaves in boiling salted water; drain. Add with a thin slice of lemon to each cup of broth.

Sliced Fresh Mushrooms: Simmer for a minute or two in the broth itself.

Fresh, Dried, or Frozen Pasta, or Rice: Simmer small or broken-up noodles, macaroni, tortellini, pastina, or rice in the finished broth until tender.

Mixed Vegetables: A julienne or dice of carrot, turnip, leek, mushroom, pepper, celery, or whole peas, simmered in the soup, adds a crunchy, flavorful touch. Combine two or three of these as you wish.

Gremolata (page 174): Sprinkle mixture of finely grated citrus rind and minced parsley and garlic on the soup just before serving to add a sharp, clean note.

SOUP-STEWS FOR A HEARTY MEAL

HOT AND SOUR SOUP WITH CABBAGE, PORK, AND MUSHROOMS

Cabbage is a mainstay ingredient of soups throughout the world. This soup is inspired by Irene Kuo, whose authoritative book, *The Key to Chinese Cooking* (Knopf), is heartily recommended. Be sure to make the soup both hot and sour.

Cooking Tip: Prepare all the ingredients before starting to cook, as total cooking time is a matter of moments once you begin. To shred pork and bamboo shoots, first cut them into ¼-inch-thick slices, then crosswise

into ¼-inch-thick shreds, about 1½ inches long. To make the meat easier to shred, place in freezer about 30 minutes, until firm but not frozen. Some shredded bean curd added with the soy sauces will lend additional texture. If you are feeling industrious or can buy good ones, serve Chinese steamed buns to accompany this soup. For the less industrious, bread or sesame bread sticks are just fine.
Serves 4

3 Tablespoons vegetable oil

4 to 6 ounces lean pork (butt or loin), shredded into ¼-inch pieces

4 ounces mushrooms (about 10 medium), thickly sliced

½ pound Chinese cabbage or romaine lettuce, trimmed, shredded into ½-inch pieces

¼ cup shredded bamboo shoots (¼-inch pieces)

1 Tablespoon light soy sauce plus 1 Tablespoon dark soy sauce, or

2 Tablespoons all-purpose soy sauce such as Kikkoman

4½ cups cold water

2 teaspoons rice wine vinegar, or more to taste

½ teaspoon freshly ground black pepper

¼ teaspoon red pepper flakes

2 Tablespoons cornstarch, dissolved in 3 Tablespoons water

1 teaspoon oriental sesame oil

Chopped scallions

1. Heat oil over medium heat in wok or large soup pot. Add pork; stir-fry until meat is no longer pink, about 45 seconds.
2. Add mushrooms, cabbage, and bamboo shoots; stir-fry until cabbage begins to wilt, about 30 seconds.
3. Add light and dark soy sauces; toss to combine. Add water. Bring to boil, reduce heat; simmer, covered, until cabbage is crisp-tender, about 5 minutes.
4. Add rice wine vinegar, black pepper, and red pepper flakes. Taste; add more soy sauce, pepper, or vinegar, as you like. Mix the cornstarch mixture with the sesame oil; add to the soup. Continue to stir until the soup thickens slightly and is smooth. Serve in warm soup bowls. Garnish with the chopped scallions.

JEWISH SWEET AND SOUR CABBAGE SOUP

This is an adaptation of an old family recipe for stuffed cabbage, but without the laborious job of stuffing the leaves. In an evocative little volume entitled *Cuisine Juive, Ghettos Modernes* (*Jewish Cooking in Modern Ghettos*), 1929, Edouard de Pomiane notes that one of the characteristics of the Jewish cuisine that transcends national boundaries is the use of sugar in otherwise savory dishes. This soup, which illustrates Pomiane's observation, can best achieve a good balance between sweet and sour if made the day before; and don't be afraid to underscore the balance with additional lemon juice, if necessary.
Serves 4 to 6

3 Tablespoons vegetable oil
2 medium onions, halved
   lengthwise, sliced crosswise
1 medium head cabbage, outer
   leaves removed
½ cup golden raisins
⅓ cup freshly squeezed lemon juice
   (2 small lemons), or more as
   needed
2 Tablespoons brown sugar
1 Tablespoon honey
1 ½ teaspoons minced garlic
2 teaspoons salt

1 teaspoon Hungarian paprika
1 can (2 pounds, 3 ounces)
   imported whole plum tomatoes,
   with their liquid
3 or 4 leftover cooked beef bones,
   with some meat on the bones, or
   3 or 4 leftover cooked short ribs
3 ½ cups water, or more as needed
¼ cup gingersnap cookie crumbs (4
   or 5 cookies)
Freshly ground black pepper
Chopped fresh parsley (optional)

1. Heat oil to rippling in large pot over medium heat. Add onion; sauté, stirring often, until onion is soft, 10 to 15 minutes.
2. Meanwhile, quarter cabbage through core. Remove and discard core; slice quarters into ¼-inch-wide strips.
3. In small bowl, stir together raisins, lemon juice, brown sugar, and honey. Reserve.
4. Add cabbage, garlic, and salt to onion. Toss to coat cabbage with oil. Cover pot; steam cabbage over medium heat until slightly wilted, stirring occasionally, about 6 minutes. Add paprika and tomatoes with their liquid; toss to combine. Tuck in bones; add water to just cover ingredi-

ents. Stir in raisin/lemon juice mixture. Bring to boil. Skim and discard froth. Simmer, partially covered, stirring occasionally, until everything is tender, 1 to 1½ hours.

5. Remove bones and skim soup. Stir in cookie crumbs. Shred meat from bones and add to soup. Simmer another 5 to 10 minutes to blend flavors. Correct seasonings. Add pepper and an extra squeeze of lemon juice, if you wish; garnish with chopped parsley.

ALSATIAN CREAM OF CHICKEN SOUP WITH RIESLING

Eating our way through the superb cuisine of Alsace several years ago and sampling the traditional main dishes of chicken, pike, and frogs' legs, all lightly sauced with Riesling and fresh cream, David and I were inspired to concoct this rich but subtle soup. Alsatian wines, of which the Riesling used here is the most esteemed, are little explored by Americans, and are frequently a good value.

Cooking Tip: Be sure to sauté the chicken properly and to deglaze the pan thoroughly in order to maximize the warm poultry flavor.

Serves 4

1 ½ to 2 pounds chicken parts (whole breast with ribs, split in half, and 2 leg and thigh portions or any other meaty combination)

2 Tablespoons unsalted butter

1 Tablespoon vegetable oil

1 teaspoon salt

6 ounces medium mushrooms

4 or 5 shallots, chopped, or ¼ cup chopped onion

1 clove garlic, minced

1 ½ cups Alsatian Riesling, or other dry, full-bodied white wine

2 ½ cups Chicken Broth (page 6)

Pinch dried thyme

1 ¼ cups heavy cream

2 egg yolks

Pinch freshly grated nutmeg (optional)

Freshly ground white pepper

Chopped fresh parsley and/or snipped chives

1. Trim away excess fat from chicken parts. Pat pieces dry with paper towels.

2. Heat butter and oil together in large noncorrosive skillet over medium heat. Arrange chicken pieces in one layer in the skillet. If necessary, work in batches. Sauté until golden on one side, 6 to 8 minutes. Turn; add salt. Continue to sauté until golden, another 6 to 8 minutes.

3. Meanwhile, trim mushroom stems flush with caps. Chop stems coarsely; reserve caps.

4. Remove chicken from skillet, allowing excess fat to drip back into skillet. Arrange chicken pieces in bottom of large noncorrosive casserole. Pour off and discard all but 2 Tablespoons of fat from skillet. Sauté shallots in skillet over medium heat, stirring occasionally, until soft, about 2 minutes. Add garlic and chopped mushroom stems; sauté, stirring occasionally, about 2 minutes.

5. Add wine to skillet, scraping up browned bits from bottom and sides of skillet with wooden spoon. Boil, uncovered, for 5 minutes to concentrate flavor. Add broth; boil until liquid is full-flavored and pale gold, about 5 minutes. Pour liquid over chicken in casserole. Sprinkle with thyme. Simmer, partially covered, until chicken is tender, 30 to 35 minutes.

6. Thinly slice reserved mushroom caps. Skim fat from surface of broth. Remove chicken. Add mushroom slices and ¾ cup of the cream. Stir; boil gently for 4 to 5 minutes to mingle flavors. Remove from heat.

7. Meanwhile, carefully remove skin from flesh and flesh from bones. Discard skin, fat, and bones. Cut flesh into bite-size pieces; return pieces to soup.

8. In small bowl, gently beat egg yolks with remaining ½ cup cream. Add a few spoonfuls of the hot soup to yolk mixture; stir. Add a few more spoonfuls. Return soup to very low heat. Slowly stir yolk mixture into soup. Add pinch of nutmeg, if you wish. Correct seasonings; add salt if necessary and white pepper. Stir until soup is heated through and slightly thickened; do not allow to boil or the eggs will curdle. Serve in warm soup bowls. Garnish with chopped parsley and/or snipped chives.

MUSHROOM BARLEY SOUP

This recipe is adapted from one my mother has been preparing for years. Dried mushrooms are underused by most of us; a small amount provides lots of flavor and can be kept on hand indefinitely. While this soup simmers a bit longer than the others, it requires almost no supervision. *Cooking Tip:* Whenever you soak dried mushrooms, be sure to use the flavorful soaking liquid in your recipe. Just strain the liquid first, through a paper coffee filter or dampened paper towel. Because the barley absorbs liquid, this soup may be a lot thicker the second or third time you serve it; thin as needed with water or broth.
Serves 4 to 6

1 ounce dried mushrooms (porcini, cèpes, or other)*

Warm water

8 ounces fresh mushrooms

2 ½ to 3 pounds short ribs, or meaty soup bones, cut into 2-to-3-inch pieces

Salt

2 to 3 Tablespoons vegetable oil

2 medium onions, coarsely chopped

1 or 2 cloves garlic, chopped

3 carrots, trimmed, peeled, thickly sliced

2 ribs celery (leafy tops reserved), chopped

½ cup barley

⅓ cup dried lima beans

7 to 8 cups water, or more as needed

Parsley stems (optional), tied in a bundle

Freshly ground black pepper

Chopped fresh parsley

1. Soak dried mushrooms in warm water to cover until softened, about 20 minutes.
2. Trim fresh mushroom stems. Coarsely chop stems. Thickly slice caps; refrigerate, covered.
3. Trim any excess fat from meat. Pat meat dry with paper towels. Salt lightly. Heat oil in large pot over medium heat. Add the bones; sauté, turning frequently, until brown, 10 to 15 minutes.
4. Remove bones from pot to platter; reserve. Add onion, garlic, one-

*Mail-order source: H. Roth and Son, 1577 First Avenue, New York, N.Y. 10028 (212-734-1110).

third of the carrot slices, one-half of the chopped celery, and chopped mushroom stems to the pot. Sauté over medium heat, tossing frequently, until vegetables are softened and lightly golden, 6 to 8 minutes. 5. Meanwhile, drain dried mushrooms over small bowl, allowing liquid to go through sieve lined with paper coffee filter or dampened paper towel. Rinse mushrooms under cold running water to remove any grit; drain. Trim and discard tough stems; coarsely chop mushrooms. Reserve soaking liquid.

6. Return bones and any accumulated juices to pot. Add barley, lima beans, dried mushrooms, and reserved soaking liquid. Toss to combine, scraping up any browned bits from bottom and sides of pot with wooden spoon. Add 7 to 8 cups of water or enough to cover all the ingredients. Bring soup to boil; skim and discard froth. Reduce to simmer. Add salt to taste, reserved leafy celery tops, and optional parsley stems. Simmer, partially covered, until meat is almost tender, about 2 hours. Adjust heat to maintain simmer. Skim occasionally. Add cold water if necessary to keep ingredients covered.

7. Add remaining sliced carrot and chopped celery, and sliced fresh mushroom caps. Stir to combine. Add water if needed. Simmer, partially covered, until carrots are tender, about 35 to 45 minutes.

8. Remove bones from pot with slotted spoon. Remove meat from bones; cut meat into bite-size pieces. Return meat to soup. Remove and discard bundled parsley stems. Add pepper and salt if needed. Serve in warm soup bowls. Sprinkle with chopped parsley.

Note: If using short ribs, leave meat on some of the bones, and place one bone with meat in each soup bowl.

CHRIS STYLER'S MINESTRONE

Chris Styler, a talented young chef with whom I have worked happily for years, grew up cooking for his large Italian family. By the age of thirteen, he was already preparing the traditional Italian feast of thirteen fish dishes (among much else) for Christmas. You'll want to keep Chris's minestrone in your repertoire.

Serves 6 to 8

2 Tablespoons olive oil

2 Tablespoons unsalted butter

2 large onions, cut into ¼-inch slices

2 carrots, trimmed, peeled, cut into ¼-inch slices

2 ribs celery, cut into ¼-inch slices

2 ham hocks

1 cup shredded green cabbage

2 cloves garlic, crushed

Rind of Parmesan cheese (2 × 4 inches)

1 can (1 pound, 12 ounces) imported whole plum tomatoes, drained, liquid reserved, seeded

1 large zucchini, trimmed, cut into ¼-inch dice

1 large yellow squash, trimmed, cut into ¼-inch dice

5 cups Mixed Meat and Poultry Broth (page 8), or Chicken Broth (page 6), or more as needed

1 can (20 ounces) cannellini beans, drained

4 ounces green beans, cut into ½-inch lengths

1 medium mealy potato, peeled, cut into ½-inch dice

Chopped fresh basil, or pinch dried

Chopped fresh tarragon, or pinch dried

Chopped fresh oregano, or pinch dried

Salt

½ cup small pasta, such as ditalini, tubetti, pastina, etc.

Freshly ground black pepper

Freshly grated Parmesan cheese

1. Heat oil and butter in large soup pot. Add onion; toss to coat with fat. Sauté over medium heat, 2 minutes. Add carrot and celery; toss to coat. Sauté 2 minutes. Lower heat to very low. Add ham hocks. Cover pot; sweat vegetables, stirring occasionally, until softened, about 15 minutes.

2. Meanwhile, blanch cabbage in large saucepan of boiling water, 5 minutes. Drain.

3. Add cabbage, garlic, cheese rind, tomatoes and reserved liquid, zucchini, and yellow squash to pot. Add enough broth to cover ingredients. Simmer, partially covered, until the vegetables are just tender, about 1 hour.

4. Remove ham hock from soup with slotted spoon. Remove meat from hocks; cut into ¼-inch cubes. Return meat to pot with cannellini beans, green beans, potato, basil, tarragon, oregano, and salt. Simmer, uncovered, until potatoes are tender, about 20 minutes. Add water if necessary to keep ingredients just covered.

5. Meanwhile, cook pasta in large saucepan of boiling salted water until al dente. Drain; rinse under cold water.

6. Just before serving, stir pasta and pepper into soup. Gently simmer until heated through; remove rind. Pass grated Parmesan separately.

RIBOLLITA (TUSCAN VEGETABLE BREAD SOUP BAKED WITH CHEESE)

Native to the hills of Tuscany, this soup is a layered mixture of brightly colored vegetables, beans, and toasted bread topped with olive oil and freshly grated cheese, and all baked until golden and crusty. This is a reconstruction of the spectacular version served at the Cave di Maiano, a rustic country inn outside Florence.
Serves 8

9 Tablespoons olive oil, or more as needed

2 large onions, halved, thickly sliced crosswise

3 carrots, trimmed, peeled, thickly sliced

2 ribs celery, trimmed, thickly sliced

3 cloves garlic, minced

2 small zucchini, trimmed, sliced

1 red bell pepper or small fresh hot red pepper, cored, seeded, diced (optional)

4 or 5 dried rosemary spikes

1 ½ pounds fresh spinach, stemmed, washed

1 can (20 ounces) cannellini beans, drained, rinsed

6 fresh plum tomatoes, cut into long strips, or 1 can (17 ounces) imported whole plum tomatoes, drained, halved

2 teaspoons salt

12 thin slices Italian or French bread

2 ½ to 3 cups Chicken Broth (page 6), or Mixed Meat and Poultry Broth (page 8), or Mixed Vegetable Broth (page 9)

2 cloves garlic

⅓ cup freshly grated Parmesan cheese

Freshly ground black pepper

1. Heat 3 Tablespoons of the olive oil in large casserole over medium-high heat. Add onion; sauté until wilted, stirring often, 6 to 9 minutes. Add carrot, celery, and garlic; toss to coat with oil; sauté about 2 minutes. Add zucchini, red pepper, and rosemary; toss until zucchini wilts slightly, 4 to 5 minutes. Scrape mixture into bowl.
2. Place spinach with water clinging to its leaves in casserole. Steam, covered, over medium heat, until leaves are wilted, 4 to 5 minutes. Turn leaves over with wooden spoon after 3 minutes to ensure even steaming.

Remove spinach with slotted spoon, allowing spinach to drain briefly over casserole. Place spinach in colander or large sieve; pour spinach cooking liquid into bowl with vegetable mixture. Rinse spinach under cold running water. Squeeze spinach dry in small clumps. Chop spinach into coarse shreds; add to vegetable mixture. Add beans, tomato, and salt; toss lightly to combine. Correct seasonings if necessary; taste should be assertive. Reserve casserole.

3. Heat broiler.

4. Arrange bread slices in single layer on baking sheet. Toast bread until golden on both sides, turning once, about 1 minute per side.

5. Lower oven heat to 400°.

6. Arrange layer of vegetable mixture on bottom of casserole to cover. Arrange 6 of the toasted bread slices in one layer over the vegetables. Spread half the remaining vegetable mixture evenly over the toast. Add remaining toast in one layer. Top with remaining vegetable mixture, smoothing evenly.

7. Add enough stock to come almost to the top of the vegetables, but leaving the top dry.

8. Heat 4 Tablespoons of the olive oil in a small skillet over medium heat until fragrant. Add garlic cloves. Simmer until the garlic is golden, about 5 minutes. Remove and discard garlic. Drizzle some of the oil over the top of the casserole. Sprinkle top evenly with grated Parmesan. Drizzle remaining oil over all.

9. Bake casserole uncovered until top is golden, 30 to 45 minutes. Allow ribollita to stand 5 minutes before serving. Serve in large shallow soup bowls, sprinkling more olive oil and freshly ground black pepper over the top. Though not traditional, more grated cheese may be added to each serving if you wish.

CHILI-BEAN SOUP WITH CHEDDAR CHEESE AND SOUR CREAM

The garnishes of cheese and sour cream mellow this soup, but not to the point where you forget what you are eating. Serve this soup steaming hot on a cold night, with cornbread, biscuits (page 209) or crackers, a salad, and plenty of cold beer.

Serves 4 to 6

4 Tablespoons vegetable oil

1 ½ pounds boneless chuck, fat trimmed, cut into ½-inch cubes

2 medium onions, chopped

2 small red peppers, cored, seeded, diced

2 small green peppers, cored, seeded, diced

3 or 4 cloves garlic, minced

1 quart water

2 cans (2 pounds, 3 ounces each) imported whole plum tomatoes, with their liquid

3 to 5 teaspoons chili powder

¼ to ½ teaspoon cayenne pepper

2 teaspoons salt

1 Tablespoon light brown sugar

3 to 4 teaspoons Worcestershire sauce

1 3-inch strip lemon rind

1 ¼ pounds cooked red kidney beans, fresh or canned

1 teaspoon dried red pepper flakes

Grated zest of 1 or 2 lemons

Grated Cheddar cheese

Thinly sliced scallions (optional)

Sour cream

1. Heat 2 Tablespoons of the vegetable oil in large skillet over medium heat. Brown chuck without crowding, working in batches if necessary, until meat is deep caramel color, 10 to 15 minutes.

2. Meanwhile, heat remaining 2 Tablespoons of vegetable oil in large pot over medium heat. Sauté onions and red and green peppers, stirring often, until onion is translucent, about 5 minutes. Stir in garlic; sauté until fragrant, about 2 minutes. Remove from heat.

3. Transfer browned meat with slotted spoon to pot. Deglaze skillet with a little water; add to pot. Stir in tomatoes, crushing slightly. Add remaining water, chili powder, cayenne, salt, brown sugar, Worcestershire sauce, and lemon rind. Bring to a boil; skim and discard froth. Lower heat; simmer, partially covered, 1 hour.

4. Skim and discard froth. Simmer, partially covered, until meat is nearly tender, about another 1¼ hours.

5. Add kidney beans, red pepper flakes, and lemon zest. Correct seasonings. Simmer another 15 minutes to heat beans and to mingle flavors. Serve hot, garnished with grated Cheddar cheese, scallions, if you wish, and sour cream.

HEARTY SOUPS MADE FROM LEFTOVERS

When you've gone beyond following recipes, you realize that the fun of cooking is in making something from nothing—combining a leftover chop, a few vegetables, a cupful of gravy to come up with something better than any of its parts. And you learn: never, never throw away leftovers.

❖ A Few General Principles ❖

- Most leftover foods can be thinned down into a soup merely by adding an appropriate liquid. A few vegetables left over from the night before, coarsely chopped, and a cut-up baked potato can be moistened with stock or milk, simmered briefly, and seasoned, for a quick soup.
- You can maximize flavors by quickly sautéeing some fresh aromatic vegetables (for example, carrots, onions, celery), deglazing with a liquid, adding the leftovers with enough liquid to cover, and then simmering. Garnishes added later can add new flavor and textural interest.
- It is important to recognize that leftover meats should be treated differently, depending on whether they were first cooked by *moist-* or *dry-*heat methods:
- *Moist-cooked meats,* those that have been *braised* or *simmered,* need no further cooking. More liquid is added along with additional leftovers, and then all is simmered.
- *Dry-cooked meats,* such as leftover *roast* or *broiled* meats, can become tough if simply reheated in liquid. These are best cut up, browned in fat, and then simmered in the soup until tender (in essence you are braising them). Roast poultry, however, is an exception: omit the browning step, and simmer for a much shorter time.

BASIC METHOD FOR SOUPS MADE FROM LEFTOVER MEATS

Here is a basic method, but keep in mind that the process for soup-making is endlessly variable.

Makes about 10 cups

FAT:

2 to 3 tablespoons fat (leftover congealed meat fat from a stew, or a mixture of butter and oil)

FOR DRY-COOKED MEAT:

6 to 8 ounces (or more) leftover roast or grilled meat, cut into bite-size chunks or strips

AROMATICS:

2 to 3 cups onion, chopped or sliced
2 to 3 cloves garlic, minced (optional)
1 or 2 ribs celery, sliced
2 or 3 carrots, sliced
Herbs to taste

SAUTÉED VEGETABLES:

1 cup (approximately) red or green peppers, zucchini, or any other vegetable that is to be sautéed before simmering

LIQUID:

Leftover gravy or sauce, plus enough other liquid to measure

3 ½ to 4 ½ cups (use water, stock, wine, tomato or other vegetable juices, chopped tomatoes, or a mixture of any appropriately flavored liquids)

STARCH ELEMENT:

1 ½ cups potatoes, cubed, or other starch, such as soaked dried beans, noodles, barley, or rice (Use less of products that swell when cooked—for example, rice)

FOR MOIST-COOKED MEAT:

6 to 8 ounces (or more) leftover braised or simmered meat cut into bite-size chunks or strips

SIMMERED VEGETABLES:

½ cup vegetables that require relatively long simmering, cut up, such as turnips, celery root, parsnips
1 to 2 cups vegetables that require brief simmering, such as mushroom slices, sliced green

beans, fresh or defrosted frozen
peas, snow peas, fresh fava
beans, small pieces of broccoli or
cauliflower

TO FINISH:

Salt and freshly ground pepper
Chopped fresh herbs

1. Heat the fat in large pot or kettle. If using wine or tomato in your soup, use a noncorrosive pot. Brown the meat, if you are using dry-cooked (hold moist-cooked meat until step 4, below), and remove and reserve. Sauté the onion until softened. Add the optional garlic, celery, carrot, and any herbs you like, and toss gently in the fat until softened.
2. Add any vegetables to be sautéed; toss for a few minutes until softened.
3. Add liquid, scraping up browned bits in the pan. Tomatoes make a good contribution at this point. Bring the liquid to a boil, skim and discard foam, and lower heat to a simmer. Skim occasionally during simmering.
4. Add all the ingredients requiring long simmering: potatoes or other starch elements, cut-up moist-cooked meat, reserved browned meat, and vegetables requiring longer cooking. Simmer, partially covered, for a half-hour or longer, until everything is tender.
5. Add cut-up vegetables that require only brief cooking, and simmer until they are tender and the flavors have combined and mellowed a bit, about 15 minutes or so. Then skim off any traces of fat from the soup's surface.
6. Season with salt and pepper, add fresh herbs such as chopped parsley or snipped chives, and serve hot.

SCOTCH BROTH

A Scotswoman in London tells me that in Scotland this soup is known simply as "broth." English upper-class hunters gave it the name "Scotch broth." This version is based on a traditional recipe, with the Scottish cook's recommended addition of the shredded tender heart of a cabbage. Accompany it with buttermilk biscuits.

Cooking Tip: If the soup becomes too thick on reheating, thin with water or broth.

Serves 4 to 6

6 to 12 ounces leftover roasted or broiled lamb (see Note)

2 to 4 Tablespoons fat from leftover lamb gravy, or vegetable oil

Leftover lamb bones (optional)

2 small onions, thinly sliced

1 medium leek, white only, cleaned, thinly sliced

3 to 5 slender carrots, trimmed, peeled, quartered lengthwise, thickly sliced

2 small turnips, peeled, cut into ½-inch dice

1 rib celery, sliced

Mushroom stems, coarsely chopped (optional)

⅔ to 1 cup leftover lamb gravy, or

Mixed Meat and Poultry Broth (page 8)

2 ripe tomatoes, peeled, seeded, chopped, or 1 can (14 ounces) imported whole plum tomatoes, drained, chopped

4 cups cold water

1 ½ teaspoons salt

4 parsley stems, tied together

⅔ cup barley

1 to 1 ½ cups shelled fresh or thawed frozen peas

¾ cup shredded tender heart of cabbage (optional)

Freshly ground black pepper

2 to 3 Tablespoons chopped fresh parsley leaves

1. Trim any excess fat from lamb. Cut lamb meat away from any bones; reserve bones. Cut meat into ½-inch dice.

2. Heat 2 Tablespoons of lamb gravy fat or vegetable oil in a large, heavy flameproof casserole over medium-high heat. Add meat and optional bones; sauté, tossing occasionally to prevent sticking, until well browned, 8 to 12 minutes. Remove meat and bones. Add more fat or oil if necessary. Add onion and leek; toss to combine; sauté over medium heat until onion and leek begin to soften, about 6 minutes.

3. Add carrot, turnip, celery, and optional mushroom stems. Toss to combine; sauté until vegetables begin to brown, about 5 minutes. Add gravy or broth, scraping up any browned bits from bottom of pot. Add tomato, water, salt, and parsley stems. Return meat and bones to casserole. Stir, bring to boil; skim. Add barley; lower heat and simmer, partially covered, until meat and barley are tender, about 30 minutes. Add water if necessary to keep ingredients covered with liquid.

4. When meat is tender, add peas, optional cabbage, and ground pepper. Simmer until cabbage is tender, 10 to 15 minutes. Skim. Remove and discard parsley stems and bones. Correct seasoning. Ladle into warmed soup bowls; sprinkle with chopped parsley.

Note: Two small 1-inch thick lamb chops may be substituted for leftover lamb. Brown the chops in vegetable oil in a small skillet.

HEARTY CORN CHOWDER

When preparing this hearty chowder, keep each ingredient separate and visible by coarse, careful chopping, and avoid overcooking. The finished chowder should not be a mush.

Cooking Tip: If fresh corn is not available, used canned niblet corn. This is one of the times when canned seems to provide more flavor than frozen.

Serves 4 to 6

½ pound bacon, thickly sliced, cut into ½-inch squares

1 Tablespoon vegetable oil

1 large onion, coarsely chopped

2 ribs celery, coarsely chopped

2 carrots, trimmed, peeled, thickly sliced

¾ pound boiling potatoes, peeled, cut into ½-inch dice

2 cups cold water, or more as needed

¾ teaspoon salt

1 sprig fresh thyme, or large pinch dried

1 cup milk

⅔ cup heavy or light cream

5 ½ cups fresh corn kernels (8 to 9 ears), or four cans (12 ounces each) niblet corn, drained

Unsalted butter (optional)

Paprika

Pilot crackers or biscuits

1. Place bacon and oil in large pot. Slowly bring up to heat; cook bacon over medium heat, tossing often, until light golden but not crisp, and fat is rendered, about 10 minutes. Remove bacon with slotted spoon to paper towels to drain. Reserve.

2. Sauté onion in bacon fat over medium heat, tossing often, until light golden, about 8 minutes. Add celery and carrot; toss for another 2 or 3 minutes.

3. Add potato, enough cold water to cover ingredients, salt, and thyme. Bring to boil; lower heat and gently boil, uncovered, until potatoes are just tender but not mushy, 20 to 25 minutes. Skim.

4. Heat milk and cream together in saucepan until almost boiling. Stir into soup along with corn kernels. Simmer gently, partially covered, for 5 minutes.

5. Remove 2 cups of solids with slotted spoon. Purée coarsely in blender or food processor. Stir back into soup. Add reserved bacon. Correct seasonings. Simmer, uncovered, 5 to 7 minutes.

6. Serve hot with a pat of butter, if you wish, a sprinkling of paprika, and pilot crackers or biscuits.

HEARTY BEEF SOUP WITH HUNGARIAN PAPRIKA AND SOUR CREAM

Those interested in exploring the cuisines of Eastern Europe would do well to visit Hungary, where local specialties are still authentically prepared. This lightened version of a traditional soup is thickened only with a purée of its aromatic vegetables. It makes a beautiful appearance at the table: each chunky ingredient visible in a thick rosy broth, topped with a small peak of sour cream and chopped fresh parsley.

Cooking Tip: Be sure to use enough paprika to give this soup a real bite, as it will be cooled down by the sour cream at the end. If possible, use only imported Hungarian paprika; I prefer the *félédes* paprika, or medium-hot variety. A good mail-order source is H. Roth and Sons, 1577 First Avenue, New York, N.Y. 10028 (212-734-1110).

Serves 4 to 6

5 Tablespoons fat (lard, bacon fat, or vegetable oil)

6 to 12 ounces leftover dry-cooked beef (such as broiled or roasted beef), cut into ½-inch dice (see Note)

2 or 3 medium onions, coarsely chopped

3 carrots, trimmed, peeled, sliced into ¼-inch rounds

1 rib celery, sliced

1 medium red pepper, cored, seeded, cut into ½-inch dice

1 Tablespoon minced garlic

2 to 4 Tablespoons imported Hungarian paprika

2 cups drained imported canned plum tomatoes

⅔ to 1 cup leftover beef gravy, or Mixed Meat and Poultry Broth (page 8)

2 medium potatoes, peeled, cut into ½-inch dice

3 cups water

1 teaspoon salt, or more as needed

4 ounces green beans, cut into 1 ½-inch lengths

3 to 4 ounces mushrooms, cut into thick slices

¾ to 1 cup sour cream

Freshly ground black pepper

Chopped fresh parsley

1. Heat 2 Tablespoons of the fat in heavy skillet over medium heat. Add meat; sauté until browned on all sides, about 5 minutes. Reserve.

2. Heat remaining 3 Tablespoons of fat in large flameproof casserole or soup kettle over medium heat. Add onion; sauté until soft, but not brown, about 15 minutes. Add carrot, celery, red pepper, and garlic. Stir to combine; sauté until all vegetables are slightly softened, about 10 minutes. Add paprika; stir; cook another 2 minutes. Add tomato and gravy; stir, cook another 2 minutes. Add potatoes, 3 cups water, salt, and reserved meat. Stir to combine. Bring to boil; skim. Lower heat; simmer, partially covered, until potatoes and carrots are tender but still slightly firm, about 35 minutes.

3. Remove 1½ cups of the vegetables from soup with slotted spoon. Purée vegetables in food processor or blender. Stir purée back into soup. If soup is not thick enough (the soup liquid should be very hearty and robust), remove and purée a small amount of vegetables; stir back into soup. If necessary, repeat to reach desired consistency.

4. Add beans and mushrooms; simmer until beans are tender, about 10 minutes. Remove from heat.

5. Reserve a few spoonfuls of sour cream as a garnish for each soup serving. Stir remaining sour cream into soup. Correct seasonings. Add pepper. Serve soup in warmed soup bowls. Top each serving with dollop of reserved sour cream; sprinkle with chopped parsley.

Note: If the meat has been moist-cooked first (braised or simmered), omit step 1 and proceed with step 2.

FLEMISH BEER SOUP

Curnonsky, the twentieth-century "Prince of Gastronomes," tells of "this strange soup, so highly esteemed in Flanders and Germany," and details a recipe that includes sugar, coriander seeds, thinly sliced bread, and egg yolks.

This beer soup is an idiosyncratic version of the soul-warming Flemish dish *carbonnades* (page 196). It can be made of any sort of leftover beef and unites all the elements of the stew on which it is based: the rich, slightly sweet brown sauce, the meat and vegetables, and even the accompanying potatoes.

Serve this soup with the same dark beer you use to make it and nothing more than a crisp salad and dark bread. Fruit and cheese are welcome afterwards.

Cooking Tip: The amount of sugar added will vary according to the degree of bitterness of the dark beer used.

Serves 4 to 6

2 Tablespoons leftover beef cooking fat, or 1 tablespoon oil plus 1 tablespoon unsalted butter, or more as needed

3 onions, halved, thickly sliced

6 ounces medium mushrooms

4 thin carrots, trimmed, peeled, halved lengthwise, cut into 1 ½-inch lengths

2 teaspoons minced garlic (2 small cloves garlic)

1 bay leaf

1 teaspoon salt

¾ teaspoon brown sugar (optional)

¼ teaspoon dried thyme, crumbled

¼ teaspoon dried marjoram, crumbled

2 bottles (12 ounces each) dark beer

½ to ⅔ cup leftover defatted beef cooking juices, gravy, or Mixed Meat and Poultry Broth (page 8)

6 to 8 ounces leftover moist-cooked beef (such as braised or simmered beef), cut into ½-inch cubes

2 medium-large boiling potatoes, peeled, cut into ½-inch dice

¾ cup water, or as needed

Freshly ground black pepper

2 Tablespoons chopped fresh parsley (optional)

1. Heat fat in a large flameproof casserole over medium heat. Add onion and toss to coat with fat. Cook, covered, stirring occasionally, until onion softens, about 5 minutes.

2. Meanwhile, remove stems from mushrooms. Coarsely chop stems. Halve caps; thickly slice caps across.

3. Add carrot, garlic, and chopped mushroom stems to onion; toss to combine. Add more fat if necessary. Sauté over medium-low heat until onions are soft and golden, but not brown, 12 to 15 minutes (see Note).

4. Add bay leaf, salt, brown sugar, thyme, marjoram, beer, and leftover meat juices. Bring to boil; lower heat, simmer uncovered, until flavors begin to develop, about 10 minutes.

5. Add reserved mushroom slices, beef, potato, and enough water to cover ingredients. Bring to boil, lower heat. Simmer gently, partially covered, until potatoes are tender, about 30 to 35 minutes.

6. Skim. Add pepper. Correct seasonings. Ladle into individual warmed soup bowls; sprinkle with chopped parsley.

Note: If using leftover roast beef rather than braised or simmered meat, sauté cubes of roast beef in large skillet with a little oil over medium-high heat until light brown; reserve. Proceed with recipe.

PURÉE SOUPS

Purée soups, usually made from vegetables, can be concocted from a single main ingredient (for example, carrot or asparagus) or can combine several ingredients in subtle blends. The soups can be served cold or hot, enriched (with butter, cream, buttermilk, yogurt, or sour cream) or not. Since all the ingredients will be puréed beyond recognition, this is an excellent opportunity to use up any collected trimmings from carrots, potatoes, mushrooms, etc.

While I prefer these soups thickened with only the puréed vegetables themselves, some may require more binding. Such starch-free vegetables as tomatoes and broccoli can separate into small bits of solids floating in an unpleasantly watery liquid. Adding a little thickener before puréeing, in the form of a cut-up peeled potato, or a couple of spoonfuls of cooked rice, results in a perfectly smooth soup, with a more palatable flavor and texture than that achieved with the more customarily used flour-based *roux*.

❖ Basic Procedure for Vegetable Purée Soups ❖

1. *Sweat the vegetables.* Trim the vegetables to uniform size for even cooking. Sweat the vegetables in butter or other fat with a small amount of chopped onion, shallot, or leek over low heat, covered, to release their juices.

2. *Add liquid.* Add stock, water, or a combination, and simmer, partially covered, until the vegetables are thoroughly tender.

3. *Purée.* First, strain the mixture, reserving the liquid. Purée the solids, using a blender, food processor, or food mill, or by simply pushing the solids through a sieve. Add a little of the liquid to each batch, if necessary, to facilitate the puréeing process. Add enough of the strained liquid back into the final purée to achieve the consistency you desire. Remember that you can make the purée as smooth or as coarse as you like.

4. *Strain.* For a more refined soup, pass the purée through a fine sieve.

5. *Enrich.* You may now add cream, milk, and/or a little butter for added smoothness. Yogurt or sour cream marry particularly well with chilled soups, and can be stirred in or used as a cool topping. I prefer to store the purée in the refrigerator without any enrichment added. This avoids possible souring during storage. I then add the desired enrichment only to the amount I am serving; this allows me to change the enrichment each time I serve the soup.

Cooking Tip: If you'd like to use these purées as a vegetable course, do not add the strained liquid back into the puréed solids in step 3. Just enrich the purée with a little cream and some chunks of butter at serving time.

CARROT SOUP WITH ORANGE

This straightforward soup illustrates the Basic Procedure for Vegetable Purée Soups.
Serves 4

2 Tablespoons unsalted butter	Salt
1 small onion, chopped (or substitute leek, shallot, or scallion)	1 bay leaf
	1 large strip orange zest
	Freshly grated nutmeg
1 pound carrots, trimmed, peeled, cut up evenly	½ cup heavy cream
	Freshly ground black pepper
1 ½ to 2 cups Chicken Broth (page 6)	Chopped fresh parsley or other herbs

1. Heat butter in heavy saucepan. Add onion. Sweat, covered, until soft, about 3 minutes. Add carrots; sweat until soft, about 4 minutes.
2. Add enough broth to cover carrots. Add salt, bay leaf, orange zest, and nutmeg. Simmer, partially covered, until carrots are tender, about 20 minutes.
3. Strain solids through sieve over large bowl; reserve liquid. Purée solids until very smooth in food processor or blender. Return purée to rinsed saucepan. Stir in enough of the reserved liquid to thin purée to desired consistency. Add cream. Bring to a simmer. Add freshly ground pepper. Correct seasonings. Serve sprinkled with chopped fresh parsley or other herbs.

Variations

Cream of Fresh Asparagus Soup: Substitute 1½ to 2 pounds asparagus, trimmed, peeled, for the carrots. Cut asparagus into small pieces. Add 1 small potato, peeled, cut into small pieces, with the chicken broth. Omit orange zest. Substitute a pinch of tarragon for orange zest and nutmeg. Garnish with blanched asparagus tips and a nut of butter.

Cream of Fresh Pea Soup: Substitute 5½ to 6 cups peas for carrots. Sweat 3 or 4 parsley sprigs, shredded, and 1 cup shredded lettuce leaves with peas. Omit orange zest. Enrich with a nut of butter.

Cream of Broccoli Soup: Substitute about 1¼ pounds broccoli for carrots. Trim, cut into 1-inch pieces. Add 3 tablespoons cooked rice to chicken broth before simmering. Omit orange zest. Enrich with a nut of butter.

CELERY ROOT, ONION, AND POTATO SOUP

This cold-weather vegetable combination can also be made as a thick purée to accompany a roast.
Serves 4

2 Tablespoons unsalted butter, plus more for garnish

2 medium onions, sliced

4 medium leeks, white part only, cleaned, sliced

1 teaspoon salt

4 medium bulbs celery root (about 2½ pounds)

Fresh lemon juice

1 small boiling potato, peeled, sliced

3½ cups water or Chicken Broth (page 6), or more as needed

1½ cups milk, or more as needed

Pinch ground mace

½ cup heavy cream

Chopped fresh parsley

1. Heat butter in large casserole over medium heat. Add onion, leek, and salt. Toss well to coat vegetables. Cover and sweat until vegetables are tender, 12 to 15 minutes. Stir occasionally to prevent sticking.
2. Meanwhile, prepare celery root. With a sharp knife, peel off and discard skin and any blemished areas. Quarter lengthwise; drop into bowl of cold water with a bit of lemon juice added to prevent discoloration. Cut each quarter lengthwise into thin slices; return to water.
3. When onion mixture is tender, add drained celery root, potato, water or broth, milk, and mace. Stir to combine. Cover; bring to a simmer over low heat. Let simmer, partially covered, until all ingredients are tender, 45 to 60 minutes. Skim.
4. Drain soup in colander set over large bowl; reserve liquid. Purée solids in batches in blender or food processor, making either coarse or smooth purée, as you prefer. Return purée to rinsed casserole. Whisk enough

reserved liquid into purée to achieve desired consistency. Whisk in heavy cream. Bring to simmer; correct seasonings. Thin, if necessary, with broth or milk. Simmer 5 to 10 minutes. Serve in warmed soup bowls. Enrich each serving with a nut of butter. Sprinkle with parsley.

Variation

Cream of Jerusalem Artichoke Soup: Substitute 2 pounds of Jerusalem artichokes, peeled, for celery root. Simmer 25 to 35 minutes. Season with freshly ground white pepper and fresh lemon juice. Garnish with chopped fresh parsley.

PUMPKIN SOUP WITH APPLES

The pumpkin purée used in this soup also makes a particularly smooth filling for pumpkin pies. Prepare this purée in quantity, without seasonings, when the supply of pumpkins is plentiful, then freeze it; you'll enjoy pies (and this soup) all through the winter.
Serves 4

2 medium tart apples, such as Granny Smith	¾ cup milk
1 teaspoon fresh lemon juice	¼ cup heavy cream
2 Tablespoons unsalted butter	Pinch ground allspice
2 small onions, chopped	Pinch ground cinnamon
2 ½ cups Chicken Broth (page 6)	1 to 2 Tablespoons bourbon,
1 to 1 ½ cups pumpkin purée (see Note)	brandy, or whisky (optional)
1 teaspoon salt	Freshly ground white pepper
1 teaspoon brown sugar	Freshly grated Parmesan or
¼ teaspoon freshly grated nutmeg, or to taste	Gruyère cheese (optional)

1. Peel, core, and chop the apples. Toss with lemon juice in medium bowl to prevent discoloration.

2. Heat butter in large saucepan over medium-low heat. Sauté onion until very soft and caramel in color, about 10 minutes. Do not over-brown.

3. Add chicken broth, chopped apples, pumpkin purée, salt, sugar, and nutmeg. Stir to combine. Slowly bring to a boil. Reduce heat, simmer, covered, until apples are tender, about 30 minutes. Stir occasionally.

4. Strain liquid into bowl. Purée solids in blender or food processor. Return liquid and purée to rinsed saucepan; whisk together. Stir in milk, cream, allspice, and cinnamon. Simmer another 5 to 10 minutes. Add bourbon and white pepper. Simmer soup another 5 minutes to blend flavors. Serve in warmed soup bowls; sprinkle with Parmesan or Gruyère, if you wish.

Note: To make fresh pumpkin purée, break off pumpkin stem, cut pumpkin in half, and scoop out seeds and stringy material. Place halves, cut side up, on foil-lined baking sheet, and cover and seal each half with foil. Bake in preheated 350° oven until flesh is very tender, about 1½ hours. Cool slightly. Scoop out flesh and mash with potato masher or in food processor. You may substitute canned unsweetened plain solid-pack pumpkin purée.

FRUIT SOUPS

Fruit soups can be unusual and refreshing, or they can be ghastly. (I have not included the recipe a chef I know uses "in emergencies": melted strawberry ice cream mixed with whipped cream . . .) The trick is to keep these soups subtle; play down the sweetness, and serve well chilled.

CREAM OF CANTALOUPE SOUP

This light, unusual soup makes a refreshing opening to a hot-weather meal. It takes no time to prepare, since there's no cooking involved.

Try varying this recipe by using other melons, and for additional appeal, garnish with thin slivers of prosciutto or fresh mint leaves. Serves 4

2 ripe cantaloupes
3 Tablespoons white wine
2 to 3 Tablespoons fresh lemon
   and/or lime juice
1 ½ Tablespoons Cointreau
2 to 3 Tablespoons Coco López or

other canned sweetened coconut
   cream, or to taste
3 to 4 Tablespoons heavy cream
Salt
Freshly grated nutmeg
Freshly ground white pepper

1. Cut cantaloupes in half. Scoop out and discard seeds and stringy material. Remove flesh; purée in food processor or blender until very smooth. Pour purée into bowl.
2. Add wine, lemon juice, Cointreau, Coco López, and heavy cream to purée. Season with salt, nutmeg, and white pepper; chill well. Serve in chilled soup bowls.

CHILLED PLUM SOUP

This easy soup has remarkable depth of flavor and color.
Cooking Tip: Taste carefully as you prepare this soup, as you may need to adjust for the plums' acidity or sweetness.
Serves 4 to 6

12 ripe plums (about 2 ½ pounds),
   stems removed
1 ½ oranges
¾ cup dry red wine
⅓ cup (packed) brown sugar
¼ cup cold water

¼ cup red currant jelly
Pinch salt
1 cinnamon stick (3 inches)
1 or 2 cloves
Fresh lemon juice, if needed
Sour cream

1. Rinse plums; halve, dropping halves, with stones, into large wide noncorrosive saucepan. Cut 2 or 3 wide strips of rind, avoiding white pith, from the one orange. Squeeze the juice from the one orange into casserole. Add wine, brown sugar, water, jelly, salt, cinnamon stick, and cloves. Stir to combine. Cover pot and bring to a boil. Stir again to combine; lower heat, simmer briskly, covered, stirring and mashing the fruit occasionally, until plums are very tender, about 40 minutes.

2. Strain mixture through sieve over large bowl; push plum flesh through sieve with wooden spoon; discard stones, skins, orange rind, and spices. Cool to room temperature. Stir in juice of ½ orange. Refrigerate, covered, until well chilled. Correct seasoning if necessary with fresh lemon juice. Top each serving with a dollop of sour cream.

A GAMUT OF FISH SOUPS

Almost everywhere in the world, the freshest local catch is combined with local seasonings, producing soups ranging from the utmost delicacy, such as Belgian *Waterzooi,* to the palate-searing spiciness of Thai fish soups.

These soups are a meal in themselves, served with warm crusty bread and white wine.

SCALLOPS À LA NAGE

Fish "in the swim"—lightly poached with just a few aromatics and served immersed in its own broth with vegetables. Any fillet or shellfish can be treated this way. This soup is a version of the recipe served at the Hotel Plaza-Athénée in Paris, where it is accompanied by a silky *Beurre Blanc* (page 122) on the side.
Serves 4

3 cups dry white wine
1 teaspoon salt
1 bay leaf
Freshly ground white pepper
½ small onion, sliced, separated into rings
1 carrot, trimmed, peeled, scored lengthwise, thinly sliced

1 ½ pounds bay scallops, or sea scallops sliced in half horizontally
2 Tablespoons chilled unsalted butter, cut into bits
1 Tablespoon Cognac or brandy

1. Combine wine, salt, bay leaf, and white pepper in wide noncorrosive saucepan. Bring to a boil. Add onion rings and carrot. Reduce heat; simmer until vegetables are just crisp-tender, about 5 minutes.

2. Add scallops to saucepan. Simmer until opaque, about 3 minutes. Remove from heat; swirl in cold butter a few bits at a time. Sprinkle a few drops Cognac into each of four warmed shallow soup dishes. Add scallops and vegetables; pour broth over.

MIXED SEAFOOD À LA NAGE WITH FENNEL AND HERBS

I first prepared this at an impromptu supper in the seaside kitchen of friends on Chappaquiddick, Martha's Vineyard, where I used the ingredients they offered me: vegetables and herbs grown in their garden, seafood that had been caught that morning, and most surprisingly, a lobster and fish stock prepared earlier that day. Serve this dish with boiled small potatoes, drained, and buttered.
Serves 4 to 6

2 Tablespoons unsalted butter, and 4 Tablespoons cut into small pieces, cold

1 Tablespoon olive oil

1 medium onion, halved, sliced crosswise

1 or 2 leeks, halved, sliced

½ cup chopped fresh fennel

1 or 2 shallots, sliced

½ teaspoon salt

1 carrot trimmed, peeled, sliced

Chopped mushroom stems (see mushrooms in next column)

2 or 3 live lobsters (about 1 ¼ pounds each)

4 to 5 cups Fish Broth (page 11)

2 pounds cod fillet

2 or 3 branches fresh thyme, or ¼ teaspoon dried

3 sprigs parsley

½ pound fresh mushrooms, stemmed, caps thickly sliced

¼ cup chopped fresh parsley

Fresh lemon juice

Freshly ground white pepper

1. Heat the 2 Tablespoons butter and oil in large, wide pot over medium-low heat. Add onion, leek, fennel, and shallot. Sweat covered, stirring occasionally, until onion is soft, 5 to 7 minutes. Sprinkle salt over vegetables. Add carrot and mushroom stems; cover and sweat until carrot is tender, about 5 to 10 minutes. Remove from heat.

2. Meanwhile, boil lobsters in fish broth in large pot for 2 minutes. Remove lobsters from broth. Arrange cod fillets over vegetables in pot. Place lobsters on top. Add broth from lobster pot, thyme, and parsley sprigs. Cover and steam for 10 minutes. Four minutes before done, add mushrooms, burying them in the pot.

3. Remove lobster and cod fillets with slotted spoon. Cut lobsters in their shells into serving pieces. Keep lobster and fish fillets warm. Remove vegetables with slotted spoon; keep warm.

4. Reduce cooking liquid in saucepan over medium-high heat to about 3 cups. Remove from heat. Whisk in the 4 Tablespoons of cold butter, one piece at a time, adding another piece just when the previous piece has liquefied; do not let the butter melt completely. The broth should be frothy. Stir in chopped parsley, fresh lemon juice, and pepper to taste.

5. Divide fillets and lobster pieces among warmed wide, shallow soup bowls. Ladle broth and vegetables over fish.

NEW ENGLAND CLAM CHOWDER

One of my happiest memories is when David and I ran a restaurant on the island of Martha's Vineyard, where from an open kitchen we could watch the sun set on the bay as we prepared dinner each evening. In season, we served over a hundred gallons of chowder per week and thought we'd never be able to look at another bowlful.

This superbly simple recipe is based on traditional colonial formulas (in New England, it is prepared with the large hard-shell clams called quahogs—pronounced *co-hogs.*) The soup is lightly thickened with a purée of its own vegetables rather than flour.

Serves 6

¼ pound salt pork, cut into
½-inch cubes
Vegetable oil if necessary
2 medium onions, sliced
1 rib celery, sliced
3 to 4 dozen clams (if using
quahogs, use 3 dozen), scrubbed
½ cup water, or more as needed

1 ½ pounds boiling potatoes,
peeled, diced
Freshly ground black pepper
1 cup light cream, or ½ cup each
heavy cream and milk
½ cup milk
Unsalted butter
Paprika

1. Heat salt pork in saucepan over medium heat to render fat, 10 to 15 minutes. If salt pork sticks to pan, add about 1 Tablespoon oil. Remove cubes with slotted spoon to paper towels to drain.

2. Add onions and celery to rendered fat. Sweat covered over medium heat until vegetables are wilted, about 10 minutes.

3. Add the clams and water to the pot; steam covered, shaking pot occasionally, until clams open, about 5 to 10 minutes.

4. Strain through sieve lined with double thickness of dampened cheesecloth over a large measuring cup. Discard any clams that don't open. Add water if necessary to strained cooking liquid to make 2 cups.

5. Remove meat from clams and chop coarsely. Reserve.

6. Add potato and the 2 cups of the cooking broth to saucepan. Boil, covered, until potatoes are quite tender but still hold their shape, 25 to 30 minutes.

7. Remove about 2 cups of the vegetables with slotted spoon. Coarsely mash with a potato masher or coarsely grind in food processor or blender. Do not overprocess. Return to pot with reserved salt pork, clams, and freshly ground black pepper. Heat over medium-low heat until heated through.

8. Combine light cream and milk in a saucepan; heat. Stir into soup.

9. Serve soup in warm soup bowls; top each with pat of butter. Dust with paprika. Serve with oyster crackers.

FISH CHOWDER WITH CREAM AND TOMATOES

As I learned from my time on Martha's Vineyard, mention chowder, and you'll soon hear someone argue that his or her version is the only true one. Tomatoes, the hallmark of the peppery Manhattan-style chowder, combine nicely with the cream in this otherwise New England-style recipe.

Serves 4 to 6

¼ pound salt pork, cut into
   ½-inch cubes
Vegetable oil if necessary
1 ½ cups sliced onion (about 2
   medium)
1 rib celery, trimmed, sliced
1 ½ pounds boiling potatoes,
   peeled, cut into ½-inch cubes
Fish frame and tail from non-oily
   fish (optional)
2 cups water
2 sprigs fresh thyme, or ¼
   teaspoon dried, crumbled

3 sprigs parsley
2 pounds sea bass or other firm,
   non-oily fish fillet with skin, cut
   into 1-to-1 ½-inch cubes
1 ½ cups light cream, or ¾ cup
   each heavy cream and milk
½ cup milk
¾ to 1 cup drained canned
   imported plum tomatoes, coarsely
   chopped
Unsalted butter
Freshly ground black pepper
Paprika

1. Place salt pork cubes in large saucepan. Heat over medium heat until fat is rendered and cubes are browned, about 15 minutes. Add vegetable oil, if necessary, to prevent sticking. Remove cubes with slotted spoon; drain on paper towels. Reserve.

2. Add onion and celery to rendered fat. Sweat covered until vegetables are softened, stirring occasionally, about 10 minutes.

3. Add potato, optional fish frame and tail, water, thyme, and parsley. Bring to boil; gently boil covered until potatoes are slightly tender, 20 to 25 minutes. Remove frame and tail.

4. Add fish cubes. Simmer covered until fish is almost cooked, 5 to 8 minutes.

5. Meanwhile, heat light cream, milk, and tomatoes together in another saucepan. Add to soup with salt pork; stir to combine. Simmer for a few minutes to combine flavors.

6. Let soup mellow off heat 1 hour, if you wish. Check seasonings; add salt and pepper if necessary.

7. Serve soup hot. Top each serving with a pat of butter and a sprinkling of pepper and paprika. Pass pilot or oyster crackers separately.

BOULLINADA (CATALÁN FISH STEW WITH RED PEPPERS AND GARLIC)

This is the Catalán version of garlic-scented *bourride,* popular along the Mediterranean coast of Spain where it meets France. Based on an old recipe of the great chef Prosper Montagné (best known as the author of the *Larousse Gastronomique*), this soup adds an accent of roasted red peppers. Montagné notes, by the way, that locals insist on slightly *rancid* lard for this dish. I decided to go against tradition here, but suit yourself. Serves 4 to 6

4 medium red peppers (about 1 ½ pounds)

1 Tablespoon olive oil

3 ounces bacon (about 4 slices), cut into ¼-inch dice

1 medium onion, cut into square chunky pieces

4 cloves garlic, minced

1 to 2 Tablespoons plus ¼ cup chopped fresh parsley

½ pound boiling potatoes, peeled, halved, and sliced crosswise

4 cups Fish Broth (page 11)

Large pinch saffron

1 ½ pounds thick non-oily fish fillets, or steaks such as halibut

steak, white snapper, cod, sea trout, bass

Dry white wine, as needed

½ pound thin non-oily fish fillets, such as red snapper or flounder

LIAISON:

6 to 8 cloves garlic, chopped

2 egg yolks, lightly beaten

⅓ cup olive oil

Freshly ground black pepper

Cayenne pepper

Fresh lemon juice

Salt

1. Preheat broiler.

2. Broil red peppers until blackened, turning occasionally, about 8 minutes. Place peppers in brown paper bag until cool. Peel; remove stem and seeds. Cut peppers into 1-inch dice, reserving any juices.

3. Heat the 1 Tablespoon olive oil over medium heat in casserole. Add bacon; sauté until lightly golden, 8 to 10 minutes. Add onion. Toss to combine. Sauté until slightly wilted, 4 to 5 minutes. Add garlic, about two-thirds reserved diced red pepper, and the 1 to 2 Tablespoons chopped parsley; sauté until fragrant, about 2 minutes.

4. Add potato, fish broth, the reserved pepper juices, and saffron. Bring to boil, covered. Boil gently until potatoes are tender, about 15 minutes.
5. Add thick fish fillets or steaks to casserole. Add more stock, white wine, or water, if necessary, to just cover ingredients. Simmer, covered, 5 minutes. Add thin fish fillets. Simmer, covered, until all fish is just cooked through, about another 5 minutes.
6. Remove fish and potato with slotted spoon to warmed platter. Spoon a little of the cooking liquid over the fish and potato to keep them moist; keep warm.
7. Boil broth vigorously until slightly reduced, about 5 minutes.
8. Combine remaining diced red pepper, a little of the cooked potato, garlic, and egg yolks in blender or processor. Purée until smooth. Add the ⅓ cup olive oil slowly while blender is running. Slowly blend in a ladleful of the hot soup. Stir purée back into soup in casserole.
9. Gently heat soup, stirring, until thickened. Do not boil. Add black pepper, cayenne, a few drops lemon juice, and the ¼ cup chopped parsley. Correct seasonings; add salt if necessary.
10. Arrange fish fillets and potatoes in individual shallow soup bowls with broth; or serve broth and potatoes in individual soup bowls, and pass the fish fillets, sprinkled with chopped parsley, separately.

FRESH SALMON SOUP WITH SPINACH NOODLES

The pale pink and green colors make this soup a subtle prelude or light main course for a special meal. The fresh pasta can be replaced with dried; just be sure not to overcook the noodles or any other ingredient in this delicate soup.
Serves 6

3 Tablespoons unsalted butter

3 Tablespoons chopped shallot

1 cup dry white wine

4 cups Fish Broth (page 11)

2 pounds salmon steaks or fillets

1 cup heavy cream

3 or 4 ounces mushrooms, halved, thickly sliced crosswise

6 ounces fresh spinach noodles, tagliatelle, or thinner noodles, or

4 ounces dried, cut into 3-inch lengths

2 Tablespoons chopped fresh parsley

2 Tablespoons snipped fresh chives

Salt

Freshly ground white pepper

Pinch cayenne pepper

Fresh lemon juice

1. Cut 2 Tablespoons of the butter into small pieces; chill.

2. Heat remaining 1 Tablespoon of butter over low heat in large flameproof noncorrosive casserole. Add shallot; sauté until soft but not brown, about 4 minutes.

3. Add wine to casserole; heat to boiling. Reduce heat; simmer uncovered until reduced by one-third, about 4 minutes. Add 4 cups fish broth; heat to boiling. Reduce heat to gentle simmer. Carefully arrange salmon in single layer in casserole. If liquid does not cover fish, lay piece of buttered waxed paper or kitchen parchment paper over fish. Cover casserole; simmer until salmon is just cooked through, 4 to 9 minutes, depending on thickness of fish. Fish should be opaque in the center and slightly springy to the touch.

4. Meanwhile, heat large pot of salted water to boiling for the noodles.

5. Carefully transfer salmon with slotted spatula to platter. Keep warm. Boil cooking liquid, uncovered, until reduced by one-third, about 5 minutes. Add cream; heat to boiling; boil for 3 minutes. Add mushrooms; simmer, uncovered, 4 to 5 minutes.

6. Divide salmon into 6 portions. Remove and discard skin and any bones. Place piece of fish in each of 6 warmed shallow soup bowls.

7. Cook noodles in boiling water until just *al dente,* about 45 seconds or longer if dried. Drain well in colander. Add noodles to broth in casserole; remove from heat. Swirl in reserved chilled butter piece by piece. Add parsley and chives; season to taste with salt, white pepper, cayenne, and lemon juice. Gently stir to combine. Correct all seasonings. Ladle broth and noodles over each portion of salmon to serve.

HERBED SEAFOOD BISQUE

Through its long history, the term *bisque* has described a variety of preparations: purées of crayfish or game birds (*Le Vray Cuisinier François*, by La Varenne, 1651, gives a recipe for bisque of pigeon); or rounds of toast dipped in consommé and spread with crayfish butter.

Bisque is used today to indicate all sorts of rich seafood soups, though one occasionally finds reference to tomato bisque. This recipe, made with a variety of shellfish (use whatever you can get, as long as total weight of the flesh is the same), is based on a classic formula of Escoffier. The rice with which he bound the soup has been eliminated, however, and replaced by a sieved purée of shellfish flesh and shells, and aromatic vegetables.

Serves 4 to 6

2 Tablespoons unsalted butter	3 Tablespoons Cognac or brandy
1 Tablespoon olive oil	1 cup dry white wine
1 small onion, chopped	3 Tablespoons thick tomato purée
1 leek, white part only, cleaned, sliced	4 cups Fish Broth (page 11)
2 or 3 shallots, chopped	½ teaspoon salt
1 small rib celery, chopped	⅓ to ½ cup heavy cream (or crème fraîche)
1 small carrot, trimmed, peeled, chopped	¼ cup chopped fresh parsley
½ teaspoon dried thyme, crumbled	2 or 3 Tablespoons snipped chives (optional)
1 bay leaf	Freshly ground white pepper
3 or 4 parsley stems	Cayenne pepper
1 or 2 cloves garlic, sliced (optional)	Few drops fresh lemon juice
8 to 10 ounces shrimp, with shells	2 or 3 Tablespoons chilled unsalted butter, cut into small pieces
8 ounces sea scallops	

1. Heat 2 Tablespoons butter and oil in large noncorrosive saucepan over medium heat. Add onion, leek, shallot, celery, carrot, thyme, bay leaf, and parsley stems. Sauté, tossing occasionally, until vegetables begin to soften, about 6 minutes. Add optional garlic; sauté 2 minutes. Add shrimp; sauté until shrimp begin to turn pink, about 2 minutes. Add scallops; sauté, tossing until outside edges are white, about 2

minutes. Add Cognac. Ignite with long kitchen match. When flames go out, add white wine. Reduce gently 3 to 4 minutes. Add tomato purée, 3 cups of the broth, and salt. Bring to boil, stirring. Simmer, covered, over low heat until shrimp and scallops are very tender, about 10 minutes.

2. Remove shrimp and scallops with slotted spoon to plate. When cool enough to handle, shell shrimp. Add shells and any exuded juices from shellfish back into saucepan. Devein shrimp.

3. Cut ¼ to ⅓ cup of the shrimp and scallops into large dice. Reserve for garnish. Return remaining shellfish to saucepan.

4. Purée soup, including shrimp shells, in batches in food processor or blender. Strain through sieve over large bowl to eliminate shells. Press shells with wooden spoon to release any liquid.

5. Return soup to rinsed saucepan. Reheat. Add cream and enough of the remaining 1 cup fish broth to bring soup to medium consistency. Heat through. Stir in reserved diced shellfish, most of the parsley and chives (reserve 2 Tablespoons for garnish), and salt, pepper, cayenne, and lemon juice to taste. Add enough cayenne to give soup a bite. Return to boil; remove from heat. Stir in cut-up pieces of butter one piece at a time, waiting until each piece is just incorporated before adding the next.

6. Serve in warmed bowls. Sprinkle remaining chives and parsley over each serving.

PASTA
AND RICE

I like enormously to lie in bed reading, getting up later and going into the kitchen where Giulietta prepares excellent nocturnal spaghetti.

—FEDERICO FELLINI

One might like or dislike Mussolini, but one thing is nearly certain: no gourmet could fail to appreciate one of the dictator's favorite dishes, *Il Duce's Risotto* [which simulates the Italian flag, with strips of green pepper, and red and white sauces].

—PAUL BOUILLARD, *La Cuisine au Coin du Feu* (1928)

PASTA

HOW TO COOK, SERVE, AND PORTION PASTA

QUICKLY SAUCED PASTA DISHES

PASTA WITH BUTTER AND FRESHLY GRATED CHEESE
PASTA WITH GARLIC AND HERBS
PASTA WITH ARTICHOKE AND WALNUT SAUCE WITH FRESH HERBS
PASTA WITH CREAM AND CHEESE
   PASTA WITH VEGETABLES AND CREAM
   PASTA WITH CREAM, PROSCIUTTO, MUSHROOMS, AND PEAS
   PASTA WITH CREAM, FRESH BASIL, AND TOMATOES
PASTA *QUATTRO STAGGIONI* (PASTA WITH VEGETABLES, PINE NUTS, AND CREAM)
PASTA WITH FOUR-CHEESE SAUCE
PASTA WITH SAUSAGE AND WILD MUSHROOM SAUCE
A TOMATO PRIMER
BASIC CHUNKY TOMATO SAUCE
UNCOOKED TOMATO SAUCE FOR PASTA
PASTA WITH UNCOOKED TOMATOES AND MOZZARELLA
PASTA WITH TOMATO-RICOTTA SAUCE
PASTA WITH TOMATO, MUSHROOM, AND ANCHOVY SAUCE

BAKED PASTA GRATINS

GRATIN OF PASTA WITH TOMATOES, HAM, AND CHEESE
SPINACH AND CHEESE LASAGNE
   CANNELONI WITH SPINACH, MUSHROOMS, AND TWO SAUCES

RICE

BOILED RICE IN MUCH WATER
CHINESE-STYLE FRIED RICE

RICE PILAFS

BASIC METHOD FOR PILAFS
   SIMPLE VEGETABLE-SCENTED PILAF
PILAF WITH LEFTOVER MEATS AND VEGETABLES

RISOTTO

BASIC TECHNIQUE FOR RISOTTO
   RISOTTO-STUFFED TOMATOES
RISOTTO WITH WILD MUSHROOMS
RISOTTO PRIMAVERA

PASTA AND RICE SALADS

BASIC CONSIDERATIONS FOR PASTA AND RICE SALADS
PENNE SALAD WITH FRESH ASPARAGUS
   TORTELLINI SALAD WITH VEGETABLES AND PROSCIUTTO
COLD ORIENTAL NOODLES WITH GINGER, SESAME, AND FRESH VEGETABLES
RICE SALAD WITH PEAS, PROSCIUTTO, AND BASIL

❖ ❖ ❖ ❖ ❖ ❖ ❖ ❖ ❖ ❖ ❖ ❖ ❖ ❖ ❖ ❖

*P*asta and rice, both staple elements of Eastern and Western cuisines, are inexpensive, easy to cook, and surprisingly nutritious. Pasta is non-fattening; it's the sauces that carry the calories. Both provide a hearty meal in a matter of minutes, making them ideal for after work or for improvised suppers with friends.

Best of all, I think of pasta (and rice as well) as a soft, neutral bed for other ingredients and sauces; a sort of artist's canvas awaiting your ingenuity in devising variations: earthy sausages and wild mushrooms, devastatingly rich cheese mixtures, or subtle and soigné vegetable and seafood creations. With all these possibilities, I could easily eat pasta every day and be perfectly happy.

Pasta is now everywhere: American cities have seen the arrival of fresh noodles in a myriad of shapes in many corner shops, and pasta bars now dispense plates of steaming noodles to those pasta junkies who need their hit on the spot.

Here is a limited repertoire of treatments for both pasta and rice, most of them quick and easy. Learn which shapes of pasta combine best with which sauces: flat noodles for smooth sauces; stubby macaroni, penne, or shells to catch bits of the chunkier blends.

However you prepare these starchy staples, you can't go wrong: like bread and ice cream, these foods seem to be loved by nearly everyone.

PASTA

Freshly made egg noodles are incomparably tender and full of flavor, and a pasta machine for rolling can be a worthwhile investment if you use it often. However, because this chapter is designed to provide you with ideas that are quick and manageable, I assume that you'll usually be using a good brand of dried pasta, preferably imported. If you do have a nearby source for fresh pasta, use it by all means. And if you want to learn the basics of the homemade product, have a look at *The Fine Art of Italian Cooking* by Giuliano Bugialli (Times Books), *The Classic Italian Cook Book* by Marcella Hazan (Knopf), and *Better Than Store-Bought* by Helen Witty and Elizabeth Schneider Colchie (Harper & Row).

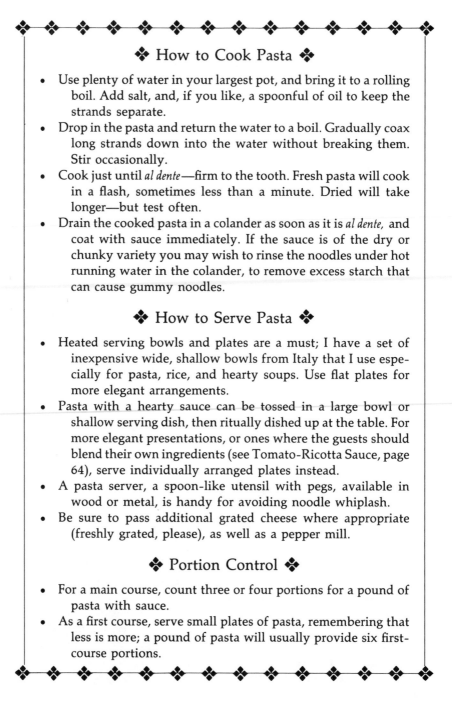

❖ How to Cook Pasta ❖

- Use plenty of water in your largest pot, and bring it to a rolling boil. Add salt, and, if you like, a spoonful of oil to keep the strands separate.
- Drop in the pasta and return the water to a boil. Gradually coax long strands down into the water without breaking them. Stir occasionally.
- Cook just until *al dente*—firm to the tooth. Fresh pasta will cook in a flash, sometimes less than a minute. Dried will take longer—but test often.
- Drain the cooked pasta in a colander as soon as it is *al dente,* and coat with sauce immediately. If the sauce is of the dry or chunky variety you may wish to rinse the noodles under hot running water in the colander, to remove excess starch that can cause gummy noodles.

❖ How to Serve Pasta ❖

- Heated serving bowls and plates are a must; I have a set of inexpensive wide, shallow bowls from Italy that I use especially for pasta, rice, and hearty soups. Use flat plates for more elegant arrangements.
- Pasta with a hearty sauce can be tossed in a large bowl or shallow serving dish, then ritually dished up at the table. For more elegant presentations, or ones where the guests should blend their own ingredients (see Tomato-Ricotta Sauce, page 64), serve individually arranged plates instead.
- A pasta server, a spoon-like utensil with pegs, available in wood or metal, is handy for avoiding noodle whiplash.
- Be sure to pass additional grated cheese where appropriate (freshly grated, please), as well as a pepper mill.

❖ Portion Control ❖

- For a main course, count three or four portions for a pound of pasta with sauce.
- As a first course, serve small plates of pasta, remembering that less is more; a pound of pasta will usually provide six first-course portions.

QUICKLY SAUCED PASTA DISHES

PASTA WITH BUTTER AND FRESHLY GRATED CHEESE

The easiest and one of the most satisfying treatments. Be sure to use only very freshly grated Parmesan cheese, or a blend of Parmesan and Romano.

Serves 4

1 pound fettuccine or tagliatelle, or other pasta
Salt
6 Tablespoons unsalted butter, cut into bits

Freshly grated Parmesan cheese
Freshly ground white or black pepper

1. Cook pasta in large pot of boiling salted water until just *al dente.* Drain well.
2. Place pasta in warmed serving bowl with butter. Sprinkle generously with Parmesan. Toss everything together, lifting gently, until blended. Top with additional cheese and pepper. Serve immediately.

PASTA WITH GARLIC AND HERBS

Try adding 2 Tablespoons drained capers with the herb for a sharper flavor.
Serves 4

1 pound linguine or spaghetti	½ cup shredded fresh basil, sage,
Salt	or parsley, or a combination
⅓ cup olive oil	Freshly grated Parmesan cheese
4 to 6 cloves garlic, minced	

1. Cook pasta in large pot of boiling salted water until just *al dente.* Drain well.
2. While pasta is cooking, heat olive oil in skillet over medium heat until rippling. Add garlic. Sauté until lightly golden, about 4 minutes. Add herbs; toss for a moment.
3. Pour sauce over pasta in warmed serving bowl or platter; add a bit more oil if dry. Sprinkle with cheese.

PASTA WITH ARTICHOKE AND WALNUT SAUCE WITH FRESH HERBS

A delicious topping, sautéed in minutes. With a bit more lemon juice, this pasta can also be enjoyed at room temperature as a pasta salad, or on a picnic. Try to use green noodles with this sauce, or the combination of green and egg noodles called *paglia e fieno* ("straw and hay").
Serves 4

Salt

¼ cup olive oil, plus more as needed

1 package (9 ounces) frozen artichoke hearts, thawed, each half cut into 2 pieces, wiped dry with paper towels

1 pound green fettuccine or linguine

3 cloves garlic, minced

1 cup walnuts, coarsely crumbled

1 ½ to 2 cups fresh basil leaves, wiped clean with paper towels, cut into chiffonade

½ cup chopped fresh parsley

Freshly ground black pepper

Freshly grated Parmesan cheese

1. Bring large pot of water to boil; add salt.
2. Heat olive oil in large skillet over medium heat until rippling. Add artichoke hearts; sauté, tossing occasionally, until lightly golden, about 5 minutes.
3. Cook pasta until just *al dente.*
4. Meanwhile, add garlic and walnuts to skillet; toss until walnuts are lightly toasted, 3 to 4 minutes.
5. Add basil, parsley, salt and pepper; toss to heat through.
6. Drain pasta. Toss pasta in warmed serving bowl with small amount of oil to coat. Top with artichoke mixture. Sprinkle with small amount of Parmesan. Pass additional cheese and pepper.

PASTA WITH CREAM AND CHEESE

This "Alfredo" without eggs or flour is a suave blend of butter, cream, and grated cheese, which melts together as it reduces and thickens. Consider this a basic recipe, one that welcomes the addition of many other ingredients.

Cooking Tip: Try sautéing a clove of garlic, minced, in the butter before adding the drained pasta.

Serves 4 to 6

Salt

1 pound fettuccine or other flat
noodles (green, white, or a
combination)

4 Tablespoons unsalted butter

1 ½ cups heavy cream

¾ cup milk, plus more if needed

¾ to 1 cup freshly grated
Parmesan cheese, plus more for
topping

Freshly ground black pepper

1. Cook pasta in boiling salted water until *al dente*. Drain.

2. In same pot, melt butter over medium heat. Add pasta; toss. Add cream, milk, and cheese. Toss until cheese melts and sauce boils for a minute or so. If too thick, add a splash of milk. If too thin to coat the noodles, even after boiling, add a bit more cheese.

3. Season with salt and pepper. Serve immediately. Pass Parmesan and pepper mill.

Variations

Pasta with Vegetables and Cream: Add 1½ to 2 cups cut-up cooked broccoli, asparagus, or zucchini once the sauce has thickened. A bit more cream and cheese may be needed.

Pasta with Cream, Prosciutto, Mushrooms, and Peas (Pasta della nonna, *or "Grandma style"*): Substitute tortellini, meat-filled rings, for fettuccine. Add ¾ cup each cooked fresh peas and sautéed mushroom slices, and ½ to ⅔ cup slivered prosciutto when the cream sauce has barely thickened. Alternatively, sauté partially thawed frozen peas in the butter before adding the drained pasta; then proceed as above.

Pasta with Cream, Fresh Basil, and Tomatoes: Sauté 3 ripe tomatoes, peeled, seeded, and coarsely chopped, in 1 Tablespoon each of olive oil and butter. Reserve. Toss pasta with butter, cream, milk, and cheese as above. Toss in 1 large bunch shredded fresh basil, 1 to 1½ cups, at the end. Serve with the reserved tomatoes and a little extra basil sprinkled over the top.

PASTA QUATTRO STAGGIONI (PASTA WITH VEGETABLES, PINE NUTS, AND CREAM)

A few years back, Jean Vergnes, chef at New York's Le Cirque restaurant, had Manhattanites clamoring for his Spaghetti Primavera, a colorful and inspired blend of pasta, fresh vegetables, cream, and toasted pine nuts. You can toss this type of dish together with whatever fresh produce is available. This version was developed with vegetables available nearly year-round; hence the name—four seasons.

Serves 4 to 6

Salt

1 ½ to 2 cups broccoli flowerets

3 carrots, trimmed, peeled, quartered lengthwise, cut into 1 ¼-inch lengths

1 small zucchini, trimmed, cut into 1 ¼-inch lengths, each piece halved lengthwise, then laid flat side down and sliced lengthwise into ¼-inch-thick strips

1 long slender yellow squash, cut in same manner as zucchini

1 or 2 red peppers, cored, seeded, cut into thin strips

1 green pepper, cored, seeded, cut into thin strips

1 pound thin flat noodles, such as linguine, tagliarini, preferably fresh green and white mixed

4 Tablespoons unsalted butter

1 cup sliced mushrooms (about 3 ounces)

2 cloves garlic, minced

2 cups heavy cream, or substitute Chicken Broth (page 6) for small part of cream

1 ¼ cups milk, or more as needed

1 ½ to 2 cups freshly grated Parmesan cheese, or a mixture of Parmesan and Romano, plus more for garnish

Freshly ground black pepper

½ cup chopped fresh parsley

2 Tablespoons olive oil

3 plum tomatoes, seeded, cut into long slivers, or 1 can (14 ounces) imported plum tomatoes, drained, cut in long slivers

¼ cup shredded fresh basil (optional; do not substitute dried)

½ cup toasted pine nuts, or coarsely crumbled walnuts

1. Bring large pot of water to boil; add salt. Add broccoli and carrots. Return to boil, stirring; boil 20 seconds. Add zucchini, squash, red and

green peppers; return to boil, stirring. Immediately drain in colander. Rinse under cold water until cool; pat dry on paper-towel-lined platter. Set aside.

2. In large heavy pot, cook pasta in boiling salted water until not quite *al dente*. Drain; rinse very briefly with hot water. Set pasta aside.

3. In same pot, heat butter over medium-high heat. When foam subsides, add mushrooms. Sauté 3 minutes. Add garlic; sauté 2 minutes. Add drained pasta, cream, milk, and cheese. Toss gently, lifting, until smooth and boiling. If sauce is too thick, add splash of milk; if too thin, even after boiling, add a bit more cheese.

4. Lower heat slightly. Add reserved vegetables, salt and pepper to taste, and half of the parsley; toss until heated through. Arrange on warmed wide serving dish.

5. While the vegetables are heating, heat olive oil in small skillet over high heat until fragrant. Add tomato strips; toss over high heat until hot, about 2 minutes. Add salt and pepper. Scatter tomatoes and optional basil over center of pasta. Sprinkle with pine nuts and remaining chopped parsley. Serve immediately, passing extra Parmesan and pepper mill.

PASTA WITH FOUR-CHEESE SAUCE

Quattro Formaggi on an Italian menu heralds a combination of cheeses at once unctuously smooth and wickedly pungent. This easy version, with a sauce prepared separately, then tossed with flat noodles, is based on a recipe of Andy Frisari, an Italian cook working in New York. Serves 4

Salt
3 Tablespoons unsalted butter
1 cup grated Fontina cheese
1 cup freshly grated Parmesan
  cheese
¾ cup ricotta cheese
¼ cup crumbled Gorgonzola cheese

2 Tablespoons milk
⅓ to ½ cup heavy cream
Splash of brandy (optional)
Freshly ground black pepper
1 pound fettuccine or other flat
  noodles

58

1. Heat large pot of water to boiling; add salt.
2. Melt butter in saucepan over low heat. When foam subsides, add cheeses. Heat gently, stirring with wooden spoon, until just melted. Stir in milk, and enough cream for medium consistency. Add optional brandy, salt, if needed, and pepper.
3. While stirring sauce, cook pasta in boiling water until *al dente.* Drain; place in warmed pasta bowls. Pour sauce over. Serve immediately.

PASTA WITH SAUSAGE AND WILD MUSHROOM SAUCE

A rich, robust dish prepared in just minutes.
Serves 4

*1 ounce dried mushrooms, such as
   porcini, cèpes, morels**
Warm water
2 Tablespoons olive oil
1 medium onion, chopped
*¾ pound sweet Italian sausage,
   casings removed, meat crumbled*
Salt
Freshly ground black pepper
Pinch dried thyme

4 cloves garlic, minced
Pinch freshly grated nutmeg
2 Tablespoons dry white wine
*1 can (14 or 17 ounces) imported
   whole plum tomatoes, drained*
½ cup heavy cream
⅓ cup chopped fresh parsley
*1 pound short pasta, such as
   shells, ziti, penne, fusilli*
Freshly grated Parmesan cheese

1. Soak mushrooms in warm water to cover until soft, 15 to 20 minutes.
2. Heat oil in large skillet over medium heat until rippling. Add onion; sauté until softened, about 6 minutes. Add sausage meat; sauté, breaking up meat with wooden spoon, until meat loses raw look, about 6 minutes. Season with salt, pepper, and thyme.
3. Heat large pot of water to boiling; add salt.
4. Meanwhile, drain mushrooms, reserving soaking liquid. Rinse mushrooms in sieve under cold water. Remove tough stems. Dry mushrooms

*Mail-order source: H. Roth and Son, 1577 First Avenue, New York, N.Y. 10028 (212-734-1110)

with paper towels. Coarsely chop. Strain soaking liquid over small bowl through sieve lined with dampened paper towel or coffee filter. Reserve liquid. Add mushrooms, garlic, and nutmeg to skillet. Toss 2 minutes. Drain off any excess oil.

5. Add wine to skillet; boil until nearly dry. Add mushroom liquid and tomatoes, scraping up any browned bits from bottom and sides of skillet and breaking up tomatoes. Reduce until thickened, 5 to 8 minutes. Add cream; reduce slightly. Correct seasonings. Stir in parsley.

6. Boil pasta until just *al dente;* drain well. Pour sauce over pasta in heated serving bowl; pass Parmesan and pepper mill.

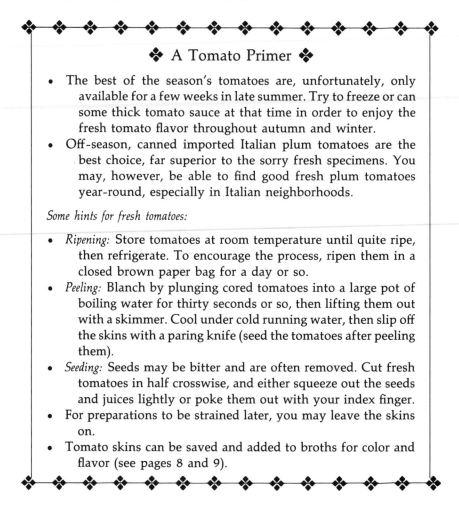

❖ A Tomato Primer ❖

- The best of the season's tomatoes are, unfortunately, only available for a few weeks in late summer. Try to freeze or can some thick tomato sauce at that time in order to enjoy the fresh tomato flavor throughout autumn and winter.
- Off-season, canned imported Italian plum tomatoes are the best choice, far superior to the sorry fresh specimens. You may, however, be able to find good fresh plum tomatoes year-round, especially in Italian neighborhoods.

Some hints for fresh tomatoes:

- *Ripening:* Store tomatoes at room temperature until quite ripe, then refrigerate. To encourage the process, ripen them in a closed brown paper bag for a day or so.
- *Peeling:* Blanch by plunging cored tomatoes into a large pot of boiling water for thirty seconds or so, then lifting them out with a skimmer. Cool under cold running water, then slip off the skins with a paring knife (seed the tomatoes after peeling them).
- *Seeding:* Seeds may be bitter and are often removed. Cut fresh tomatoes in half crosswise, and either squeeze out the seeds and juices lightly or poke them out with your index finger.
- For preparations to be strained later, you may leave the skins on.
- Tomato skins can be saved and added to broths for color and flavor (see pages 8 and 9).

BASIC CHUNKY TOMATO SAUCE

Freeze some of this rich but simple sauce when summer's tomatoes are in plentiful supply, or try in the winter with imported canned plum tomatoes. Consider this a basic recipe to which nearly anything can be added: capers, olives, diced ham, tiny sautéed sausage meatballs, or clams steamed open in the simmering sauce in a covered saucepan. Makes about 2½ cups

1 Tablespoon unsalted butter

1 Tablespoon olive oil

1 medium onion, coarsely chopped

2 to 3 cloves garlic, minced

2¾ to 3 pounds fresh tomatoes, peeled, seeded, coarsely chopped, or 2 cans (1 pound, 12 ounces or 2 pounds, 3 ounces each) imported whole peeled plum tomatoes, drained, seeded, coarsely chopped

1 teaspoon salt

½ teaspoon sugar, if needed

¼ cup shredded basil leaves, or ½ teaspoon dried basil, crumbled

1 bay leaf

Pinch dried thyme or oregano (optional)

Freshly ground black pepper

2 Tablespoons chopped fresh parsley

1. Heat butter and oil in heavy saucepan over medium heat. When foam subsides, add onion. Sauté until wilted, 4 to 5 minutes. Add garlic; sauté 2 minutes.

2. Add tomatoes, salt, sugar if tomatoes are acid, 2 Tablespoons of the fresh basil or ½ teaspoon dried, bay leaf, and optional thyme or oregano. Boil, uncovered, over medium-high heat until liquid has reduced to thick purée and binds chunks of tomato, 10 to 20 minutes. Stir often to prevent scorching. Remove bay leaf.

3. Just before serving, add pepper, salt if needed, parsley, and the remaining 2 Tablespoons fresh basil.

UNCOOKED TOMATO SAUCE FOR PASTA

An old Italian idea, newly rediscovered, often referred to as pasta *al santo* or *alla carretera*. Use only the season's reddest, ripest specimens for this special treat.
Serves 4

SAUCE:

4 to 5 ripe tomatoes (about 1 ½ pounds)

2 teaspoons salt

½ teaspoon freshly ground black pepper

⅓ cup olive oil, plus more if needed

2 Tablespoons finely chopped red or yellow onion, or scallions (optional)

2 or 3 cloves garlic, sliced very thin

½ cup shredded fresh basil or parsley, or more

1 pound spaghetti, vermicelli, or capelli d'angeli (angel hair)

Splash good wine vinegar or fresh lemon juice, if needed

1. Core tomatoes. Halve crosswise; seed. Cut into even ½-inch dice with serrated knife. You should have 3 to 4 cups. Place in bowl with any exuded juices.
2. Add salt, pepper, and oil; toss. Add optional onion, garlic, and basil or parsley. Toss gently, adding oil if dry. Cover with plastic wrap. Let sit 1 to 2 hours at room temperature, or refrigerate, if longer. Bring to room temperature before serving. Toss occasionally.
3. Cook pasta in large pot of boiling salted water until *al dente*. Drain. Place in large warmed serving bowl.
4. Pour off excess liquid from tomatoes, reserving for salad dressing. Correct seasoning. Add vinegar or lemon juice if tomatoes are not acid enough. Toss with hot pasta. Add more basil or parsley to taste.

PASTA WITH UNCOOKED TOMATOES AND MOZZARELLA

Inspired by Vincenzo Buonassisi, the Italian food authority whose book *Pasta* (Lyceum Books) contains a wealth of ideas for pasta dishes. This dish is a play of hot noodles, a cool chunky tomato sauce, and barely melted cheese.

Serves 4 to 6

1 pound ripe tomatoes
½ cup olive oil
¼ cup fresh basil leaves, coarsely chopped; or 2 teaspoons dried basil, crumbled, plus 3 Tablespoons chopped fresh parsley
½ cup oil-cured black olives, pitted, cut into thin slivers

¼ cup freshly grated Parmesan cheese
Salt
Freshly ground black pepper
8 ounces mozzarella cheese, in 1 piece
1 pound pasta, such as conchiglie, shells, or linguine

1. Core tomatoes. Halve lengthwise; seed. Cut into ¼-inch strips. In medium bowl toss tomatoes with oil. Add basil, olives, Parmesan, and salt and pepper; toss. Cover. Marinate, refrigerated, 2 hours or more.
2. Just before serving, cut mozzarella into ⅜-inch cubes. Place in large serving bowl.
3. Cook pasta in large pot of boiling salted water until *al dente*. Drain. Add to mozzarella; toss to lightly melt cheese. Add marinated tomato mixture. Toss everything together. Serve immediately.

PASTA WITH TOMATO-RICOTTA SAUCE

Brightly colored red, white, and green, this treatment is best arranged on individual plates or in individual bowls so each guest can blend his or her own portion. If you already have tomato sauce on hand, this dish can be prepared in about the time required to boil the noodles. Served with a crisp green salad, it makes a festive supper for three or four close friends.

Serves 3 to 4

2 cups Basic Chunky Tomato
Sauce (page 61)
1 container (15 ounces) ricotta
cheese, at room temperature
¾ teaspoon salt
Freshly ground black pepper
¼ teaspoon freshly grated nutmeg,
or more to taste

1 pound wide noodles, such as
green tagliatelle or fettuccine
3 Tablespoons unsalted butter
1 ½ to 2 cups thickly sliced
mushrooms (5 to 6 ounces)
2 Tablespoons chopped fresh basil
or parsley
Freshly grated Parmesan cheese

1. Heat tomato sauce in medium saucepan over medium heat, stirring occasionally. Keep warm.
2. Beat ricotta, salt, pepper, and nutmeg with wooden spoon until fluffy. Add more seasonings if needed. Reserve.
3. Cook noodles in large pot of boiling salted water until just *al dente.* Drain. Rinse quickly under hot water. Drain. While noodles are cooking, heat butter in large skillet over medium heat. When foam subsides, add mushrooms. Sauté until lightly browned, 3 to 4 minutes. Remove from heat.
4. Divide pasta among individual warmed serving bowls. Ladle tomato sauce, dividing evenly, over center of each portion of noodles. Gently spoon ricotta mixture into center of sauce. Scatter mushrooms, dividing evenly, over ricotta. Sprinkle with basil or parsley.
5. Serve immediately. Pass cheese and pepper mill.

PASTA WITH TOMATO, MUSHROOM, AND ANCHOVY SAUCE

A pungent sauce that is welcome in cold weather. This works well with imported canned plum tomatoes.
Serves 4

2 to 3 Tablespoons olive oil	½ teaspoon dried oregano,
1 medium onion, coarsely chopped	crumbled, or more to taste
2 or 3 cloves garlic, minced	1 tin anchovy fillets (2 ounces),
¾ to 1 pound medium mushrooms,	drained, coarsely chopped
quartered	2 Tablespoons capers, drained
3 Tablespoons dry white wine	Freshly ground black pepper
1 can (2 pounds, 3 ounces)	1 pound green fettuccine
imported whole peeled tomatoes,	¼ cup chopped fresh parsley, or
drained, liquid reserved, coarsely	more to taste
chopped	Freshly grated Parmesan cheese
Salt	

1. Heat oil in large skillet over medium heat until rippling. Add onion; sauté until wilted, 4 to 5 minutes. Add garlic; sauté 2 minutes. Add mushrooms; toss to coat. Sauté until lightly golden, 2 to 3 minutes.
2. Add wine, scraping up any browned bits from bottom and sides of skillet. Reduce 1 to 2 minutes.
3. Add drained tomatoes and half the reserved tomato liquid. Cook over medium-high heat, stirring to prevent scorching, until sauce thickens, 10 to 15 minutes. If sauce becomes too thick, add a little more reserved tomato liquid.
4. Meanwhile, heat large pot of water to boiling; add salt.
5. Add oregano and anchovies to skillet. Cook 2 minutes. Add capers, salt, if needed, and pepper. Simmer gently.
6. Cook pasta in boiling salted water until just *al dente*. Drain well. Arrange pasta in four warmed individual pasta bowls. Stir parsley into sauce. Spoon sauce over pasta. Pass Parmesan and a pepper mill.

BAKED PASTA GRATINS

A short sampler of hearty baked items, which require a bit more time but are well worth the effort, especially for entertaining.

GRATIN OF PASTA WITH TOMATOES, HAM, AND CHEESE

A quick noodle-and-cheese dish, with a mellow combination of tomatoes and cream.
Serves 6

Salt

2 Tablespoons unsalted butter

1 pound tube-shaped pasta, such as penne, rigatoni, or ziti

2 to 2 ½ cups Basic Chunky Tomato Sauce (page 61)

1 ½ cups heavy cream, or more as needed

3 ounces sliced prosciutto, cut into ½-inch squares

1 to 1 ¼ cups freshly grated Parmesan cheese

3 Tablespoons chopped fresh parsley, plus more for garnish

1. Heat large pot of water to boiling; add salt.
2. Butter 6-to-8-cup gratin dish or other shallow baking dish with 1 Tablespoon of the butter. Cut other Tablespoon of butter into bits; chill.
3. Preheat oven to 400°.
4. Cook pasta in boiling water until barely *al dente,* about 6 minutes. Drain; rinse briefly. Set aside to drain.
5. Stir together about ½ cup tomato sauce and about 3 Tablespoons cream in small bowl; set aside.
6. Drizzle a little tomato sauce in bottom of buttered dish. Arrange an even layer of pasta over bottom of pan. Layer tomato sauce, ham, cream, cheese, and parsley, using one-third of each ingredient. Repeat layering two more times, reserving some pasta and cheese.
7. Arrange an even layer of pasta over top. Pour reserved tomato-cream mixture evenly over all. Sprinkle with reserved cheese and bits of butter. Bake until lightly golden and bubbly, about 30 minutes. For a deeper gratin, briefly place dish under preheated broiler until golden. Sprinkle with chopped parsley. Serve immediately.

SPINACH AND CHEESE LASAGNE

A lightened lasagne, popular with vegetarians, but no less luscious for its lack of meat. The glazed topping, a bright blend of greens, reds, and golds, makes this a spectacular dish for a crowd.
Cooking Tip: If whole sheets of green pasta are unavailable, dried packaged lasagne or sheets of regular egg noodles can be substituted; just keep them all very *al dente*.
Serves 12

FILLING:

- 2 pounds fresh spinach, stemmed, or 2 packages (10 ounces) frozen leaf spinach, thawed
- 1 container (15 ounces) ricotta, pushed through a sieve
- 8 ounces mozzarella, grated
- 2 egg yolks
- ⅓ cup chopped fresh parsley
- 1½ teaspoons salt, plus more for spinach
- ½ teaspoon freshly ground black pepper, plus more for spinach
- ¼ teaspoon freshly grated nutmeg, plus more for spinach
- 10 Tablespoons unsalted butter
- 2 cups coarsely chopped onion (about 1½ medium onions)
- 5 cloves garlic, minced
- 8 to 10 ounces mushrooms, coarsely chopped or sliced
- 3 Tablespoons dry white wine

PARMESAN CREAM SAUCE:

- 2 cups heavy cream
- 2 cups freshly grated Parmesan cheese
- 2 Tablespoons flour
- ¼ cup milk
- 2 Tablespoons brandy or Cognac

- 2 Tablespoons olive oil
- 2 cans (1 pound, 12 ounces each) imported whole plum tomatoes, drained well; tomatoes halved lengthwise if large
- Salt
- Freshly ground black pepper
- 3 sheets fresh green pasta or substitute 1 package (16 ounces) dried lasagne

1. *Filling:* Wash fresh spinach in several changes of lukewarm water; drain. In large pot, cook spinach covered, over medium-high heat with just the water that clings to the leaves. Stir once or twice. Cook just until wilted, about 4 minutes. Drain. Work in batches if necessary. Rinse spinach under cold water to stop cooking. If using frozen spinach, omit this step.

2. Squeeze all excess moisture from spinach. Coarsely chop; set aside.

3. In large bowl combine sieved ricotta, mozzarella, egg yolks, parsley, salt, pepper, and nutmeg. Beat with wooden spoon until blended and fluffy. Set aside.

4. Heat 2 Tablespoons of the butter in large skillet over medium heat. When foam subsides, add onions. Sauté until wilted, 5 to 6 minutes. Add garlic; sauté 2 minutes. Transfer onion mixture to bowl with ricotta mixture.

5. Heat 3 Tablespoons of the butter in same skillet over high heat. When foam subsides, add spinach. Season with salt, pepper, and nutmeg. Toss over high heat until dry, 4 to 5 minutes. Add to bowl with ricotta mixture.

6. Heat 3 Tablespoons butter in same skillet over medium heat. When foam subsides, add mushrooms. Sauté until light golden, 2 to 3 minutes. Add wine; stir until moisture has evaporated. Add mushroom mixture to bowl. Mix to make sure all ingredients are evenly distributed. Set aside.

7. *Parmesan Cream Sauce:* Boil cream gently in heavy saucepan over medium heat, 5 minutes. Add Parmesan, reserving about 3 Tablespoons. In small bowl whisk together flour and milk until smooth. Strain into sauce. Cook over medium heat until cheese has melted and sauce has thickened slightly. Add brandy; simmer 1 minute. Set aside, with waxed paper laid directly on surface of sauce.

8. Heat oil in skillet over medium heat until rippling. Add tomatoes; toss without breaking until slightly dried out, about 3 minutes. Transfer to plate. Season with salt and pepper. Reserve.

9. Heat large pan of water to boiling. Add salt. (A roasting pan set over two burners works well for this.) Gently boil sheets of pasta until *al dente.* If using fresh pasta, this will take about 30 seconds. Carefully drain pasta with 2 large slotted spatulas. Gently pat dry with paper towels.

10. *Assembly:* Butter a 14 × 10 × 2½-inch baking dish with 1 Tablespoon of the butter. Preheat oven to 400°.

11. Dribble a little of the cream sauce in bottom of pan. Lay sheet of pasta over; allow edge of sheet to go up sides of pan and overhang. Correct seasonings in filling mixture. Carefully spoon half the filling

evenly over pasta. Arrange half the tomatoes over the filling; top with about one-third of the cream sauce. Lay second sheet of pasta over; top with remaining filling and the second one-third of the sauce. Lay third pasta sheet over. Trim edges of top sheet to fit pan. Trim overhanging edges of bottom two layers, leaving a ¾-inch border. Fold border over onto top sheet. Top with remaining tomatoes, sauce, and the reserved 3 Tablespoons Parmesan. Dot with the remaining 1 Tablespoon butter cut into bits.

12. Bake 40 to 45 minutes, or until golden. Let sit 10 minutes before cutting into squares.

Variation

Canneloni with Spinach, Mushrooms, and Two Sauces: Prepare half quantities of the filling, the Basic Chunky Tomato Sauce (page 61), and Parmesan Cream Sauce in the Spinach and Cheese Lasagne. Cut two sheets of fresh green pasta dough into 4 × 4-inch squares. (Egg noodle or commercial canneloni dough can be substituted.) Blanch dough just until softened. Drain and pat dry. Roll each square neatly around several Tablespoons of filling. Arrange rolls in buttered shallow baking dish. Top with alternating rows of tomato sauce and Parmesan Cream Sauce. Sprinkle 2 Tablespoons Parmesan cheese and a few bits of butter over the top. Bake in preheated 375° oven until golden brown and bubbly, about 30 minutes. Let sit a few minutes before serving two canneloni to each person.

RICE

Perfectly cooked rice is often the mark of a fine cook. Use any of these methods for fluffy rice with firm, separate grains.

BOILED RICE IN MUCH WATER

A good method when separate grains are important, as for a rice salad or stuffing. No measuring is involved.

Cold water
Salt

Long-grain white rice

1. Fill large pot, at least 4 to 6 quarts, with water. Add about 1 teaspoon salt, or more as needed. Cover. Heat to boiling.
2. Scatter in rice (about 1½ cups makes 4 cups cooked rice). Stir until water boils again. Boil vigorously, uncovered, 12 minutes or until just tender.
3. Drain through sieve. Rinse briefly under hot water.

CHINESE-STYLE FRIED RICE

Here is another technique that transforms a few leftover bits to quick and delicious advantage. Remember this easy recipe whenever you find leftover meats, fish, or vegetables on hand. Try substituting soy sauce to taste for salt.
Serves 4

1 Tablespoon sesame seeds
3 Tablespoons peanut oil, plus more if needed
2 cloves garlic, finely minced
2 to 3 teaspoons finely minced peeled fresh ginger
½ cup sliced mushrooms
½ red or green pepper, cored, seeded, cut into thin strips
1 ½ cups cooked shredded meat or seafood

1 teaspoon salt
3 cups cooked white rice
2 eggs
3 Tablespoons thin diagonal slices scallions, both green and white parts
Pinch dried red pepper flakes (optional)

1. Heat small dry skillet over medium heat. Add sesame seeds. Toast, stirring occasionally, until light gold, 2 to 3 minutes. Reserve.

2. Heat oil in large skillet or wok over medium-high heat. Add garlic and ginger; toss until fragrant, 30 seconds. Add mushrooms and pepper; toss 1 minute. Add shredded meat and salt; toss until heated through, about 2 minutes. Add rice; toss until heated through, adding oil if pan is dry.

3. Break eggs into center of pan. Immediately stir to combine. Toss with rice until eggs have scrambled lightly. Remove pan from heat before egg is completely dry.

4. Add scallion, sesame seeds (reserving 1 teaspoon for garnish), and optional dried red pepper flakes. Correct seasonings. Serve hot from pan or large platter. Scatter reserved sesame seeds over top.

RICE PILAFS

Probably Turkish in origin, the word pilaf can be found in numerous alternate spellings: *pilav, pilaw, pilaff,* and *pullao,* among others. This technique, which produces perfect, tender grains full of flavor, is characterized by two simple steps: (a) rice is first sautéed in butter or oil; and (b) then cooked in a relatively small amount of liquid, usually a flavorful broth, just until the liquid is absorbed.

BASIC METHOD FOR PILAF

Serves 4 to 6 (about 4 cups cooked rice)

2 ¼ cups Chicken Broth (page 6)
or water
2 Tablespoons unsalted butter
3 Tablespoons chopped onion
1 ½ cups long-grain white rice

¼ cup dry white wine
½ teaspoon salt
Freshly ground black pepper
1 to 2 Tablespoons chopped fresh
parsley (optional)

1. Heat broth or water to boiling in covered pan.
2. Meanwhile, heat 1 Tablespoon of the butter in saucepan over medium heat. Add onion; sauté until onion begins to wilt, about 2 minutes. Add rice; stir to coat. Cook, stirring, until grains begin to turn translucent, 2 to 3 minutes. Add wine; stir. Cook until nearly dry, 2 to 3 minutes. Stir in hot liquid and salt. Heat to boiling. Lower heat to lowest possible setting. Stir rice with fork. Cook, partially covered, until liquid has been absorbed and rice is tender, about 17 minutes. If after 15 minutes rice is tender but liquid still surrounds rice, continue to cook uncovered. If rice is not yet tender but the liquid has been absorbed, add a bit more water or broth, and cook, covered, until tender.
3. Off heat, add remaining 1 Tablespoon butter, pepper, and optional parsley. Fluff rice with fork. Serve immediately.

Variation

Simple Vegetable-Scented Pilaf: This pilaf is excellent with a sauced dish or stew; the rice allows you to catch every last drop of the juices. Try different combinations of diced vegetables and other liquids, such as Fish Broth (page 11) when the pilaf is to be served with a fish dish.

Sauté 1 minced garlic clove, 1 rib celery, 1 or 2 carrots, finely diced, and ¼ cup diced mushroom trimmings with the onion in step 2 of Basic Method for Pilaf (above). Add parsley and other fresh herbs at end.

PILAF WITH LEFTOVER MEATS AND VEGETABLES

A wonderful main dish, which extends a few bits of leftover meat into a meal for a small crowd. This is a basic recipe; experiment with your own blend of ingredients. Diced cooked seafood can be substituted for the meat.

Cooking Tip: A small pinch of saffron added to the broth is a pleasant addition.

Serves 4 to 6

6 Tablespoons plus 1 Tablespoon
(optional) unsalted butter

1 large onion, coarsely chopped

2 cloves garlic, minced

3 carrots, trimmed, peeled, halved
lengthwise, thickly sliced

2 ribs celery, trimmed, halved
lengthwise, thickly sliced

Other vegetables, such as diced
zucchini, peppers, scallions,
broccoli, or peas, raw or cooked
(optional)

1 ½ cups long-grain white rice

¼ cup dry white wine

2 ¼ cups Chicken Broth (page 6),
or mixture of broth and water

1 teaspoon salt

⅓ cup slivered almonds (1 ½ ounces)

1 ½ cups sliced mushrooms (5
ounces)

1 to 2 cups cooked meat, such as leftover lamb, chicken, beef, ham, seafood, or a combination, cut into
bite-size pieces

¼ cup chopped fresh parsley or other
herbs

Freshly ground black pepper

Juice of ½ lemon, or more

1 ripe tomato, cored, halved lengthwise, seeded, cut into strips or
wedges (optional)

1. Heat 2 Tablespoons of the butter in large saucepan over medium heat. When foam subsides, add onion; toss to coat. Sauté, stirring occasionally, until slightly wilted, about 3 minutes. Add garlic, carrots, celery, and other vegetables (if cooked leftovers, add at the end); toss 2 minutes. Add rice; toss until slightly translucent, 2 to 3 minutes. Stir in wine; reduce slightly, tossing occasionally, about 2 minutes. Stir in broth and salt. Cover pan. Increase heat; heat to boiling. Lower heat to bare simmer. Simmer, leaving pot lid slightly ajar, 17 minutes, or until liquid is nearly absorbed.

2. Meanwhile, heat 1 Tablespoon of the butter in large skillet over medium heat. Add almonds; sauté, stirring almost constantly, until almonds are light gold, about 4 minutes. Be careful not to burn the almonds. Drain on paper towel; reserve.

3. Heat another 2 Tablespoons of the butter in skillet over high heat. When foam subsides, add mushrooms; toss until slightly wilted, about 2 minutes. Add meat. Sauté briefly while the rice is cooking. Sprinkle with parsley and pepper. Reserve.

4. When rice has cooked through, add 1 Tablespoon of the butter and pepper. Stir gently. Add lemon juice; correct seasonings. Spoon rice into warmed shallow serving dish or platter. Top with mushroom-meat mixture, scattering over rice. Sprinkle almonds over center.

5. Heat tomato strips in skillet, adding the optional 1 Tablespoon of butter if needed; do not cook the tomato. Arrange strips around edges of dish. Serve hot.

RISOTTO

The perfect risotto has firm, separate grains, bathed in a creamy liquid. For best results, use the small round-grained Arborio rice, available in specialty shops, in Italian markets, and by mail from Manganaro Foods, 488 Ninth Avenue, New York, N.Y. 10018 (212-563-5331).

BASIC TECHNIQUE FOR RISOTTO

Once a risotto begins to cook, you must stay with it, and serve it at once when done. The additions of small amounts of simmering broth, which evaporate and are absorbed quickly, result in the distinctive risotto texture. The amount of broth needed will vary depending on several factors; pot size, heat, evaporation rate, quality of rice. When you feel comfortable with this technique, try adding fresh peas, mushrooms, saffron and beef marrow, zucchini, asparagus, broccoli, mixed seafood, or whatever. Ingredients that can withstand 20 minutes or so of cooking can be sautéed in the same pan before the rice and left in; those ingredients that would overcook are best added at the end, usually precooked separately.
Serves 6

1 pound Arborio rice (about 2 cups)
6 to 8 cups Chicken Broth (page 6) or Mixed Meat and Poultry Broth (page 8), or a combination
3 Tablespoons unsalted butter

½ small onion, chopped
¾ to 1 cup freshly grated Parmesan cheese, plus more for garnish
Salt
Freshly ground black pepper

1. Remove any dark grains from the rice. Heat broth to boiling. Adjust heat to maintain steady simmer. Cover if not used immediately.
2. In heavy medium saucepan, melt 2 Tablespoons of the butter over medium-high heat. When foam subsides, add onion. Sauté until onion begins to wilt, about 3 minutes. Add rice, stir with a wooden fork until

grains are coated with butter and begin to turn translucent, about 3 minutes.

3. Add ladleful or about ¾ cup broth to rice; broth should just cover rice. Lower heat to medium; broth should simmer as soon as it is added to rice, but not boil away immediately. Stir constantly. When liquid is almost but not quite evaporated, 4 to 5 minutes, add enough broth to just cover rice, another ¾ cup or so; continue to stir. Repeat simmering process, adding enough liquid to just cover rice each time the mixture has become nearly dry. Adjust heat as you go to maintain simmer.

4. After 20 to 25 minutes, most of the broth should have been added. Test rice; it should be nearly tender, with a firm center. Add most of the cheese, reserving some for later. Add another ladleful of broth. Continue to cook, stirring, until rice is *al dente*, slightly firm but not hard. There should be creamy "sauce" between the grains. Add a bit more liquid if needed; use water if all the broth has been used.

5. Add the remaining Tablespoon butter, and salt and pepper to taste. Sprinkle cheese on top. Serve at once. Pass additional cheese and pepper mill.

Variation

Risotto-Stuffed Tomatoes: See page 103.

RISOTTO WITH WILD MUSHROOMS

The dried mushrooms impart their rich woodsy flavor to this risotto.
Serves 6

*1 ounce dried mushrooms (about 1
cup), such as porcini, cèpes,
morels**

*2 cups warm water, or more as
needed*

*1 pound Arborio rice (about 2
cups)*

*4 to 6 cups Chicken Broth (page
6) or Mixed Meat and Poultry
Broth (page 8)*

5 Tablespoons unsalted butter

1 Tablespoon olive oil

*1 ½ cups sliced fresh mushrooms
(5 ounces)*

*2 Tablespoons chopped onion or
scallions*

*1 cup freshly grated Parmesan
cheese plus more for garnish*

Salt

Freshly ground black pepper

*2 Tablespoons chopped fresh
parsley (optional)*

1. Soak dried mushrooms in the 2 cups warm water or enough to cover,
until softened, 15 to 20 minutes.
2. Remove any dark grains from rice.
3. Drain mushrooms through sieve lined with coffee filter or dampened
paper towel; reserve soaking liquid. Remove and discard tough stems
from mushrooms. Rinse mushrooms in sieve under cold water. Drain on
paper towels. Coarsely chop. Reserve.
4. Heat broth and strained mushroom liquid to boiling. Adjust heat to
maintain steady simmer.
5. Heat 2 Tablespoons of the butter and olive oil in large skillet over
high heat. When foam subsides, add sliced fresh mushrooms. Toss until
lightly golden, 3 to 5 minutes. Reserve.
6. Melt 2 Tablespoons of the butter in large saucepan over medium-high
heat. When foam subsides, add onion. Sauté until wilted, 2 to 3 minutes.
Add chopped dried mushrooms; sauté 1 minute. Add rice; stir with
wooden fork until grains are coated with butter and begin to turn
translucent, about 3 minutes.
7. Add ladleful or about ¾ cup of the simmering broth; liquid should

*Mail-order source: H. Roth and Son, 1577 First Avenue, New York, N.Y. 10028
(212-734-1110).

just cover rice. Lower heat to medium; broth should simmer with rice, and not boil away immediately. Stir constantly. When liquid is almost but not quite evaporated, 4 to 5 minutes, add enough broth to just cover the rice, another ¾ cup or so; continue to stir. Repeat simmering process, adding enough liquid to just cover the rice each time the mixture has become nearly dry. Adjust the heat as you go to maintain a simmer.

8. After 20 to 25 minutes, most of the broth should have been added. Test the rice; it should be nearly tender with a firm center.

9. Add reserved sautéed fresh mushrooms and most of the cheese, reserving some for a final sprinkle. Add another ladleful of broth. Continue to cook, stirring until rice is just *al dente,* slightly firm but not hard. There should be a creamy "sauce" between the grains. Add a bit more liquid if needed; use water if all the broth has been used.

9. Add the remaining Tablespoon of butter, and salt and pepper to taste, and the optional parsley. Sprinkle cheese on top. Serve at once. Pass additional cheese and a pepper mill.

RISOTTO PRIMAVERA

Like its pasta counterpart, this lovely spring dish unites several fresh vegetables, toasted pine nuts, and lots of grated cheese. Use one or all of the green vegetables in this recipe. Plan to serve this dish as a main course, perhaps with a green salad, crusty bread, and a light dessert such as a sorbet or fruit.
Serves 4 to 6

1 cup 2-inch zucchini batons (1 medium zucchini)

4 Tablespoons unsalted butter, plus more if needed

1 cup 2-inch lengths string beans

Salt

¾ cup broccoli flowerets

4 asparagus spears, trimmed, peeled, stalks diagonally cut into 2-inch lengths, tips reserved

5 to 7 cups Chicken Broth (page 6) or Mixed Vegetable Broth (page 8)

2 cups coarsely chopped onions (2 medium onions)

2 cloves garlic, minced

1 ¼ cups 2-inch carrot batons (about 3 carrots)

1 pound Arborio rice (about 2 cups)

½ cup dry white wine

1 cup thickly sliced mushrooms

1 ripe tomato, peeled, seeded, cut into wedges

1 cup freshly grated Parmesan cheese

2 Tablespoons unsalted butter, cut into chunks

¼ cup chopped fresh parsley, plus more for garnish

Freshly ground black pepper

Toasted pine nuts or crumbled toasted walnuts

1. Sauté zucchini batons in 1 Tablespoon unsalted butter in skillet over medium heat until crisp-tender, about 2 minutes. Remove to bowl and reserve.
2. Blanch string beans in large pot boiling salted water until crisp-tender, 3 to 4 minutes. About 1 minute before end of cooking time, add broccoli flowerets and asparagus tips. Drain; rinse under cold water to stop cooking; drain again. Reserve string beans and broccoli with zucchini in bowl; reserve asparagus tips separately.
3. Heat broth to boiling; adjust heat to maintain simmer.

4. Heat 2 Tablespoons of the butter in large skillet over medium heat. When foam subsides, add onion. Sauté until slightly softened, about 3 minutes. Add garlic, carrot batons, and asparagus stalks; sauté another 3 minutes.

5. Add rice and stir until translucent, about 3 minutes. Add the wine and reduce by one-half.

6. Add about ¾ cup of the broth, or enough to just cover the rice. Adjust heat so the broth boils very gently. Stir constantly until the liquid is almost but not quite evaporated, about 4 to 5 minutes. Continue adding more broth until nearly all the broth has been added and the rice is nearly tender, 20 to 25 minutes.

7. While the rice is cooking, sauté the mushrooms in 1 Tablespoon of the butter until very lightly browned, about 2 minutes. Transfer to small bowl. Sauté tomato wedges, adding more butter if necessary, until just heated through, about 2 minutes. Reserve.

8. About 5 minutes before the rice is done, add another ¾ cup of broth, the reserved zucchini, string beans, and broccoli flowerets, ¾ cup of the Parmesan cheese, and the 2 Tablespoons of butter cut into chunks. Add the parsley, and salt and pepper to taste.

9. Mound the cooked risotto, which should be still rather moist, onto a warmed earthenware platter or other serving dish. Arrange blanched asparagus spears and toasted pine nuts over center. Scatter the sautéed mushrooms around the edges and the tomato around the center. Sprinkle the ¼ cup cheese and chopped parsley over all. Serve immediately; pass extra cheese and a pepper mill.

PASTA AND RICE SALADS

Though recently embraced as the latest food rage, salads based on pasta and rice have been around for years. Perfect buffet and party dishes, where they disappear quickly, these cool, hearty salads are also a good choice for warm weather eating.

❖ Basic Considerations for Pasta and Rice Salads ❖

- Keep the pasta and rice quite firm when cooking.
- After cooking and draining, toss the pasta or rice with oil (or for sour cream- or yogurt-based dressings, with a splash of milk) in order to keep the pieces separate.
- Dressings range from light vinaigrettes and oil-and-citrus-juice mixtures to more substantial versions based on home-made mayonnaise, sour cream, yogurt, or *crème fraîche,* often used in combination. Play with different blends for different uses.
- A little chopped scallion, red onion, or shallot always helps.
- Add crunch with diced or sliced raw celery, carrots, peppers, toasted nuts, or blanched vegetables such as green beans, broccoli, asparagus, or sugar-snap peas.
- More substantial ingredients include slivered or diced meat, shellfish, smoked fish or poultry.
- Season assertively with salt and pepper and other seasonings, since pasta will absorb a great deal of flavor.
- Use fresh herbs and a squeeze of fresh lemon juice to give a welcome lift.
- Arrange the salad generously and attractively in a large bowl, garnishing with additional vegetables, wedges of ripe tomatoes, hard-cooked eggs, cucumbers, small oil-cured black olives, more chopped parsley, and other fresh herbs.
- Try serving pasta and rice salads with an assortment of several other salads, such as mixed green salad (page 105), ripe to-mato slices dressed with oil and fresh basil or tarragon, or marinated blanched or steamed vegetables (page 108). Serve with a selection of breads, cheeses, and fruits.

PENNE SALAD WITH FRESH ASPARAGUS

A wonderful way to use the season's first asparagus and tarragon. The quill-shape penne, or ziti or rigatoni, are ideal for this salad, since they catch bits of the vegetables and dressing in their open ends. Other vegetables such as sugar-snap peas, green beans, or zucchini can be substituted.
Serves 8

*1 pound small penne, rigatoni,
    ziti, or other short pasta*
Salt
*6 to 8 ounces fresh asparagus,
    trimmed, peeled, cut diagonally
    into lengths equal to pasta*
*2 or 3 carrots, trimmed, peeled,
    halved lengthwise, thickly sliced*
¼ cup milk
2 ribs celery, cut into large dice
1 medium red onion, finely chopped
*2 red peppers, cored, seeded, cut
    into thin strips 1 ½ inches long*

Freshly ground black pepper
*1 to 1 ½ cups homemade
    mayonnaise (page 123)*
½ to ¾ cup sour cream
Juice of 1 lemon
Pinch cayenne pepper
½ cup chopped fresh parsley
*2 ripe tomatoes, cut into strips or
    wedges*
*2 Tablespoons chopped fresh basil
    or parsley or other fresh herbs*

1. Cook pasta in a large pot of boiling salted water. About 3 minutes before it is done, add asparagus and carrots. When pasta is *al dente,* drain and refresh everything under cold water until cool. Drain well.
2. In large bowl, toss pasta mixture with milk. Add celery, onion, red pepper, and plenty of salt and pepper; toss.
3. In medium bowl, whisk together mayonnaise, sour cream, lemon juice, cayenne, and chopped parsley. Add half the dressing to pasta. Toss; cover and chill. Remove salad from refrigerator 30 minutes before serving. Then add enough dressing to coat ingredients generously. Correct seasonings. Transfer salad to serving bowl. Garnish with tomatoes and chopped herbs.

Variation

Tortellini Salad with Vegetables and Prosciutto: A cold version of the *della nonna* treatment (page 56), with an interesting play of textural contrasts.

Substitute 1 pound tortellini, white or green meat-filled rings, for the penne. Use 1 rib celery instead of 2; use 1 red pepper, chopped, instead of 2. Add ¾ cup slivers or small squares of prosciutto or other ham with celery and onion in step 2. Omit other vegetables. Garnish with one package (10 ounces) frozen peas, partially thawed, tossed in 3 Tablespoons butter in a skillet over high heat until cooked through, about five minutes. Dress as in step 3 above.

PASTA WITH UNCOOKED TOMATOES AND MOZZARELLA

See page 63.

COLD ORIENTAL NOODLES WITH GINGER, SESAME, AND FRESH VEGETABLES

A pungent, strongly flavored treatment that can be featured as a summer main dish or on a buffet.
Serves 6

1 pound wide egg noodles or other
  flat pasta
Salt
2 to 2 ½ Tablespoons oriental
  sesame oil
2 Tablespoons oriental sesame paste
  or smooth peanut butter
¼ cup warm water
½ cup dry sherry
⅓ cup soy sauce (preferably
  Kikkoman)
⅓ cup peanut oil
1 heaping Tablespoon minced
  peeled fresh ginger
1 to 2 teaspoons minced garlic
2 teaspoons sugar
1 teaspoon Chinese rice wine
  vinegar or other white vinegar

1 teaspoon freshly ground black
  pepper
½ teaspoon dried red pepper flakes
  (optional)
3 or 4 scallions, trimmed, both
  green and white parts, thinly
  sliced on diagonal
2 or 3 ribs celery, trimmed, thinly
  sliced on diagonal
1 cup thinly sliced mushroom
  halves (3 ounces)
1 red pepper, cored, seeded, cut into
  thin strips
1 cup shredded cooked meat or
  shrimp (optional)

1. Cook noodles in boiling salted water until *al dente.* Drain; rinse under cold water. Drain again. Toss noodles in large bowl with sesame oil. Cover; reserve.

2. In medium bowl whisk together sesame paste or peanut butter with the warm water until smooth. Stir in sherry, soy sauce, peanut oil, ginger, garlic, sugar, vinegar, black pepper, and pepper flakes. Pour sauce over noodles.

3. Add scallions, reserving some for garnish, celery, mushrooms, red pepper, and optional meat. Toss to combine. Cover; chill.

4. Serve on wide platter. Sprinkle with reserved scallions.

RICE SALAD WITH PEAS, PROSCIUTTO, AND BASIL

Try this salad as stuffing for ripe tomatoes, served hot or cold.
Serves 4 to 6

3 Tablespoons unsalted butter
1 package (10 ounces) frozen small
   peas, partially thawed
1 ¼ cups long-grain white rice
Salt
6 ounces prosciutto, cut into slivers

Freshly ground black pepper
¾ cup olive oil, or as needed
¼ to ½ cup chopped fresh parsley
Minced fresh basil
Juice of 2 lemons

1. Heat butter in large skillet over high heat. When foam subsides, add peas. Toss until heated through, about 5 minutes. Reserve.
2. Cook rice in large pot of boiling salted water until *al dente,* about 12 minutes. Drain. Rinse under hot water. Drain again. You should have about 3 cups of cooked rice.
3. While rice is still warm, combine in large bowl with peas and prosciutto. Season with salt and pepper. Add enough oil to moisten rice. Let mixture stand at room temperature, covered, to allow flavors to blend.
4. Just before serving, mix in herbs and lemon juice. Correct seasonings. Toss well.

VEGETABLES AND SALADS

[On eating a well-prepared salad]
. . . though green turtle fail, though venison's tough,
And ham and turkey are not boiled enough,
Serenely full, the epicure may say,
Fate cannot harm me—I have dined today.

—SYDNEY SMITH, quoted in
Kettner's Book of the Table
(1877) by E. S. Dallas

86

It's time to rethink the roles we allot to vegetables and salads. In the last decade or two, we've seen tremendous growth in our "vegetable consciousness": a wide variety of fresh produce is available to nearly all of us; we aren't exposed to soggy canned peas and carrots quite as ubiquitously as we once were. (I remember the surprise of a woman friend as she ran into me buying fresh green beans at the supermarket. "What do you do with those?" she asked, puzzled. "Oh, I just eat them raw, or blanch or steam them." "That's funny—I never knew you could buy green beans except canned or frozen.")

I am not advocating vegetarian diets per se—I believe in eating *everything* in moderation—but rather, giving more due to fresh vegetables and salads in our meals. Why not dine on a baked potato, perhaps stuffed with ham, cheese, and herbs (see page 104)? Or on a plate of perfectly steamed asparagus or broccoli, with a bit of lemon and butter, served with some bread and cheese? A beautifully composed salad, incorporating neat slivers of last night's chicken and potatoes, is a meal that is not only satisfying but also nutritionally balanced. Many of the recipes in this chapter make ideal first courses or can serve as light supper or lunch main dishes.

However you serve these vegetables and salads, feature them with pride in your menus: beautifully cooked vegetables shouldn't take a back seat to anything else.

VEGETABLES

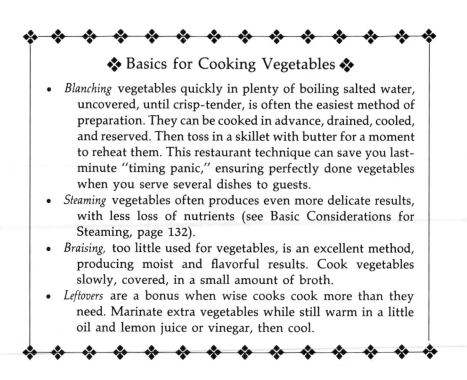

❖ Basics for Cooking Vegetables ❖

- *Blanching* vegetables quickly in plenty of boiling salted water, uncovered, until crisp-tender, is often the easiest method of preparation. They can be cooked in advance, drained, cooled, and reserved. Then toss in a skillet with butter for a moment to reheat them. This restaurant technique can save you last-minute "timing panic," ensuring perfectly done vegetables when you serve several dishes to guests.
- *Steaming* vegetables often produces even more delicate results, with less loss of nutrients (see Basic Considerations for Steaming, page 132).
- *Braising,* too little used for vegetables, is an excellent method, producing moist and flavorful results. Cook vegetables slowly, covered, in a small amount of broth.
- *Leftovers* are a bonus when wise cooks cook more than they need. Marinate extra vegetables while still warm in a little oil and lemon juice or vinegar, then cool.

GRATINS

The golden-brown glaze that characterizes these vegetable dishes makes delicious eating. In his monumental *Guide Culinaire* (1902), Escoffier differentiates types of gratins. In the *complete gratin,* raw foods and a sauce are topped with bread crumbs and butter, and each component of the dish must cook through at the same moment. A *quick* or *light gratin* consists of precooked foods that are lightly covered with a sauce and gratin topping, which browns quickly while the food is simply heated through.

GRATIN OF POTATOES WITH CREAM

The French *gratin dauphinois*, like its American cousin, scalloped potatoes, is an irresistible, if rich, accompaniment to all sorts of plain meat dishes. The authentic version relies on neither cheese nor eggs, which are often included for thickening. This simple recipe is based on the method I learned from Richard Olney.
Serves 6

1 clove garlic, halved	*2 to 2 ½ pounds boiling potatoes,*
1 Tablespoon unsalted butter,	*peeled, cut into ¹⁄₁₆-inch slices*
softened	*Salt*
¾ cup milk	*Freshly grated nutmeg*
1 cup heavy cream	*Freshly ground black pepper*

1. Rub $9\frac{1}{2} \times 1\frac{1}{2}$-inch glass pie plate or 12-inch gratin dish with cut sides of garlic. Discard garlic. Let dish dry. Rub with butter; set aside.
2. Preheat oven to 475°.
3. Heat the milk and ⅔ cup of the heavy cream in heavy-bottomed saucepan to boiling.
4. Arrange one-third of the potato slices in prepared dish in even layers. Season with salt, and sparingly with nutmeg. Repeat layering and seasoning with another one-third of the potato slices. Layer final third of potato slices in neat overlapping pattern. Sprinkle with salt. Pour enough hot milk mixture into dish to come two-thirds of the way up the potatoes. Drizzle the remaining ⅓ cup cream over the top.
5. Bake until top is lightly browned, 15 to 20 minutes. Lower heat to 375°. Continue to bake until potatoes are tender when poked with small sharp knife, and milk is absorbed, about 1 hour and 10 minutes in all; the top should be an even golden brown. Grind pepper over top.

Variations

Potato and Celery Root Gratin: Substitute peeled celery root slices for ⅓ the amount of the potatoes above, sandwiching the celery root between two layers of potatoes.

Potato Gratin with Ham and Cheese: Scatter ¾ cup diced cooked ham and ½ cup grated Gruyère cheese between the layers of potatoes, then sprinkle the top with about 2 Tablespoons of cheese. Combine this with a salad for a hearty supper.

ZUCCHINI GRATIN WITH RICOTTA AND TOMATOES

This Provençale gratin was developed by David Ricketts for *Cuisine* magazine. It makes a quick and easy light supper.
Serves 4 (makes one 9-inch gratin)

1 can (1 pound, 12 ounces)
imported whole plum tomatoes
4 Tablespoons unsalted butter
1 Tablespoon olive oil
1 ½ cups chopped onion (about ¾ pound)
3 cups thinly sliced zucchini (about ¾ pound)
1 clove garlic, finely minced

¼ teaspoon dried basil, crumbled
Pinch freshly grated nutmeg
Salt
Freshly ground black pepper
2 eggs
1 cup ricotta cheese, drained, sieved
1 cup heavy cream
¾ cup freshly grated Parmesan cheese

1. Preheat over to 450°.
2. Run knife back and forth a few times in can to slice tomatoes; drain.
3. Heat 2 Tablespoons of the butter and oil in large skillet over medium heat. Add onion; sauté until soft, about 8 minutes.
4. Meanwhile, heat remaining 2 Tablespoons butter in second large skillet over medium heat. Add zucchini; sauté until just tender, 5 to 7 minutes. Transfer zucchini to paper towels with slotted spoon; drain.
5. Add garlic to onion; toss to combine. Sauté 2 minutes. Stir in tomatoes, basil, nutmeg, and salt and pepper to taste. Cook, stirring occasionally, over medium-high heat until moisture evaporates, about 8 minutes.
6. Whisk eggs lightly in large bowl. Whisk in ricotta, heavy cream, and Parmesan; add salt to taste.
7. Arrange one-half of the zucchini slices in layer in bottom of 9-inch pie plate. Spread tomato mixture evenly over zucchini. Arrange remaining zucchini slices over tomato layer. Pour ricotta mixture over all.
8. Bake 10 minutes. Reduce heat to 375°; continue baking until top is browned and slightly puffed, about 25 minutes longer. Let stand 5 minutes before serving.

VEGETABLE RAGOUTS

In a classic *ragoût* we find ingredients first tossed in fat, then simmered in liquid. Here, sufficient liquid is provided by the vegetables themselves.

ZUCCHINI RAGOUT WITH TOMATOES AND PEPPERS

A sort of ratatouille without the eggplant, since many people find cooking eggplant problematic. The advantage of this ragout is its versatility: serve it hot with meat or fish, or on its own as a starter, either hot, or at cool room temperature, drizzled with a little olive oil, vinegar, and chopped fresh herbs. Also, note that I have used this stew as a component of several other dishes (see Variations, below), so that a cupful or two of tonight's leftovers can easily provide the basis for a delicious fish gratin or home-baked pizza tomorrow.
Serves 6

3 Tablespoons olive oil
3 medium onions, peeled, sliced
4 to 8 cloves garlic, minced
2 medium green peppers, cored, seeded, cut into ½-inch dice
2 medium red peppers, cored, seeded, cut into ½-inch dice
1 ½ pounds slender zucchini, trimmed, sliced into ¼-inch thick rounds

2 cans (1 pound, 12 ounces each) imported plum tomatoes in purée
1 ½ teaspoons salt
½ cup shredded fresh basil, or 2 teaspoons dried, crumbled
¼ cup chopped fresh parsley
Pinch sugar, if needed
Freshly ground black pepper

1. Preheat oven to 400°.
2. Heat olive oil in large casserole over medium heat. Add onion; toss to coat with oil. Sauté until slightly wilted, 8 to 10 minutes. Add garlic; sauté 2 to 3 minutes.

3. Add green and red peppers; toss to combine. Sauté until peppers begin to soften, 5 to 6 minutes. Add zucchini slices; toss to combine and coat with oil. Sauté until slightly softened, about 5 minutes.

4. Stir in tomatoes, breaking slightly, salt, about 1 Tablespoon of fresh basil, shredded, or all of the dried basil, and about 1 Tablespoon of the chopped parsley. If the tomatoes are acidic, stir in pinch of sugar. Bring mixture to boil. Place casserole, uncovered, in oven. Bake, stirring occasionally, until zucchini and peppers are very tender, but still intact, and the mixture is very thick, about 1 hour and 15 minutes. If after 25 to 30 minutes the mixture is too thick, cover for remainder of baking time. Or if mixture is bubbling very violently, lower heat to 375° or 350°, to maintain slow but steady simmer.

6. Add black pepper and the remaining fresh basil and parsley. Add more salt if necessary. Let stand 10 minutes before serving. Serve slightly warm or at room temperature.

Variations

Baked Eggs with Zucchini Ragout: Arrange the cooked ragout in an oiled gratin dish or other shallow ovenproof dish and make several indentations in the mixture with the back of a spoon. Carefully break a raw egg into each hollow, top with a little grated cheese, and bake in a preheated 400° oven until the egg whites are just set.

Gratin of Fish Fillets with Zucchini Ragout (see page 140)

Pastitsio (see page 200)

Pizza (see page 215)

CABBAGE RAGOUT WITH
JUNIPER AND CREAM

A simple blend of flavors, creamy and tender. Serve this with braised duck or chicken (see page 189).

Cooking Tip: If you prefer to omit the cream, replace it with a meat or vegetable broth.

Serves 4 to 6

4 ounces bacon, cut into ½-inch
   dice
1 Tablespoon vegetable oil
1 small head cabbage, outer leaves
   removed (1 ¼ to 1 ½ pounds)

5 juniper berries, slightly bruised,
   or 1 Tablespoon gin
½ cup heavy cream
Freshly ground black pepper

1. Slowly brown bacon with vegetable oil in medium casserole over medium-low heat until almost crisp, about 8 minutes. Remove bacon with slotted spoon to plate lined with paper towel. Reserve.

2. Quarter, core, and cut cabbage into ½-inch wide shreds. Add to bacon fat in casserole. Toss over medium-low heat to coat. Steam, covered, tossing occasionally, until cabbage is wilted, 8 to 10 minutes.

3. Add juniper berries or gin, if using, and cream. Toss to combine. Simmer, covered, until cabbage is crisp-tender, 3 to 5 minutes. Uncover; simmer until cream is reduced slightly, 3 to 5 minutes. Add reserved bacon and freshly ground pepper. Serve hot.

VEGETABLE PURÉES

A smooth vegetable purée makes an excellent accompaniment to meat or fish, and can be prepared in advance. See the Basic Procedure on page 32.

QUICHES AND CUSTARDS

Who could have envisioned, fifteen years ago, that quiche would one day be served everywhere? I used to like to serve a slice of quiche as a first course, but these days I find it too much, unless thin and delicate, such as the onion tarts served with white wine in Alsace (page 97).

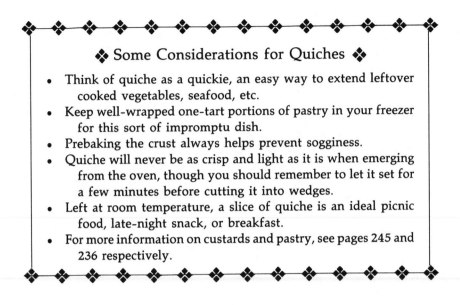

❖ Some Considerations for Quiches ❖

- Think of quiche as a quickie, an easy way to extend leftover cooked vegetables, seafood, etc.
- Keep well-wrapped one-tart portions of pastry in your freezer for this sort of impromptu dish.
- Prebaking the crust always helps prevent sogginess.
- Quiche will never be as crisp and light as it is when emerging from the oven, though you should remember to let it set for a few minutes before cutting it into wedges.
- Left at room temperature, a slice of quiche is an ideal picnic food, late-night snack, or breakfast.
- For more information on custards and pastry, see pages 245 and 236 respectively.

BASIC PASTRY FOR QUICHES AND TARTS

Makes two 9- or 10-inch shells

3 cups flour
2 teaspoons salt
Pinch sugar
12 Tablespoons unsalted butter,
  cold

2 Tablespoons plus 1 teaspoon
  vegetable shortening, cold
3 Tablespoons cold water, or more
  as needed

By Hand:
1. Sift together flour, salt, and sugar into large bowl.
2. Cut butter and shortening into small pieces over bowl, letting pieces fall into dry ingredients. Rub mixture together with fingertips, pastry blender, or two knives, until mixture forms coarse crumbs; do not over-mix.
3. Sprinkle 3 Tablespoons of the cold water over flour mixture; toss with

fork all the while. Add more water if necessary, tossing with fork, until pastry can be gently gathered together into a ball. Do not make dough too wet. Knead ball once or twice in bowl to distribute butter evenly. Gather together into ball. Cut in two portions; flatten each, wrap, and chill at least 1 hour.

With Food Processor:

1. Add flour, salt, and sugar to bowl of food processor. Mix with several on/off pulses.

2. Add large chunks of butter and shortening to bowl. Process, with on/off pulses, until mixture resembles coarse meal; do not overprocess.

3. Scrape mixture into bowl. Add water as in step 3 above; proceed with recipe.

FRESH TOMATO AND BASIL QUICHE

A celebration of summer flavors, meltingly tender. See A Tomato Primer, page 60, for more information on tomatoes and their handling. *Cooking Tip:* Be sure to drain the tomatoes thoroughly in steps 4 and 5 to prevent a soggy crust.

Serves 6 (makes one 9-inch quiche)

½ recipe Basic Pastry for Quiches and Tarts (page 94)

⅔ cup grated Swiss or Gruyère cheese

2 firm, ripe tomatoes, halved crosswise, seeded, cut into ⅜-inch thick slices

Salt for tomatoes plus ½ teaspoon

2 egg yolks

1 egg

¾ cup heavy cream, or ½ cup heavy cream plus ¼ cup sour cream

½ cup milk

¼ teaspoon freshly ground pepper, white or black

Pinch freshly grated nutmeg

2 Tablespoons minced fresh herbs, such as basil, parsley, chives, dill, or a mixture

1 Tablespoon chopped scallions, or 1 teaspoon minced garlic (optional)

1 Tablespoon unsalted butter, cut into bits, cold

Cayenne pepper

1. Roll pastry on lightly floured surface into circle slightly larger than 9-inch quiche pan with removable bottom. Line pan with pastry; trim off excess pastry. Form a decorative edge if you wish. Chill.

2. Preheat oven to 400°.

3. Line pastry with aluminum foil; fill with dried beans or rice. Place on heavy sheet pan. Bake until edges are set, 8 to 10 minutes. Remove foil and beans carefully. Prick pastry very lightly with fork, without piercing. Scatter about 1 Tablespoon of the cheese over the pastry. Bake until pastry is light golden and set, 10 to 12 minutes. Check pastry every few minutes while baking; if pastry bubbles up, prick again. Remove pastry from oven.

4. While the pastry is baking, arrange tomato slices on plate; sprinkle with salt to help drain excess juices. Whisk together egg yolks, egg, heavy cream, milk, ½ teaspoon salt, pepper, and nutmeg.

5. Sprinkle half the remaining cheese over the pastry. Drain the tomato slices on paper towels. Arrange slices in ring on pastry against outer edge, overlapping very slightly if necessary to make the slices fit. Scatter the remaining cheese, minced fresh herbs, and optional scallions over tomatoes.

6. Place quiche, still on sheet pan, on oven rack. Carefully pour custard mixture into pan, being careful not to let any of the mixture overflow the sides of the pastry; this prevents a soggy crust. Quickly scatter cold butter bits over surface. Sprinkle with cayenne.

7. Bake 5 minutes. Lower heat to 375°. Bake until golden and puffed, another 25 to 30 minutes.

8. Let quiche cool slightly before unmolding; serve as soon as possible.

Variations

Asparagus or Broccoli Quiche: Substitute 1 to 1½ cups crisply blanched or steamed asparagus or broccoli for the tomatoes and basil. Toss the vegetable quickly in a small amount of butter in a skillet to dry it out and enhance the flavor, then scatter in the crust with the cheese and custard.

Scallop and Mushroom Quiche: Suitable for brunch or a late supper, this quiche can also be prepared with lightly cooked flaked crabmeat, shrimp, lobster, smoked salmon, or a combination of seafood ingredients.

Substitute 4 ounces scallops (cut up if large) for tomatoes and basil. Sauté in butter with ¾ cup sliced mushrooms, just until the scallops are opaque, 3 to 4 minutes. Flavor with garlic and parsley. Remove solids from pan with slotted spoon. Reduce any pan liquids until syrupy. Whisk reduced liquid into custard mixture to heighten scallop flavor.

ALSATIAN ONION TART

The sweet, slow-cooked onions make this a particular favorite. Though this is served throughout Alsace, the best version I've had was that of Pierre Gaertner, whose restaurant Aux Armes de France in Ammerschwihr is worth a journey. Chef Gaertner is the author of *The Cuisine of Alsace* (Barron's). Here is my version, which uses a sour cream pastry. Serves 6 to 8 as a first course, 4 as a main course
(makes one 10-inch tart)

1 recipe Sour Cream Flaky Pastry (page 206)	2 eggs
	½ cup heavy cream
2 to 3 Tablespoons unsalted butter	½ cup milk
1 Tablespoon vegetable oil	Salt
1 ¼ pounds onions, halved lengthwise, thinly sliced lengthwise	Freshly ground black pepper
	Freshly grated nutmeg
	Cayenne pepper
1 ½ Tablespoons flour	

1. Roll pastry thinly on lightly floured surface into circle slightly larger than 10-inch quiche pan with removable bottom. Line pan with pastry. Trim overhang. Prick pastry lightly with fork without piercing. Refrigerate 20 to 30 minutes to allow pastry to rest.
2. Heat butter and oil in skillet over low heat. Add onion slices; toss to coat. Sauté, tossing occasionally, until soft but not brown, about 25 minutes. Sprinkle flour over onions. Toss over heat to mix and cook flour, 2 to 3 minutes. Set aside.
3. Preheat oven to 400°.
4. Meanwhile, line pastry with aluminum foil; weight with dried beans or rice. Bake crust in 400° oven on baking sheet 10 minutes. Remove weights and foil. Prick pastry lightly again; bake until very lightly golden brown, another 10 to 12 minutes. Remove pastry from oven. Lower heat to 375°.
5. Spread onions in cooked pastry shell. Beat together eggs, cream, milk, salt and pepper, nutmeg, and cayenne. Place quiche pan in oven on baking sheet. Pour custard mixture into pan. Bake until quiche is set in center, 30 to 40 minutes. Cool slightly before unmolding.

VEGETABLE TIMBALES WITH BEURRE BLANC

A colorful first course in the *nouvelle cuisine* style.
Cooking Tip: Be sure to let the baked custards set for 3 or 4 minutes before unmolding them.
Serves 4

CARROT MOUSSELINE:	GREEN BEAN MOUSSELINE:
1 pound carrots, trimmed, peeled,	*½ pound green beans, trimmed*
cut into small even pieces	*Salt*
Salt	*1 Tablespoon unsalted butter*
1 Tablespoon unsalted butter	*Freshly grated nutmeg*
Freshly grated nutmeg	*Cayenne pepper*
Cayenne pepper	*Freshly ground black pepper*
Freshly ground black pepper	*1 egg, lightly beaten*
2 eggs, lightly beaten	*¼ cup heavy cream*
½ cup heavy cream	
	Unsalted butter, softened
	Beurre Blanc (page 122)

1. Cook carrots and green beans separately in two large saucepans of boiling salted water until very tender, about 15 to 20 minutes. Drain. Purée vegetables separately in food processor or blender. Force each purée through a sieve.

2. Heat 1 Tablespoon of butter in each of two saucepans over medium heat. Add one purée to each pan; dry purées, stirring frequently, about 4 minutes. Season each purée well with nutmeg, cayenne, and salt and pepper. Transfer each purée to a bowl and chill.

3. Stir 2 eggs into carrot purée; stir 1 egg into bean purée. Chill both purées.

4. Add small amount of cream to each purée to lighten. Lightly whip remainder of the ½ cup cream; fold into carrot purée. Lightly whip remainder of the ¼ cup cream; fold into bean purée.

5. Preheat oven to 375°.

6. Butter 4 timbale molds. Place half of carrot mousseline in bottoms of each of the 4 molds, dividing evenly; smooth the surfaces. Layer green

bean mousseline over carrot, dividing evenly. Layer remainder of carrot mousseline over green beans, dividing evenly. Smooth the tops.

7. Place molds in roasting or baking pan; lay buttered parchment or wax paper over tops of molds. Pour enough hot water into pan to come halfway up sides of molds. Bake until mousseline mixture is set and puffed, 30 to 35 minutes. Remove molds from *bain-marie.* Let stand 3 or 4 minutes. Invert molds, carefully draining out any excess liquid while holding mousseline mixture in mold with spatula. Carefully unmold timbales on small individual plates. Surround with *beurre blanc.*

SPINACH PÂTÉ

I was getting nowhere developing a vegetable pâté without a meat binder or flour thickener. Then, while unsuccessfully retesting another recipe, I realized I had stumbled on the vegetable pâté I had been looking for.

Makes one 8½ × 5-inch loaf (about 12 first-course servings)

2 pounds fresh spinach, stemmed, trimmed, or 2 packages (10 ounces each) frozen leaf spinach, thawed

5 Tablespoons unsalted butter, plus more for pan

⅔ cup thinly sliced scallions, green and white parts

1 clove garlic, minced (optional)

1 ½ teaspoons salt, or more to taste

½ teaspoon freshly ground black pepper, or more to taste

½ teaspoon freshly grated nutmeg, or more to taste

6 eggs

1 cup ricotta cheese

½ cup sour cream

½ cup chopped fresh parsley

½ cup chopped fresh dill (optional; do not use dried)

¾ cup grated Gruyère or Swiss cheese

¼ cup freshly grated Parmesan cheese

1. Wash fresh spinach in several changes lukewarm water; drain. Steam, covered, in large pot over medium-high heat, with just the water that clings to leaves. Stir once or twice. Cook just until wilted, about 4 minutes. Drain; rinse under cold water to stop cooking. (If using frozen spinach, omit this step.)

2. Squeeze all possible moisture from fresh or frozen spinach. Chop coarsely; set aside.

3. In large skillet, heat butter over medium heat. When foam subsides, add scallions and optional garlic. Cook for 1 to 2 minutes. Increase heat; add spinach, salt and pepper, and nutmeg. Toss until excess moisture has evaporated and spinach is dry, 4 to 5 minutes. Reserve off heat; cool slightly.

4. Preheat oven to 375°. Bring kettle of water to boil for *bain-marie*. Butter loaf pan. Cut piece of parchment or waxed paper to fit bottom and two long sides of pan with some overhang. Arrange paper in pan; spread with butter. Set pan aside.

5. In large mixing bowl, whisk eggs lightly. Add ricotta and sour cream; whisk until completely smooth. Add parsley, dill, and reserved spinach mixture. Mix with large spatula until combined. Stir in Gruyère and Parmesan. Correct all seasonings; mixture should be assertively seasoned.

6. Place prepared loaf pan in roasting pan. Scrape spinach mixture into loaf pan. Fold paper overhangs loosely over top of mixture. Place roasting pan on center rack in oven. Pour in enough hot water to come one-third to one-half way up sides of loaf pan. Bake until center is firm, 50 to 60 minutes. Remove loaf pan from water bath; cool on wire rack. Unfold paper and turn out pâté on platter. Wrap in plastic wrap and chill.

7. Slice pâté into thin slices with serrated knife. Serve with tomato vinaigrette, made by stirring 2 diced, cored, seeded ripe tomatoes into basic vinaigrette (page 106).

Variation

"Gnocchi" Gratin: Leftover pâté, similar in texture and flavor to spinach gnocchi, can be transformed into an easy and delicious supper dish.

Serves 4 to 6

Dribble a little tomato sauce (page 61) into bottom of buttered shallow baking dish. Arrange pâté slices, overlapping, in dish. Top with tomato sauce and freshly grated Parmesan cheese; dot with butter. Bake in preheated 400° oven until bubbly and lightly golden, about 25 minutes. If desired, increase oven heat to broil; briefly run dish under broiler until browned, 30 to 60 seconds.

STUFFED VEGETABLES

STUFFED RED PEPPERS WITH RICE AND ANCHOVIES

I love the taste of sweet red peppers for this dish, though green peppers work fine too. Be sure to keep both peppers and rice firm in the precooking stage. You can omit the anchovies, if you are so inclined.
Serves 4

4 medium to large red (or green) peppers, well shaped, with flat bottoms if possible
Salt
¾ cup long-grain white rice
3 Tablespoons olive oil
1 small onion, chopped
2 cloves garlic, minced
1 teaspoon dried basil, crumbled, or ¼ cup chopped fresh basil
Freshly ground black pepper
¼ cup chopped fresh parsley
4 ounces Italian Fontina or mozzarella cheese, cut into ½-inch cubes

¼ cup freshly grated Parmesan cheese
1 Tablespoon fresh lemon juice or wine vinegar
6 to 8 anchovy fillets, packed in oil, drained, coarsely chopped (see Note)
½ cup Chicken Broth (page 6)

TOPPING:

2 Tablespoons bread crumbs
2 to 3 Tablespoons freshly grated Parmesan cheese
Olive oil

1. Cut lids off peppers. If you wish to have pepper in the filling, stem lids and coarsely chop; reserve. Scoop out ribs and seeds from peppers; rinse peppers under cold running water to remove any hidden seeds. If necessary, slice off paper-thin slivers from bottoms so peppers stand upright.
2. Add peppers to large pot of boiling salted water; boil just until crisp-tender, about 7 minutes. Drain in colander, rinsing with cold water to stop cooking. Place peppers, cut side down, on paper-towel-lined plate to drain.

3. Cook rice in large pot of boiling salted water, stirring occasionally, until just firm-tender, 11 to 13 minutes. The boil should be steady, not vigorous. Drain rice; mix warm rice with 1½ Tablespoons of the olive oil in a bowl to keep grains separate.

4. Heat 1½ Tablespoons of the olive oil over medium heat in small skillet. Add onion; sauté until onion begins to wilt, about 4 minutes. Add reserved chopped pepper at this point if you wish to include in filling. Add garlic; toss 2 minutes. Add contents of skillet to bowl of rice. Add basil, salt and pepper, and chopped parsley; toss to combine. Set aside to cool.

5. Preheat oven to 375°.

6. Add Fontina and ¼ cup Parmesan cheese, lemon juice, anchovies, and broth to rice; toss to combine. Fill peppers with rice mixture, mounding mixture about ⅛ inch above rims. Arrange peppers in shallow casserole or ovenproof dish. Combine bread crumbs and the 2 to 3 Tablespoons Parmesan cheese; scatter over top of each pepper. Drizzle a few drops of olive oil over topping. Pour hot water to depth of ½ inch in casserole. Bake in upper third of oven until tops brown and filling is hot, 20 to 25 minutes. Serve warm or at room temperature for a buffet.

Note: Three to four whole anchovies preserved in salt can be substituted. Soak in cold water 20 to 30 minutes. Pat dry. Remove fillets and any small bones. You can also substitute ½ cup chopped cooked ham, chicken, shrimp, or shellfish for the anchovies. Adjust seasonings.

MICHAEL BATTERBERRY'S STUFFED TOMATOES WITH RICE AND THREE CHEESES

Michael Batterberry, the urbane founding editor of *Food & Wine* magazine, devised these creamy stuffed tomatoes. Prepare them in the cool of a summer morning, then leave them at room temperature until lunch or dinner. They are equally good hot or cold.
Serves 8

8 large ripe firm tomatoes

Salt

2 Tablespoons olive oil, plus more
as needed

½ cup sliced scallions

2 cloves garlic, minced

1 cup long-grain white rice

2 Tablespoons dry white wine

1 ½ cups Chicken Broth (page 6)

½ cup chopped fresh basil or 1
teaspoon dried basil, crumbled

4 ounces mozzarella cheese, cut into
½-inch cubes

4 ounces Fontina cheese, cut into
½-inch cubes

Fresh lemon juice

Freshly ground black pepper

Freshly grated Parmesan cheese

1. Heat oven to 350°.

2. Slice tops from tomatoes. Scoop out flesh; remove and discard seeds. Coarsely chop flesh; reserve. Salt insides of tomatoes, then invert on paper-towel-lined platter to drain.

3. Heat olive oil in large skillet over medium heat until rippling. Add scallions and garlic; sauté 2 minutes. Add rice and white wine; toss until nearly dry. Add broth. Simmer, partially covered, until rice is firm-tender, about 14 minutes.

4. Transfer rice mixture to bowl; toss with tomato pulp, basil, and the cheeses. Season with lemon juice, salt and pepper. Mound rice filling into tomato shells. Sprinkle grated Parmesan, then olive oil, over each.

5. Bake until heated through, about 20 minutes. Serve hot or at room temperature.

Variation

Risotto-Stuffed Tomatoes: Prepare a plain cheese or mushroom risotto (page 74), leaving it slightly wet. Spoon it carefully into the tomatoes as indicated above. Proceed with the topping and baking instructions in step 6 of the stuffed peppers, on page 102. These can also be made as finger food, using cherry tomatoes.

STUFFED POTATOES IN THEIR JACKETS

Serves 4

*4 large baking potatoes (2 to 2 ½
pounds)*
*4 teaspoons unsalted butter,
softened*
⅓ cup sour cream or yogurt
*½ cup heavy cream or milk, or as
needed*
1 teaspoon salt, or more as needed
*½ teaspoon freshly ground black
pepper*

*1 cup plus 1 Tablespoon grated
Gruyère or Swiss cheese*
*⅓ cup diced cooked ham
(preferably Westphalian or
Black Forest)*
*2 Tablespoons chopped fresh
parsley*

1. Preheat oven to 400°.
2. Scrub and dry potatoes; rub with butter. Place on baking sheet. Roast until skin is crisp and potato is tender when poked with thin knife, 1 hour to 1 hour 10 minutes.
3. Split potatoes in half lengthwise. Let cool slightly.
4. Scoop out pulp with spoon; place pulp in bowl. Reserve skins. Mash pulp gently with fork until coarsely broken up. Add sour cream, ⅓ cup heavy cream, and salt and pepper; blend until just combined. Add more cream if mixture is not creamy enough. Add 1 cup of the cheese, the ham, and parsley. Stir gently to mix; keep mixture coarse. Correct seasonings if necessary.
5. Lightly pack mixture back into skins. Arrange halves on baking sheet or in baking dish. Sprinkle remaining 1 Tablespoon of cheese over tops of the potatoes. Dribble remaining cream over center of each potato half. Bake until lightly golden, 10 to 20 minutes.

S A L A D S

The ability to throw together fine salads is an estimable talent, for the ingredients must be expertly prepared, combined, and dressed. Following are some guidelines.

❖ Basic Considerations for Green Salads ❖

Selecting the Greens:

- Develop a knack for combining two, three, or four main greens for a salad. Don't combine several bitter varieties, such as endive, chicory, and arugula. Instead, toss one of these with a soft lettuce such as Boston, a crisp one such as Romaine, a red-leafed variety for color, and fresh sprigs of watercress for added crunch.
- Other welcome additions to the salad bowl include radishes, cucumbers, peppers, blanched green vegetables, potatoes, slivers of meat (see composed salads on page 111), hard-cooked eggs, olives, and much else. Ripe tomatoes are perhaps better in a salad of their own, sliced thickly and left to sit for an hour or so after sprinkling with salt, fresh basil or tarragon, and olive oil, with a small splash of good wine vinegar.

Preparing and Serving the Greens:

- Wash the greens very thoroughly in a colander or several changes of cold water; nothing is worse than a gritty salad.
- Cut or tear the greens into largish bite-size pieces (but not so large that the mouth can't cope with them).
- Dry the greens thoroughly.
- Roll up the greens compactly in paper or cloth towels, place in plastic bags, and let crisp in the refrigerator for at least an hour. This process results in perfectly dry, crisp leaves that will keep for two days or so. Just be sure to pack the greens so that each bag has a selection of all the varieties.
- Toss greens with dressing just before serving. Use just enough dressing to coat greens. Go easy; you can always add more dressing. Serve on chilled plates.

BASIC MUSTARD VINAIGRETTE

This remains the best all-around choice, flavored with Dijon mustard, a mixture of lemon juice and wine or other vinegar, and a blend of rich olive oil with a lighter oil. Remember the basic ratio of 2 or 3 parts oil to 1 part acid.
Makes about ⅓ cup, to serve 4 to 6

*1 Tablespoon red wine vinegar, or
more
2 teaspoons fresh lemon juice
½ teaspoon freshly ground black
pepper
¼ teaspoon salt*

*1 clove garlic, minced
1 teaspoon Dijon mustard
Pinch mixed herbs
2 Tablespoons olive oil
1 Tablespoon vegetable oil*

1. Whisk together vinegar, lemon juice, pepper, salt, garlic, mustard, and mixed herbs until blended and smooth.
2. Whisk in oil drop by drop. When dressing begins to thicken, add oil in thin steady stream. Continue until all the oil is incorporated and the dressing is thick and blended. Correct all seasonings if necessary.

CREAMY GARLIC VINAIGRETTE

When you want to prepare a dressing in advance, or one with a creamy consistency that will coat leaves evenly, a bit of egg yolk added to the acid in the beginning will bind the sauce, much like a mayonnaise (of which this is actually a very thin version). This is a deliciously pungent dressing that will keep refrigerated for two or three days, and is often my choice for marinated vegetable salads.
Cooking Tips:

• Taste the dressing if you've prepared it in advance, especially if you've marinated vegetables in it. It may need to be spiked with a bit more lemon juice, vinegar, and/or mustard.

106

- If the sauce appears to have separated, whisk it for a moment, and it will quickly come back together.
- Add a few paper-thin slivers of red pepper and a bit of chopped parsley to this dressing, and let it steep for an hour or two before serving.

Makes 1 scant cup

Half an egg yolk	*2 or 3 cloves garlic, thinly sliced*
Juice of 1 lemon	*1 Tablespoon Dijon mustard*
2 to 2 ½ Tablespoons red wine vinegar	*½ cup olive oil*
	¼ cup vegetable oil
½ teaspoon salt	*Pinch cayenne pepper*
½ teaspoon freshly ground black pepper	*¼ cup chopped fresh parsley (optional)*
½ teaspoon dried basil, crumbled	

1. Whisk together egg yolk, lemon juice, vinegar, salt, pepper, basil, garlic, and mustard until blended and smooth.
2. Combine oils and add a drop at a time. When dressing begins to thicken, add oils in thin steady stream. Continue until all the oil has been incorporated. Add the cayenne and the optional parsley. Correct all seasonings if necessary; this dressing should be quite tart.

Vinaigrette Variations

Create your own special vinaigrettes by experimenting with the wide range of flavored vinegars and oils now available. For added interest, try making your own herbal-flavored vinegars; the technique is quite straightforward. Pour scalded vinegar over the coarsely chopped fresh herb or other flavoring agent. Let cool and allow to stand, covered, two to three weeks. Strain if you like. Try vinegars made with basil, tarragon, chives, rosemary, mint, shallots, garlic, hot chilies, and fresh berries.

MARINATED VEGETABLE SALADS

These are excellent light first courses or "sitting-around food": when friends drop by, set out a platter of tart vegetables, bread or crackers, and a cheese or two. Many of these dishes transform winter's meager produce offerings into something more intriguing. When preparing hot vegetables, remember to cook a bit extra for use in these salads.

MARINATED GREEN BEANS IN CREAMY GARLIC VINAIGRETTE

Consider this a master recipe, equally suitable for other vegetables such as broccoli, cauliflower, leeks, carrots, and mushrooms (usually left raw) used singly or in combination.

Cooking Tips:

- Keep the vegetables slightly undercooked.
- Keep the dressing quite tart.
- Try other herbs: dill or fennel fronds, chives, tarragon, or a combination.

Serves 4 to 6

1 ¼ pounds green beans, ends trimmed on bias
Salt
1 or 2 red peppers, cored, seeded, cut into long, very thin slices

¼ cup chopped fresh parsley (optional)
Creamy Garlic Vinaigrette (page 106)

1. Cook beans in large pot boiling salted water until crisp-tender, 7 to 8 minutes. Drain well; pat dry on paper towels.
2. Add beans, red pepper, and optional parsley to dressing. Marinate 20 minutes or longer. Toss, and serve at room temperature.

Variation

Fennel with Lemon and Herbs: Toss rounds or strips of crisply blanched or steamed fennel with fresh lemon juice and herbs. Marinate as above.

THREE-COLOR WINTER SALAD

Serves 4 to 6

1 large bunch broccoli
1 bunch carrots, trimmed, peeled
Creamy Garlic Vinaigrette (page 106)
2 red peppers, cored, seeded, cut into long thin slivers

2 cloves garlic, sliced in thin slivers (optional)
¼ cup chopped fresh parsley

1. Trim broccoli-stem bottoms. Cut stems from flowerets; cut stems diagonally into 1-inch lengths. Divide broccoli head into small flowerets. Cut carrots diagonally into 1-inch lengths. Place broccoli stems and carrots in steamer over boiling water; steam 2 to 3 minutes. Add broccoli flowerets and steam until all are crisp-tender, about another 5 minutes. Drain; rinse under cold running water to stop cooking and set color. Drain well; dry vegetables on paper towels. Toss vegetables with dressing in bowl; let marinate at least 30 minutes.
2. Add peppers, optional garlic, and parsley to vegetables. Serve at room temperature.

JULIENNE SALAD WITH TWO MUSTARDS

Serves 4

3 carrots, trimmed, peeled
2 ribs celery, trimmed
2 medium celery roots
Juice of 1 lemon
2 ounces Gruyère or Swiss cheese,
   in 1 piece

POMMERY MAYONNAISE:

3 egg yolks, at room temperature
1 teaspoon Dijon mustard
1 Tablespoon Pommery mustard
Juice of ½ lemon
1 Tablespoon red wine vinegar, or
   more to taste

Salt
Freshly ground black pepper
⅔ cup olive oil
½ cup vegetable oil
⅓ cup chopped fresh parsley, plus
   additional for garnish

Several leaves soft lettuce (such as
   Boston or Bibb)

1. Cut carrots and celery into julienne strips 1½ inches long. Place strips in bowl of ice water to keep crisp. Peel celery root; remove any blemished areas from white flesh. Cut into julienne strips 1½ inches long. Place celery-root julienne strips in small bowl; toss with juice of 1 lemon to prevent discoloration. Cut cheese into julienne strips 1½ inches long; toss with celery root.
2. To make dressing, whisk together yolks, 2 mustards, juice of ½ lemon, vinegar, salt, and pepper. When blended, whisk in the combined oils a drop at a time. When mixture is thick, add remaining oil in thin steady stream, whisking continually. Adjust seasoning if necessary with lemon juice, mustards, vinegar, salt and pepper; the mayonnaise should have a sharp flavor. Add parsley.
3. Toss the celery root, cheese, and any lemon juice remaining in the bottom of the bowl with the mayonnaise; cover until ready to serve. If made more than 1 hour ahead, refrigerate.
4. At serving time, thoroughly drain carrot and celery; pat dry with paper towels. Add to celery root and mayonnaise; toss to combine. Adjust seasonings if necessary. Serve on lettuce leaves; sprinkle with chopped parsley if desired.

COMPOSED SALADS

A type of salad that serves well as a complete meal is the composed salad, or *salade composée.* A carefully arranged mixture of raw and cooked ingredients, the best-known versions of this type are the American chef's salad, with meats and cheeses grouped on a bed of greens, and the *salade Niçoise.* The best version I've had of that Provençale specialty was at a long lunch on a terrace overlooking the Mediterranean. Each component was presented separately: a large tin of flat anchovies in fruity olive oil, ripe olives, sliced red tomatoes, tiny ribs of crisp celery hearts and fennel, and a large bowl of fresh greens and pencil-thin green beans. Each of us composed our own salad on the spot; with lots of bread and a local rosé, this was a perfect way to let an entire afternoon slip by.

Some Combinations to Try:

- Breast of chicken, with strips of red pepper and toasted walnuts
- Cool rare roast lamb, with blanched leeks and slivers of carrot and ginger
- Smoked turkey with cooked cranberries and pecans
- Thinly sliced roast pork with mango, pine nuts, and freshly ground pepper (a creation of Chef Sandy Gluck at New York's Café New Amsterdam)
- Tissue-thin slices of country ham, goat cheese, and arugula
- Poached scallops, lime zest, and diced ripe tomato
- Rare roast beef, cold potatoes, and zucchini in mustard vinaigrette with grated fresh horseradish
- Smoked poultry and crab apple with apple cider vinaigrette

LUKEWARM SALADS (SALADES TIÈDES)

One of the interesting conceits of the "new" French cuisine is the play of temperatures. Some composed salads are a study in contrasts—for example, sizzling-hot sautéed chicken livers, deglazed with vinegar, then arranged over cold baby spinach leaves. Others are served luke-warm, or *tiède.*

THE CHARVET BROTHERS' SALADE TIÈDE OF CORNED BEEF AND CABBAGE

The Charvet brothers of Aix-en-Provence, while preparing a *salade tiède* of duck breast and green cabbage for *The International Review of Food and Wine* in New York, invented this recipe on a whim. When lean, hot sliced corned beef was delivered to our kitchen for a deli-style lunch, the Charvets instantly transformed their duck salad into a memorable blend of warmed corned beef and cabbage.
Serves 4

½ *pound lean cooked corned beef,*
  thickly sliced
Double recipe Basic Mustard
  Vinaigrette (page 106)

THE VEGETABLES:

½ *medium head of cabbage*
2 *ripe tomatoes*
1 *Tablespoon sherry vinegar, or*
  other wine vinegar

2 *teaspoons coarse (kosher) salt*
1 *strip (2 inches) orange zest*

GARNISH:

½ *cup coarsely chopped nuts (such*
  as hazelnuts and almonds, or
  walnuts and almonds)
2 *Tablespoons chopped fresh chervil*
  or parsley

1. Trim all traces of fat from meat. Cut into thick julienne. Marinate meat in dressing while preparing remainder of salad.
2. Heat oven to 350°. Heat large pot of water to boiling.
3. Halve cabbage; core. Cut cabbage into thin shreds. Soak in bowl of cold water 5 minutes. Drain.
4. Meanwhile, blanch tomatoes in pot of boiling water 1 minute. Remove with slotted spoon; cool.
5. Add cabbage shreds to boiling water with vinegar, salt, and orange zest. Boil until cabbage is crisp-tender, about 8 minutes. Drain.
6. Meanwhile, core and peel tomatoes. Slice in half crosswise. Squeeze out seeds and excess liquid. Coarsely chop; reserve.
7. Place nuts on baking sheet. Toast in oven, tossing occasionally, until lightly browned, 5 to 10 minutes. Heat cabbage and tomatoes in oven,

if necessary, until lukewarm. Combine cabbage and tomatoes in bowl. Drain vinaigrette from meat, reserving a small amount for garnish. Toss vinaigrette with cabbage and tomatoes. Correct seasonings. Arrange the vegetables on warmed serving plates. Arrange the meat julienne attractively over the vegetables. Top each serving with toasted nuts and chopped herbs. Drizzle the reserved vinaigrette over each.

❖ 4 ❖

FISH AND SHELLFISH

BASIC TIMING PRINCIPLE FOR COOKING FISH

A SAUCE PRIMER

STOCK REDUCTION WITH CREAM
    WATERCRESS SAUCE
    CHIVE, BASIL, OR TARRAGON SAUCE
    MUSHROOM SAUCE
    BUTTER GLAZE
BEURRE BLANC (WHITE BUTTER SAUCE)
    HERBED BEURRE BLANC
    TOMATO BEURRE BLANC
    MUSTARD BEURRE BLANC
    LOBSTER BEURRE BLANC
MAYONNAISE
    FOOD PROCESSOR OR BLENDER MAYONNAISE
    AÏOLI
    WATERCRESS MAYONNAISE
    TOMATO MAYONNAISE
    GENOA SAUCE
    FENNEL MAYONNAISE
    MOUSSELINE MAYONNAISE
    HOW TO DOCTOR COMMERCIAL MAYONNAISE
FLAVORED BUTTERS: LEMON-HERB BUTTER
    GARLIC BUTTER
    SAFFRON BUTTER
    ANCHOVY BUTTER
    FENNEL BUTTER
    BASIL BUTTER
    POMMERY MUSTARD BUTTER
    CAPER BUTTER

POACHING AND BOILING

BASIC METHOD FOR OVEN-POACHED FISH
    FISH FILLETS WITH MUSHROOMS
    FISH FILLETS WITH SHELLFISH GARNITURE
    FISH FILLETS WITH VEGETABLE JULIENNE
    FILLET OF SOLE WITH CAVIAR
FISH SALADS
EASY METHOD FOR LOBSTERS

BROILING AND GRILLING

BASIC METHOD FOR BROILED FISH FILLETS
SCALLOP BROCHETTES WITH BACON, MUSHROOMS, AND CROUTONS
BARBECUED SHELLFISH

STEAMING AND PAPILLOTES

MISCELLANEOUS METHODS

*F*ish may be today's perfect food. It cooks quickly, is lighter than meat, and is low in calories and high in protein. While fish is no longer the bargain it once was, it's still one of the best choices for a fresh, delicious meal.

This chapter offers a sampler of simple methods for cooking fish: poaching, broiling, steaming, cooking *en papillote,* baking, and others. Consider all the recipes as jumping-off points: use whatever fish you can purchase fresh, adjusting timing as indicated below.

Fish adapts easily to diverse treatments: serve it with nothing more than a squeeze of lemon juice and some chopped parsley (dieters will appreciate this), or dress it up with a sauce or garnish; the Sauce Primer will ease you through a few basics. While any of these dishes is a fine main dish, you can get a special dinner party off to an auspicious start by beginning with a small fish course: a mousseline in an individual timbale, for example, or a small, moist poached fillet with a light sauce or vegetable julienne.

Whatever cooking method you choose, keep in mind that the only secret to remember is never to overcook fish. Cook just until done, usually when opaque, and no longer (no need to keep the center raw as Parisians were doing a few years back). And have the forethought to cook a little more than you need; on the following day, you can serve a cool fillet with a dab of mayonnaise, or flake the fish to use in a salad, to stuff a tomato or a crêpe, or to flavor a quiche (page 96) or soufflé.

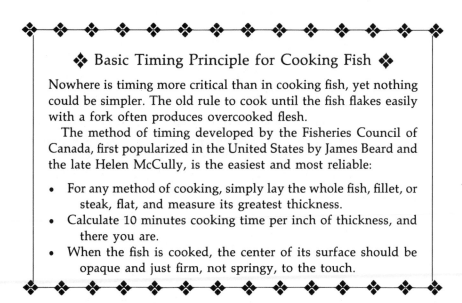

❖ Basic Timing Principle for Cooking Fish ❖

Nowhere is timing more critical than in cooking fish, yet nothing could be simpler. The old rule to cook until the fish flakes easily with a fork often produces overcooked flesh.

The method of timing developed by the Fisheries Council of Canada, first popularized in the United States by James Beard and the late Helen McCully, is the easiest and most reliable:

- For any method of cooking, simply lay the whole fish, fillet, or steak, flat, and measure its greatest thickness.
- Calculate 10 minutes cooking time per inch of thickness, and there you are.
- When the fish is cooked, the center of its surface should be opaque and just firm, not springy, to the touch.

A SAUCE PRIMER

While any fish can be served on its own, many sauces marry beautifully with the delicate flavors and textures of fish. Here is a small repertoire of light, flourless sauces; each lends itself to multiple variations and to a wide variety of uses (including, of course, nonfish items such as vegetables, meats, and poultry, substituting appropriate broths for fish broth where needed).

STOCK REDUCTION WITH CREAM

The simplest sauces are based on the concentrated fish flavor of a reduced fish broth or cooking liquid, frequently lightened with cream. Herbs and other flavor variations add interest. Serve with hot fish cooked by any method.
Serves 4 (makes about ¾ cup)

1 cup fish poaching liquid or Fish Broth (page 11)	*Few drops fresh lemon juice*
¾ cup heavy cream	*Salt*
1 to 2 Tablespoons chopped fresh parsley	*Freshly ground white pepper*

1. Boil poaching liquid or broth in wide heavy saucepan over medium heat until thickened and syrupy (about one-third of the original volume should remain). Be careful not to burn liquid as it reduces.

2. Add cream; simmer until thickened enough to coat the back of a spoon, 3 to 5 minutes. Add parsley; adjust seasonings with lemon juice, and salt and pepper as needed. Spoon around and/or over the fish.

Variations

Watercress Sauce: Substitute handful of coarsely shredded watercress leaves for the parsley.

Chive, Basil, or Tarragon Sauce: Substitute handful of coarsely chopped fresh herbs for the parsley. If you prefer a green-colored sauce rather than a pale one flecked with green, simmer herbs and watercress stems in the sauce; then purée, and pass through a sieve.

Mushroom Sauce: Add thin slices of fresh mushrooms when the sauce has reduced; simmer 1 to 2 minutes.

Butter Glaze: Omit cream. When the liquid has reduced, remove pan from heat. Cut 4 Tablespoons cold unsalted butter into small bits. Swirl a few bits into sauce until amalgamated but not completely melted; repeat with the next few bits. The sauce should be smooth and light. Correct seasonings with lemon juice, salt, and pepper. Use sauce immediately. Any fresh herbs are a welcome addition.

BEURRE BLANC (WHITE BUTTER SAUCE)

The silkiest sauce imaginable: glossy, buttery, and tart. This favorite of *nouvelle cuisine* chefs has its origins in the fine home cooking of the Loire Valley. Follow these steps, and this so-called tricky sauce will come out right every time.

Uses: Fish served hot, mousses, stuffed fillets, vegetables such as asparagus, vegetable mousses.

Cooking Tip: The reduction can be done in advance, but leave it a little wet.

Serves 4 (makes 1 scant cup)

> 2 to 3 Tablespoons chopped
> shallots
> 1/3 cup dry white wine
> 1/4 cup good wine vinegar
> 1 1/2 sticks (6 ounces) unsalted
> butter, cut into chunks, chilled
>
> Fresh lemon juice
> Salt
> Cayenne pepper

1. *The reduction:* Place shallots, wine, and vinegar in heavy noncorrosive saucepan. Boil gently over medium heat until mixture has reduced to about 2 Tablespoons of thick "marmalade." Be careful not to scorch the reduction.

2. *Mounting the sauce:* Remove the reduction from heat. Whisk a chunk or two of butter into the reduction; the butter should become "liquefied"—creamy and white, rather than melting into a clear liquid. Return the pan to low heat. Add butter, two chunks at a time, whisking. Add more when the previous chunks have almost but not quite liquefied. The sauce should become light and frothy.

3. When all the butter has been incorporated, whisk over heat for another 30 seconds or so. Season with lemon juice, salt, and cayenne; for a sharper sauce, add a couple of drops of vinegar. Serve the sauce within 30 minutes; keep warm, but not hot. Strain the sauce, if you wish.

Variations

Herbed Beurre Blanc: Add 3 to 4 Tablespoons chopped fresh herbs such as parsley and chives, tarragon, fennel, dill, or basil to finished sauce.

Tomato Beurre Blanc: Simmer ¾ to 1 cup diced peeled, seeded tomatoes, or 1 can (14 ounces) canned imported whole plum tomatoes, drained, seeded, and chopped, in 2 teaspoons butter until quite dry. Add 2 Tablespoons chopped fresh parsley and/or tarragon; stir into finished sauce.

Mustard Beurre Blanc: Add 1 teaspoon Dijon mustard or more to taste, to finished sauce. Whole-grain mustards are especially appropriate here.

Lobster Beurre Blanc: When cooking lobster on its own or for a mousseline, reserve the coral; simmer the shells in white wine to cover, 15 to 20 minutes. Strain; substitute the liquid for the white wine in the reduction. Add reserved coral and chopped fresh herbs to finished sauce for lovely red-and-green-flecked effect.

MAYONNAISE

This mayonnaise is slightly less oily than the classic formula, and includes mustard, also not strictly classic. Vary the acidity and seasonings to your taste. Note the blend of oils, for a more balanced flavor.
Uses: Cold poached fish or shellfish, salads, cold mousses, and cold meats and vegetables.
Cooking Tip: If mayonnaise separates or breaks, whisk together 1 yolk with mustard and lemon juice briefly; beat in the broken mayonnaise drop by drop. Then continue as in step 2 below, adding oil if necessary.
Makes about 2 cups

3 egg yolks, at room temperature	*1 ⅔ cups oil (half vegetable, half*
1 ½ teaspoons Dijon mustard	*olive)*
1 teaspoon salt	*Pinch cayenne pepper*
Freshly ground white pepper	*1 Tablespoon wine vinegar*
Juice of 1 lemon	*1 Tablespoon boiling water*

1. Whisk together egg yolks, mustard, salt, white pepper to taste, and 2 teaspoons lemon juice in medium bowl or in electric mixer with wire whisk attachment until yolks are slightly thickened and frothy.

2. Add combined oils one drop at a time to yolk mixture, whisking constantly until each drop is absorbed before adding the next. When about one-third of the oil has been added, add oil by teaspoonfuls, whisking all the while. When about half the oil mixture has been incorporated, add oil in a thin steady stream, whisking. Add cayenne, vinegar, remaining lemon juice if you wish, and boiling water. Correct seasonings. Refrigerate, covered, up to 3 or 4 days.

Variations

Food Processor or Blender Mayonnaise: Substitute 2 egg yolks and 1 whole egg for the egg yolks. First process yolks, egg, mustard, salt, pepper, and lemon juice together. Gradually add oil with the motor running. The result is a quickly prepared, firm-textured sauce.

Aïoli: The "butter of Provence," pungent with garlic. Add 4 to 8 cloves garlic, minced or mashed to a paste, with the yolks in step 1. Try this on grilled bluefish or swordfish, served hot.

Watercress Mayonnaise: Add a handful of coarsely shredded watercress leaves to finished mayonnaise. For a lighter version, stir in a large spoonful of sour cream or yogurt.

Tomato Mayonnaise: This is almost a cold Béarnaise. Use as a tart accent to the Seafood Sausage (page 145). Simmer ¾ to 1 cup diced peeled, seeded tomatoes, or 1 can (14 ounces) imported whole plum tomatoes, drained, chopped, in 2 Tablespoons olive oil until quite dry. Add dash of wine vinegar and 2 Tablespoons chopped fresh parsley or tarragon. Fold into finished mayonnaise.

Genoa Sauce: A pistachio-and-lime-based version based on an Escoffier formula. Process ¼ cup shelled pistachios and 2 Tablespoons pine nuts in food processor until finely chopped. Add 2 egg yolks, 1 whole egg, 1 teaspoon salt, freshly ground black pepper to taste, and 2 teaspoons fresh lime juice. Blend for about 10 seconds. Add combined oils as you would with regular mayonnaise. Stir in cayenne, ⅓ to ½ cup chopped fresh herbs, juice of ½ lemon, and more lime juice and tarragon vinegar to taste. Let sauce mellow for 2 hours before using.

Fennel Mayonnaise: Fold into basic mayonnaise the following: ½ cup chopped fennel bulb, ¼ cup chopped fennel fronds, ⅓ cup chopped fresh parsley, ½ Tablespoon Pommery mustard or to taste, and fresh lemon juice, if you wish. A dash of Pernod can't hurt.

Mousseline Mayonnaise: A lighter version of the basic mayonnaise. Whip ¼ cup heavy cream, or ¼ cup *crème fraîche* plus 2 Tablespoons milk, until almost stiff. Stir a large spoonful into basic mayonnaise. Fold in remainder. Correct seasonings.

How to Doctor Commercial Mayonnaise: Use an unsweetened variety; add a bit of lemon juice, cayenne pepper, Dijon mustard, and perhaps a dash of sherry or brandy.

FLAVORED BUTTERS

An "instant" method to lend flavor to fish, especially broiled or grilled items. Flavored butters of numerous varieties can be kept refrigerated for two weeks, or frozen indefinitely and used directly from their frozen state. Roll the butter into a cylinder in waxed paper, wrap tightly, and label. Cut off a small disk to be placed on each portion just before serving when you want to add flavor to fish, meats, or vegetables.

LEMON-HERB BUTTER

Makes about ½ cup

1 large shallot or scallion
2 Tablespoons fresh parsley leaves
Grated zest of 1 lemon
1 stick (4 ounces) unsalted butter,
softened

Juice of 1 lemon
Salt
Freshly ground black pepper

Chop shallot with parsley leaves and lemon zest in a food processor or blender. Add butter; process until smooth. Add lemon juice, and salt and pepper to taste.

Variations

Garlic Butter: Substitute 3 or 4 cloves garlic for shallots.

Saffron Butter: Simmer ½ teaspoon saffron threads, or more to taste, in 3 Tablespoons white wine for a few seconds. Process the butter with 1 Tablespoon lemon juice. Add saffron mixture, and salt and pepper to taste.

Anchovy Butter: Mash 1 can (2 ounces) anchovies, drained. Process with butter, 1 Tablespoon fresh lemon juice, and salt and pepper to taste. Sieve butter if anchovies are especially bony.

Fennel Butter: Break up 2 Tablespoons fennel seed in processor, then process with butter. Add 1 Tablespoon fresh lemon juice, and salt and pepper to taste. Force through a sieve. Add Pernod to taste, and 1 Tablespoon chopped fennel fronds, if you wish.

Basil Butter: Process 1 or 2 cloves garlic and 3 Tablespoons shredded basil leaves in the processor. Add butter, 1 teaspoon fresh lemon juice, and salt and pepper to taste; process.

Pommery Mustard Butter: Add 1½ Tablespoons Pommery mustard, 1 teaspoon fresh lemon juice, and salt and pepper to taste to butter; process.

Caper Butter: Add 3 tablespoons capers, drained and rinsed, grated zest and juice of ½ lemon, and salt and pepper to taste to the butter; process. Try this on thinly sliced dark bread with slices of smoked salmon.

POACHING AND BOILING

Quick oven-poaching is my favorite way to cook fish. It emerges firm and incomparably moist, and is equally good served hot with a sauce, or cool. (Cool the fish in the liquid before draining and refrigerating, covered. Remove the fish from the refrigerator about 30 minutes before serving; the chill masks flavor.) If nothing else in this chapter intrigues you, try cooking some fish this way.

BASIC METHOD FOR OVEN-POACHED FISH

Unsalted butter, softened
2 to 4 Tablespoons chopped
    shallots or scallions
Fish fillets
Salt

Freshly ground white pepper
1 cup dry white wine or vermouth,
    or more as desired
Water or Fish Broth (page 11)

1. Preheat oven to 375°.
2. Butter a shallow flameproof baking pan that will hold fish in a single layer. Scatter chopped shallots in bottom of pan. Season fillets with salt and pepper, then arrange carefully in pan, folding as necessary. Add wine and enough water or fish broth to come almost to top of fish. Lay a piece of buttered parchment or waxed paper on fish, buttered side down. Bring liquid almost to boil over medium heat on top of stove. Immediately remove from heat; place in oven. Bake (oven-poach) until fish is just cooked, usually 3 to 10 minutes, depending on thickness of fillet. Lift fillets from pan with slotted spoon, draining. Reserve poaching liquid for other uses. Garnish and sauce fish as you like.

Variations

Oven-poached fish can be augmented with other ingredients, as below, or can be used when precooked fish is called for as part of a larger preparation: placed on a bed of spinach and napped with sauce for a Florentine treatment; in a fish pot pie; or gratinéed on a bed of tender noodles (page 141).

Fish Fillets with Mushrooms: Top fillets with sliced mushrooms before adding wine. When cooked, lift out with slotted spatula; sauce as desired.

Fish Fillets with Shellfish Garniture: Scatter shelled shrimp or scallops around the fillets for the last 3 to 4 minutes of poaching.

Fish Fillets with Vegetable Julienne: Top fillets with a mixed vegetable julienne before adding wine.

Fillet of Sole with Caviar: Based on a recipe of Chef Jacques Manière of Paris, this is a treatment for a special occasion. Poach fillets of sole as indicated, drain well, nap with Beurre Blanc (page 122), and top each with a generous dab of caviar.

FISH SALADS

In the event there is leftover poached fish, flake it coarsely for a salad, gently fold in just enough mayonnaise to bind (preferably homemade, or one of the variations above), and add chopped celery, scallions, shallots, or red onions, and other vegetables to taste. Season with fresh lemon juice, herbs, and salt and pepper, and serve cool on lettuce leaves, garnishing, to your taste, with cucumbers, cooked potatoes, green beans, hard-cooked eggs, olives, and if possible, the ripest fresh tomatoes.

EASY METHOD FOR LOBSTERS

This is the simplest way to cook lobster, resulting in moist, tender flesh. You can first prepare a vegetable-scented broth by simmering some cut-up carrot, celery, onion, and herbs in a cup or so of white wine for 20 minutes, then straining this into a large pot of boiling salted water; or simply add a healthy splash of white wine to the water. Plunge live lobsters into the rapidly boiling water, cover, and boil as follows:

$1\frac{1}{4}$-pound lobster—7 to 8 minutes

$1\frac{1}{2}$-pound lobster—8 to 10 minutes.

Split the underside of the tail lengthwise with a chef's knife, and serve with clarified butter, fresh lemon, and sprigs of watercress.

BROILING AND GRILLING

BASIC METHOD FOR BROILED FISH FILLETS

Fish fillets
Unsalted butter, melted, or olive oil
Salt

Freshly ground pepper
Fresh lemon juice

1. Arrange broiler pan 3 to 4 inches from heat. Preheat broiler.
2. Place fish fillets on sheet of aluminum foil. Brush both sides of fillets with melted butter or olive oil. Sprinkle with salt and pepper, and squeeze of lemon juice. Lay fish, on foil, on broiler pan.
3. Broil 10 minutes per inch, or just until fish is opaque and firm, and lightly golden; baste fish once or twice with its own juices, or with more butter or oil. Don't turn fillets. When cooked, lift fillets carefully with one or two spatulas to serving dish. Top each serving with flavored butter (page 125), or with squeeze of lemon juice and sprinkling of chopped fresh parsley or other fresh herbs.

SCALLOP BROCHETTES WITH BACON, MUSHROOMS, AND CROUTONS

A succulent combination for a dinner in minutes. The brochettes can be assembled beforehand and refrigerated, covered, until needed. Bring them to room temperature before broiling; be sure your broiler is pre-heated, and watch carefully to ensure even browning. Serve this on a bed of rice pilaf (page 71).

Serves 4 (two 8-inch skewers per serving)

1 stick (4 ounces) unsalted butter
2 or 3 cloves garlic, lightly bruised
Juice of ½ lemon
Freshly ground black pepper
8 thick slices bacon, cut into
   1-inch squares
1 pound sea scallops, cut into 1 ½-
   inch chunks, if large

4 one-inch-thick slices day-old
   French or Italian bread, crusts
   trimmed, cut into 1-inch cubes
16 small to medium mushrooms,
   blanched 1 minute, drained
Chopped fresh parsley, or gremolata
   mixture of chopped parsley, garlic,
   and grated lemon zest

1. Melt butter with garlic in small saucepan over medium heat. Add lemon juice and pepper; simmer 5 minutes. Reserve.
2. Assemble brochettes as follows: bacon, scallop, bacon, bread, mush-room, bacon, scallop, bacon, bread, bacon, scallop, bacon, mushroom (the bacon insulates the scallops). Arrange skewers on foil-lined broiler pan.
3. Preheat broiler.
4. Remove and discard garlic from butter. Brush skewers with butter mixture on all sides, anointing scallops and bread generously. Grind pepper over all. Broil 4 to 5 inches from flame, 5 to 6 minutes total. Turn every minute or two, spooning cooking juices over skewers, until all sides are golden.
5. Place skewers on warmed platter. Spoon juices over; sprinkle with parsley or gremolata. Serve with rice. Garnish, if desired, with wedges of fresh lemon.

BARBECUED SHELLFISH

One of the best but least-known ways to cook oysters, clams, and mussels is on a barbecue. I learned this method from Alice Waters, the inspired chef-owner of Chez Panisse in Berkeley and author of *The Chez Panisse Menu Cookbook.* Be sure to cook the shellfish *just* until they open, and no longer; the flesh should be heated through but not toughened. Serve with plenty of Lemon-Herb Butter, gently warmed in a saucepan over low heat until creamy.
Serves 3 to 4

*2 dozen oysters in their shells, or
2 to 3 dozen mussels in their
shells, or a combination*

*Lemon-Herb Butter (page 125),
melted just until creamy
Freshly ground black pepper*

1. Wash oysters; scrub mussels and debeard. Discard any open shells.
2. Arrange shellfish on oiled grill about 3½ inches above hot coals. Cook until shellfish open: 2 to 4 minutes for oysters; 1½ to 3 minutes for mussels. Do not overcook. Carefully remove top shells, retaining juices in the bottom shells. Spoon butter over shellfish; sprinkle with pepper.

STEAMING AND PAPILLOTES

Many people mistakenly think that these two methods require special knowledge or equipment. Follow the simple guidelines below, and you'll realize that both steaming and cooking *en papillote* (in a parchment paper or foil case) not only are easy but produce extremely moist, flavorful fish.

❖ Basic Considerations for Steaming ❖

- While many good and inexpensive steamers are available, you can improvise by placing a wire rack or heatproof mug in a lidded pot, then laying an oiled plate of food on the rack. If you own a wok, you can crisscross three chopsticks in the wok, triangle fashion, and lay the plate on this "rack."
- Place enough water in the pot to come 1 inch below the plate with the food, no higher. Cover and bring to a vigorous boil, which will fill the pot with steam. Lay the fish on an oiled plate, and place in the pot. Be careful; steam can burn unexpectedly.
- Be sure the lid fits tightly, and try not to open it during cooking.
- Foods can be steamed over a flavored liquid such as a broth, or over water with a few thin slices of aromatics such as ginger, garlic, lemon, or lime in it.
- Be sure that the water does not boil away during steaming; add more boiling water during cooking if necessary, pouring it in without wetting the foods.
- Fish is not the only food that steams well by these guidelines; almost any vegetable can be steamed to advantage, as well as chicken, custards, breads, and puddings.

BASIC METHOD FOR STEAMED FISH FILLETS

Serves 4

Water
½ cup dry white wine, vermouth,
  or sherry (optional)
1 teaspoon vegetable oil
1 ½ pounds firm-fleshed white fish

such as haddock, striped bass, or
  sea trout
Juice of 1 lemon
1 Tablespoon chopped fresh parsley

1. Pour enough water, including optional wine, if you wish, into large saucepan or pot, or steamer, to come within 1 inch of bottom of plate that will sit on top of heatproof mug or rack. Cover pot; heat water to boiling over medium heat.

2. Meanwhile, place fillets on oiled plate and sprinkle with lemon juice. Carefully remove cover from pot or steamer. Place plate with fillets on mug or rack. Steam, covered, 3 to 10 minutes, depending on thickness of fish (10 minutes per inch of thickness of fish), until fish is opaque.

3. Transfer fillets with spatula to warmed serving platter. Sprinkle with parsley, or sauce and garnish as you wish. Or chill fillets; serve with homemade mayonnaise or flake into a fish salad.

Variations

Steamed Whole Fish: Follow the same steaming procedure with a whole fish. Keep the head and tail on, and if possible, have the backbone removed by your fishmonger for easy serving. A few thin slices of lemon and onion placed in the cavity will help flavor the fish. Allow 10 minutes cooking time per inch of thickness.

Steamed Fish with Ginger and Scallions: Cut slashes in a whole fish or skin sides of fillets; insert thin slivers of peeled fresh ginger and scallions. Steam as above.

Fish Steamed with Aromatic Vegetables: Scatter a julienne of mixed vegetables (page 137) over fillets or whole fish. Steam as above.

STEAMED CLAMS OREGANATA

This dish, which uses a basic procedure applicable to other shellfish, makes a tasty first course or light supper.
Serves 4

2 pounds littleneck clams	1 cup dry white wine
Cornmeal	Salt
3 Tablespoons olive oil	Freshly ground black pepper
1 medium onion, chopped	Chopped fresh parsley
2 Tablespoons dried oregano, crumbled	Lemon wedges

1. Scrub clams. Place in large bowl; sprinkle with cornmeal. Cover with cold water. Soak, stirring occasionally, at least 1 hour. Drain; rinse.
2. Heat oil in large saucepan or pot over medium heat until rippling. Add onion; sauté until wilted, but not brown, 6 to 8 minutes. Add oregano; toss. Stir in wine. Simmer until reduced by half. Season with salt and pepper.
3. Add clams to saucepan. Steam, covered, shaking saucepan occasionally, until clams open, 4 to 8 minutes. Drain.
4. Serve clams in warmed shallow soup bowls with a ladleful of the broth, avoiding any sediment at the bottom. Garnish with parsley and lemon wedges, and serve with plenty of good bread.

CHRIS STYLER'S STEAMED MUSSELS WITH TOMATO AND FENNEL

Serves 4

2 pounds mussels
Cornmeal
4 large, ripe tomatoes, peeled,
   seeded, cut into ½-inch dice
3 Tablespoons chopped shallot
2 Tablespoons dry white wine

2 teaspoons fennel seeds
Salt
Freshly ground black pepper
Dash Tabasco (optional)
Parsley sprigs

1. Scrub mussels with stiff brush; debeard. Place in bowl. Sprinkle lightly with cornmeal; cover with cold water. Soak at least 1 hour, stirring occasionally. Drain; rinse.
2. Place tomatoes, chopped shallot, wine, fennel seeds, and salt and pepper to taste in large saucepan or pot. Simmer, covered, over medium heat, shaking occasionally, until thickened slightly, 10 to 15 minutes.
3. Add mussels and optional Tabasco. Steam, covered, until mussels open, 3 to 6 minutes. Serve immediately in large soup plates with ladleful of broth. Garnish with parsley.

❖ Basic Considerations for Cooking *en Papillote* ❖

Cooking *en papillote,* an old French technique formerly used in an open hearth, is quick and easy, and seals in flavors and juices better than any other method. This method could actually be considered oven-steaming. You can also cook a sealed *papillote* in a steamer instead of the oven. Follow these guidelines:

Forming the Papillotes:

- Using parchment paper or aluminum foil, cut a heart shape large enough to accommodate a serving of fish on one-half of the heart (the word *papillote* means butterfly). Lightly brush one side with softened butter or oil. Lay the fish (or other food) on one side of the heart. Add other ingredients as directed; fold the other side of the heart over the fish, covering it somewhat loosely to allow room for steam. Fold the curved edges of the heart over tightly to seal in the juices, and then seal again, folding a series of small pleats. Place on a baking sheet.
- The sealed *papillotes* can be prepared ahead and refrigerated, but allow them to come to room temperature before cooking so that the timing in the recipes will be accurate.

Baking:

- The *papillotes* are cooked in a hot oven as directed in the following recipes; usually they will puff up with steam when ready.
- You may need to add a few minutes to the basic 10-minute timing rule.

Serving:

- Transfer each *papillote* quickly to a heated plate and serve one, unopened, to each guest. Let each person cut open his or her own package so that none of the aromatic steam escapes before serving.

FILLET OF SEA BASS EN PAPILLOTE
WITH AROMATIC VEGETABLES AND CREAM

This simple, refined dish is one of my favorites for entertaining, whether as a first or main course. You may, if you wish, omit the cream, but a couple of spoonfuls can only improve things.

Cooking Tip: If you've got leftover poaching liquid or fish broth on hand, put about ½ cup into a saucepan; reduce by two-thirds. Add the cream, garlic, and nutmeg, and proceed with the rest of step 7.

Serves 6

2 pounds bass fillets or other firm-fleshed white fish
Salt
Freshly ground pepper
4 Tablespoons unsalted butter, softened
2 Tablespoons chopped shallot
1 leek, trimmed, cut in fine julienne (⅓ to ½ cup)
1 carrot, trimmed, peeled, cut in fine julienne (about ½ cup)
1 rib celery, trimmed, cut in fine julienne (⅓ to ½ cup)

6 Tablespoons dry white wine or Fish Broth (page 11)

OPTIONAL CREAM REDUCTION:

1 cup heavy cream
2 cloves garlic
Pinch freshly grated nutmeg
Few drops fresh lemon juice
2 Tablespoons chopped fresh parsley
Salt
Cayenne pepper

1. Cut fish into 6 even pieces; season lightly with salt and pepper. Reserve.

2. Tear off 6 large squares of parchment paper or aluminum foil. Fold in half. Cut out half a heart, starting and ending with the center fold. The half heart should be large enough for the fish, with a remaining border of 4 or 5 inches all around. Unfold hearts; lay flat on work surface.

3. Lightly butter one half of each heart using 2 Tablespoons of the butter in all. Sprinkle the chopped shallot over each buttered area. Arrange portion of fish on top of the shallot, close to center fold. Mix together garniture of julienned vegetables; divide evenly among the 6 servings, scattering over the fish. Dot each fish portion with remaining 2 Table-

spoons butter cut into bits. Sprinkle 1 Tablespoon wine over each portion.

4. Preheat oven to 450°.

5. Seal packages closed by first folding unbuttered heart half over fish, joining rounded edges. Fold curved edge over once, and then a second time with a series of pleats to seal packet tightly. Place on baking sheet. Fish can be prepared in advance to this point.

6. Bake packets about 16 minutes for ¾- to 1-inch fillets, another 3 to 4 minutes if 1½ inches thick. The packets should puff.

7. Meanwhile, if preparing optional cream reduction, reduce the cream, garlic, and nutmeg by about one-third in a small skillet. Strain into small saucepan; simmer until slightly thickened. Add lemon juice, parsley, salt, and cayenne.

8. Remove the *papillotes* from the oven. Open each package; nap with small amount of optional reduced cream so juices combine.

WHOLE FISH BAKED EN PAPILLOTE

This method works well with bass, snapper, tilefish, weakfish (sea trout), and other firm-fleshed white fish. The head and tail add flavor, but if you prefer, have the fish filleted; then reassemble the two long fillets (flesh to flesh) for easy serving. The *papillote* also makes cleaning up a snap.

Serves 3 to 4

1 small onion, thinly sliced
2 carrots, thinly sliced (optional)
Salt
2 ½ to 3 pounds whole firm-fleshed fish such as bass, bluefish, snapper, or tilefish, cleaned and scaled
1 to 2 teaspoons unsalted butter,

cut into small bits, plus butter for foil
Freshly ground black pepper
½ lemon, thinly sliced
Several sprigs fresh dill or fennel
3 to 4 Tablespoons white wine (optional)

1. Preheat oven to 400°.
2. Blanch onion and carrot in large saucepan of boiling salted water 2 minutes. Drain.
3. Lay fish on piece of buttered aluminum foil large enough to enclose fish snugly; place on baking sheet. Season fish inside and out with salt and pepper. Arrange onion, carrot, butter, lemon slices, and dill inside and over top of fish. Wrap fish in foil, folding edges together to seal tightly.
4. Bake about 10 minutes per inch of thickness. Serve directly from foil, or allow to cool slightly, until warm.

MISCELLANEOUS METHODS

BAKED TROUT WITH CROUTONS AND LEMON PERSILLADE

A whole small fish, stuffed with a crunchy filling, is neatly served to each guest.
Makes 2 servings

5 slices day-old white bread, crusts trimmed, cut into ½-inch cubes
5 Tablespoons unsalted butter plus additional for baking dish
2 Tablespoons olive oil
1 small onion, finely minced
⅓ to ½ cup chopped mushrooms (optional)
4 cloves garlic, minced
Grated zest of 2 lemons

¼ cup plus 2 Tablespoons chopped fresh parsley
Salt
Freshly ground black pepper
1 Tablespoon fresh lemon juice
2 trout (about ¾ pound each), with head and tail, cleaned and boned
¼ cup dry white wine

1. Preheat oven to 450°.
2. Brown bread cubes in 3 Tablespoons of the butter and 1 Tablespoon of the olive oil in large skillet over medium heat. Toss frequently until crisp and golden, 3 to 6 minutes. Remove croutons to plate.
3. Add 1 Tablespoon of the butter to the skillet. Add onion; toss for 2

to 3 minutes. Add optional mushrooms; toss 2 minutes. Add garlic and lemon zest; toss 1 minute. Add the ¼ cup chopped parsley, salt and pepper, and croutons. Toss to combine. Add lemon juice to moisten. Remove skillet from the heat. Correct seasonings.

4. Butter shallow baking dish large enough to hold fish in one layer. Salt and pepper fish inside and out. Stuff each fish with half the stuffing; place fish in dish. Dot the remaining Tablespoon of butter over fish. Sprinkle with the remaining Tablespoon of oil and white wine.

5. Bake 5 minutes. Lower heat to 400°; bake until flesh is firm to touch, 15 to 20 minutes more. Remove from oven; let rest 3 minutes before serving.

6. To serve, remove fish to platter; sprinkle with pan juices and the 2 Tablespoons chopped parsley.

GRATIN OF FISH FILLETS WITH ZUCCHINI RAGOUT

This quick, full-flavored gratin is a perfect use for a cup or two of leftover Zucchini Ragout, or substitute a similar amount of thick tomato sauce (page 61), or Basquaise (page 192). Any fish can be used, though I like a strongly flavored one such as bluefish here. The vegetable mixture keeps the fish moist from above and below, and is topped by a crisply browned crust.

Serves 2

1 ½ cups Zucchini Ragout (page 91)

2 fish fillets or steaks (about 7 ounces each), such as bluefish, swordfish, or striped bass

Salt

Freshly ground black pepper

2 Tablespoons olive oil

5 Tablespoons bread crumbs

2 Tablespoons freshly grated Parmesan cheese

1. Reduce zucchini ragout in medium saucepan over medium heat to about 1 cup. Reserve.

2. Preheat oven to 450° and set rack in upper third of oven.

3. Lightly season fish with salt and pepper. Drizzle about 1 Tablespoon of the oil into gratin dish or shallow baking dish just large enough to hold fish in one layer. Sprinkle about 2 Tablespoons of the bread crumbs in dish; spoon a little ragout over. Arrange fish in dish in one layer. Spread remaining ragout evenly over fish.

4. Top with remaining bread crumbs and grated cheese. Sprinkle remaining oil over all. Bake until bubbly and golden brown, 20 to 25 minutes; fish should be firm when lightly pressed. If fish is cooked and the crumbs have not browned, quickly slide dish under preheated broiler.

ANDRÉ SOLTNER'S SOLE WITH NOODLES

A superb, rich dish that unites several of the above techniques. André Soltner, the gifted chef-patron of New York's famed Lutèce, has devised his own version of a traditional dish from his native Alsace.
Serves 4

Unsalted butter, softened, for
   baking dishes and parchment
   paper
1 to 1 ½ pounds sole fillets
1 Tablespoon chopped shallot
Salt
Freshly ground black pepper
1 ripe tomato, peeled, seeded,
   chopped
1 cup dry white wine
1 ⅓ cups Fish Broth (page 11)
1 cup heavy cream

HOLLANDAISE:

2 sticks (8 ounces) unsalted butter,
   cut into small bits
3 egg yolks
Juice of 1 lemon
2 teaspoons cold water
Salt
Cayenne pepper

12 ounces egg noodles or fettuccine,
   fresh if possible

141

1. Preheat oven to 375°.

2. Butter large flameproof dish. Arrange fish fillets in one layer, folding slightly to fit, if necessary. Sprinkle fish with shallot and salt and pepper. Scatter chopped tomato over all. Add wine and fish broth. Cover fish with piece of buttered parchment or waxed paper. Bring pan just to boiling on top of stove over medium heat; transfer to oven. Bake until fillets are just firm, about 6 minutes. Do not overcook.

3. Pour off cooking liquid from pan into heavy saucepan. Keep fish covered in baking dish. Reduce liquid over high heat by about three-fourths (there should be about ½ cup). Add ½ cup of the cream; boil until sauce is slightly thickened, about 3 minutes. Reserve fish-cream sauce.

4. To make Hollandaise, melt the 2 sticks butter in small heavy saucepan; reserve off heat. Whisk egg yolks with half the lemon juice and 2 teaspoons cold water in top of double boiler. When slightly thickened, place over simmering water. Whisk vigorously until mixture thickens. Slowly whisk in butter a little at a time. Mixture should remain warm; if it gets hot, remove from heat. When all the butter has been incorporated and the sauce is thick and creamy, add remaining lemon juice to taste. Season with salt and cayenne. Reserve.

5. Bring large kettle of salted water to boil. Add noodles; return to boil. Cook until *al dente.* Drain; rinse. Reserve.

6. Preheat broiler.

7. Mix noodles and remaining ½ cup cream in buttered shallow gratin dish large enough to hold fish fillets in one layer. Arrange fish over noodles, draining any exuded juices into fish-cream sauce. Whisk Hollandaise into fish-cream sauce. Correct seasonings with salt, pepper, cayenne, and lemon juice. Nap fillets evenly with sauce. Pour remaining sauce over all. Broil just until golden and bubbly. Serve immediately.

❖ Basic Seafood Mousseline and Its Varied Uses ❖

While light-as-air fish mousses are now associated with the "new French cooking," they are absolutely classic, spelled out in great detail by Escoffier. One of my favorite cooking classes consists of a demonstration of a basic mousseline, followed by nearly a dozen spin-off recipes that show its multiple uses. Some of these are indicated here.

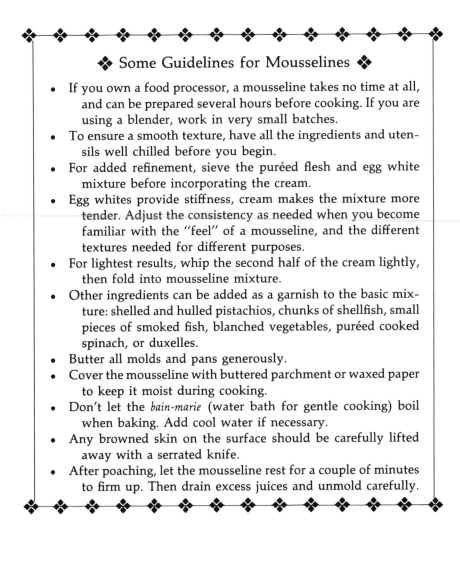

❖ Some Guidelines for Mousselines ❖

- If you own a food processor, a mousseline takes no time at all, and can be prepared several hours before cooking. If you are using a blender, work in very small batches.
- To ensure a smooth texture, have all the ingredients and utensils well chilled before you begin.
- For added refinement, sieve the puréed flesh and egg white mixture before incorporating the cream.
- Egg whites provide stiffness, cream makes the mixture more tender. Adjust the consistency as needed when you become familiar with the "feel" of a mousseline, and the different textures needed for different purposes.
- For lightest results, whip the second half of the cream lightly, then fold into mousseline mixture.
- Other ingredients can be added as a garnish to the basic mixture: shelled and hulled pistachios, chunks of shellfish, small pieces of smoked fish, blanched vegetables, puréed cooked spinach, or duxelles.
- Butter all molds and pans generously.
- Cover the mousseline with buttered parchment or waxed paper to keep it moist during cooking.
- Don't let the *bain-marie* (water bath for gentle cooking) boil when baking. Add cool water if necessary.
- Any browned skin on the surface should be carefully lifted away with a serrated knife.
- After poaching, let the mousseline rest for a couple of minutes to firm up. Then drain excess juices and unmold carefully.

BASIC SEAFOOD MOUSSELINE

1 ½ pounds sea scallops, with
    juices, or other seafood such as
    shrimp, lobster, salmon, sole,
    flounder, pike, or a combination
1 shallot (optional)
Salt
Freshly ground white pepper
Pinch cayenne pepper

Pinch freshly grated nutmeg
2 egg whites
1 cup heavy cream or crème
    fraîche, or more depending on
    use
Fresh lemon juice
Cognac or brandy

1. Keep all ingredients cold. Purée scallops and optional shallot in food processor or blender, working in batches, until very smooth. Season with salt, white pepper, cayenne, and nutmeg. Add egg whites; blend until smooth.
2. If mixture has become warm, chill. Blend in cream in food processor or blender until mixture is perfectly smooth. Add lemon juice and Cognac to taste. Correct all seasonings.
3. Use as outlined in the following recipes.

Variations

Timbales of Seafood with Beurre Blanc: An elegant beginning to a dinner party. For an even more luxurious version, top the sauced timbales with a medallion of poached lobster tail, or with a small mound of caviar.

Makes 8 to 10 4-ounce timbale molds, ramekins, or custard cups

Chill Basic Seafood Mousseline mixture (above). Whip an additional ½ cup heavy cream lightly; fold into mousseline mixture. Carefully spoon into well-buttered timbale molds; tap gently on hard surface to pack. Place in *bain-marie;* water level should come one-half to two-thirds of the way up sides of molds. Cover tops with buttered parchment or waxed paper. Bake in preheated 325° oven for 20 to 30 minutes, or until tops are firm to touch. Remove paper and any browned skin. Let stand a few minutes. Drain excess juices; carefully unmold. Serve with Beurre Blanc (page 122).

"Kugelhopf" of Seafood with Tomato Beurre Blanc: A spectacular dish that no one will suspect you prepared in minutes earlier that day. The Alsatian kugelhopf mold allows the sauce to run down in glossy rivulets. Alternatively, you can use a ring mold.

Chill Basic Seafood Mousseline mixture (above). Whip an additional ½ cup heavy cream lightly; fold into mousseline mixture. Pack half the mixture into well-buttered kugelhopf mold or other 6-cup mold. Tap to pack. Arrange thick strips of fresh salmon over surface. Top with remaining mousseline. Cover with buttered parchment or waxed paper. Bake in *bain-marie* in preheated 375° oven for 45 minutes or until top is firm to touch. Remove paper and any browned skin. Let stand a few minutes. Drain any excess juices; carefully unmold. Serve with Tomato Beurre Blanc (page 123) drizzled down sides.

Mousse-Stuffed Fillets: Vary the combinations as you like; mousselines of shellfish or salmon are especially fine wrapped in a fillet of sole or flounder.

Chill ½ Basic Seafood Mousseline mixture (above). Spoon mixture on skin side of 8 fillets of sole or flounder. Gently fold other half over to cover. Oven-poach in white wine in preheated 375° oven (page 127), covered with buttered parchment or waxed paper, just until firm, about 15 minutes. Sauce with Herbed Beurre Blanc (page 122).

Seafood Sausage: Serve this hot, two or three bias-cut slices per portion, with a Beurre Blanc (page 122), or cold with a tomato mayonnaise (page 124), or better yet with two sauces, such as fennel and watercress mayonnaises (page 124). This easy recipe uses Saran Wrap instead of sausage casings; do not substitute other brands, which may not be heatproof. And be sure to seal the "casing" tightly as directed.

Serves 8 to 12

1 pound sea scallops, with juices
1 shallot (optional)
1 teaspoon salt
½ teaspoon freshly ground white pepper
Pinch cayenne pepper
Large pinch freshly grated nutmeg
2 egg whites
1 Tablespoon fresh lemon juice, or more as needed

1 Tablespoon Cognac, or more as needed
¾ cup chilled heavy cream
Garnish: Shelled pistachios, slivers of scallop, blanched green beans and/or carrots, cut in small dice
1 Tablespoon unsalted butter

1. Make mousseline mixture using all ingredients through heavy cream, according to technique in Basic Seafood Mousseline recipe (above). Make sure mixture is very cold. Fold in optional garnish.
2. Butter two 24-inch lengths of Saran Wrap. Arrange one lengthwise on flat surface. Lay half the sausage mixture, from left to right, across center of wrap, in approximately 9-inch-long tube shape. Bring long side of wrap, farthest away from you, over the top of the mixture and around, tucking under. Press out air bubbles as you work. Lift closest side of wrap up and over mixture, forming a compact sausage, approximately 9 by 1½ inches. Twist both ends closed, sealing in the mixture; bring the twisted ends of the plastic wrap up and over the top and lay flat on top of the sausage. Gently smooth out roll. Repeat procedure with remaining wrap and sausage mixture. Wrap each sausage again tightly with a second layer of wrap. Chill, if necessary, to firm up mixture.
3. Lay sausages in wide saucepan of hot water. Place plate on top of sausages to keep them submerged. Bring slowly to a bare simmer on top of the stove over low heat. Simmer until firm and spongy, 15 to 20 minutes, turning once during the cooking. Let rest in hot water 5 minutes. Remove sausages with spatulas to paper-towel-lined wire rack. If sausage is to be served cold, cool; unwrap, and chill, covered.
4. To serve, unwrap and slice into medallions. Accompany with appropriate sauce.

Cold Seafood Terrine: This keeps well for about three days, and makes light, cool eating in hot weather. Some inlaid fillings are indicated, but use your imagination to concoct others. Serve with any of the mayonnaise variations (page 123).

Add ½ cup heavy cream to Basic Seafood Mousseline mixture (above), and chill. Butter 8 × 4-inch loaf pan. Arrange long sheet of buttered waxed paper to cover two long sides and bottom of loaf pan, with ends hanging over sides. Spoon in mousseline mixture. If forming an inlay, spoon in half the mousseline. Use the back of a spoon dipped in cold water to form a trough lengthwise down center; fill with chunks of salmon, puréed cooked spinach mixed with a bit of the mousseline, whole scallops, shrimp, etc. Spoon in remaining half of mixture. Tap pan firmly on countertop to pack mixture. Fold ends of paper over top. Poach in *bain-marie* (water level should come one-half to two-thirds of the way up side of pan) in preheated 325° oven just until firm, 45 to 60 minutes. Cool; chill thoroughly in refrigerator. Unmold; slice with serrated knife.

SAUTÉS

BASIC CONSIDERATIONS FOR SAUTÉS

SEAFOOD SAUTÉS

SCALLOPS WITH MADEIRA AND CREAM
SHRIMP SAUTÉ WITH GARLIC AND SNOW PEAS
ANDRÉ SOLTNER'S *NAVARIN* OF LOBSTER IN PERNOD CREAM SAUCE

POULTRY SAUTÉS

CHICKEN BREASTS WITH MUSHROOMS AND WHITE WINE
CHICKEN BREASTS WITH MUSTARD AND CREAM
CHICKEN BREASTS WITH VEGETABLE JULIENNE AND CREAM
CHICKEN BREASTS WITH WINE VINEGAR AND WILD MUSHROOMS
CHICKEN WITH PEPPERS AND ARTICHOKES
CHICKEN THIGHS WITH GINGER AND SNOW PEAS
CHICKEN LIVERS WITH MARSALA AND SAGE

MEAT SAUTÉS

STEAK AU POIVRE VERT
  HAMBURGERS AU POIVRE
SLICED STEAK WITH HUNGARIAN PAPRIKA AND SOUR CREAM
LAMBURGERS WITH PINE NUTS AND GARLIC
BURGERS WITH BASQUE VEGETABLES
LAMB "RAGOUT" WITH SWEET GARLIC CLOVES AND VEGETABLE GARNITURE
PORK CHOPS *CHARCUTIÈRE*
WEISSWURST WITH CIDER, APPLES, AND ONIONS
SAUSAGES WITH PEPPERS, TOMATOES, AND BASIL

VEGETABLE SAUTÉS

SAUTÉ OF SPRING VEGETABLES
BARBARA TROPP'S HOT AND SOUR HUNAN-STYLE VEGETABLES
BARBARA TROPP'S DRY-FRIED SZECHWAN EGGPLANT

*O*ne summer while I was taking courses at the Culinary Institute of America, a woman classmate informed me, "I'm here to learn how to cook the kind of food they serve at La Caravelle [an *haute cuisine* restaurant in New York City]. I've got two weeks, and I want to learn five or six recipes that will make my guests *drop dead.*" In truth, specific recipes are of no use unless one understands what is happening when food cooks, and why. The only secret to "knock 'em dead" dishes is to learn *how to cook.*

The sauté, so popular in fine restaurant cooking, is ideal for the home cook: the ingredients are simply and quickly cooked, sauced with their own pan residues, and served at once, so their fresh tastes and textures are enjoyed at their optimum. The technique of the sauté is simple: food is first cooked in a small amount of hot fat. The flavorful crusty bits left in the pan (the *sucs*) are dissolved by *deglazing,* adding a small amount of liquid to the pan. Other liquids can be added and *reduced,* or boiled down, to evaporate moisture and concentrate flavor. The resulting quick sauce can then be enriched and garnished in several ways.

These dishes are ideal for impromptu main dishes. For a dinner party, do a sauté as a first course, and have the remaining dishes ready beforehand. Once you've finished the sauté, you can sit down with your guests with little left to do in the kitchen.

❖ Basic Considerations for Sautés ❖

The basic concept in sautéing is to *seal in the juices* of the food. Keep the following in mind.

Ingredients and Equipment:

- Be sure that all *ingredients are dry*. Otherwise they will not brown, but steam and stew in their own juices.
- Have all ingredients *at room temperature* and *within convenient reach* before you begin.
- Cut ingredients to *uniform size* so they will cook evenly.
- Keep in mind the *relative amounts* of different ingredients. For example, do you want a mouthful of chicken to contain a slice each of mushroom and red pepper, or do you want the chicken showered with vegetables?
- Since quick-cooking cuts of meat are best for meat sauté dishes, use *tender, choice cuts.* To reduce expense, follow the example of the Chinese stir-fry; allow a small amount of meat to flavor a large panful of garnish ingredients.
- Use a *heavy skillet or sauté pan* that permits good browning over fairly high heat. Copper, heavy stainless steel with an aluminum core, or cast iron are good choices; enameled cast iron, I find, is uncomfortably heavy and does not always brown food well.

The Initial Browning Process:

- Some recipes call for coating the ingredients with seasoned flour before sautéing to aid in browning and in thickening the sauce. But use flour sparingly, as it can lead to a pasty sauce. I prefer to *avoid flour when possible.*
- The *fat medium* can be butter, oil, or other substances. Clarified butter allows for higher sautéing heat without burning the butter. Adding a little oil to the butter will accomplish the same result and eliminate the extra task of clarifying the butter.
- Be sure the *fat is hot* before you add the food. Oil should be rippling and butter foam should have subsided. Dry pieces of food should sizzle as they hit the pan. (*Sauter* means "to jump.") Use only enough fat to coat the bottom of the skillet.

- The *larger the item* being sautéed, the *lower the heat.* Otherwise, the outside of the food can burn before the heat penetrates to the center.
- *Don't crowd the food in the pan.* The surface of the pan should be covered with a single layer of food, with a little space between each piece. Too many pieces, and the food will steam; too few, and the fat will burn.
- Once the food is spread in the pan, let *it sit in the hot fat for about 30 seconds before tossing and stirring.* This promotes browning, and as an Austrian chef I once worked with advised, "It really gives it that sautéed flavor."
- *Regulate the heat carefully* so that the fat sizzles steadily but not so furiously that the food burns.
- *Add ingredients in order of their cooking time.*
- Once the main ingredient is cooked through, *remove it carefully,* without piercing, to a heated serving plate. *Keep warm,* loosely covered with aluminum foil, or place, covered, in a warm oven. Serve as soon as possible.

Deglazing and Finishing:

- Pour off excess fat. *Deglaze* by adding to the pan a small amount of liquid such as water, wine, liquor, beer, stock or broth, vinegar, or tomato or other juices. Quickly scrape up any browned bits from the bottom and sides of the pan. Flame any alcoholic liquid to burn off the harsh alcohol taste, or just simmer the liquid for a moment or two. These deglazing juices, slightly reduced, can now be used as a sauce.
- Once the pan is deglazed, you can add another liquid, usually stock, broth, or cream, which is then *reduced* for a subtler and slightly more abundant sauce. Several liquids can be added in this manner, reducing after each addition. This is called *stratification.*
- Pour a small amount of sauce from a spoon as it reduces to recognize the perfect *napping* consistency: sauce will coat the food lightly and evenly.
- *Enrich the sauce* by swirling in a nut of cool butter, off the heat. The final addition of butter is called *montage au beurre,* or mounting a sauce with butter.

SEAFOOD SAUTÉS

A sauté of seafood makes a fine light meal or a beguiling opener for several other courses. The secret of cooking seafood is to avoid overcooking; once liquid is added, gentle simmering, rather than boiling, is called for.

SCALLOPS WITH MADEIRA AND CREAM

This dish represents one of the simplest forms of the sauté. Note that overcooking is avoided by removing the scallops from the pan while the sauce reduces. Lobster, crabmeat, or shrimp can be prepared this way, and other fortified wines such as dry Marsala or sherry can be substituted for the Madeira. Arrange scallop mixture on bed of rice, pouring sauce over, if you wish.
Serves 4

4 Tablespoons unsalted butter	*2 Tablespoons minced shallots*
1 ½ to 2 cups sliced mushrooms (5	*½ to ⅔ cup Madeira*
to 6 ounces)	*1 cup heavy cream*
1 ½ pounds scallops, patted dry	*Salt*
with paper towels	*Freshly ground white pepper*

1. Heat 2 Tablespoons of the butter in large skillet over medium heat. When foam subsides, add mushrooms; sauté, tossing, until light brown, about 3 minutes. Remove mushrooms with slotted spoon to plate.
2. Add the remaining 2 Tablespoons butter to skillet. When foam subsides, add scallops. Sauté, tossing, until opaque, about 3 minutes. Arrange scallops and mushrooms with slotted spoon on warm individual serving plates. Keep warm.
3. Pour off any excess fat from skillet. Add shallots to skillet. Sauté 1 minute. Add Madeira; reduce over high heat by one-half, about 3 minutes. Add cream and any juices exuded by mushrooms and scallops. Reduce until thickened, about 3 minutes. Add salt and pepper to taste. Pour over scallops.

SHRIMP SAUTÉ WITH GARLIC AND SNOW PEAS

A lighter sauté, oriental in style, with a delicate, brothlike sauce.
Serves 4 to 6

2 Tablespoons unsalted butter
1 Tablespoon peanut or vegetable
  oil
4 to 6 ounces snow peas, strings
  removed
1 ¼ pounds medium shrimp,
  shelled, deveined
Salt
Freshly ground black pepper

3 cloves garlic, minced (about 2
  teaspoons)
½ cup dry white wine
Grated zest of 1 lemon
3 Tablespoons chopped fresh
  parsley
Few drops oriental sesame oil
Fresh lemon juice as needed

1. Heat butter and oil in large skillet over medium heat. When foam subsides, add snow peas; sauté until snow peas just lose their raw taste but remain crisp, 3 to 5 minutes. Meanwhile, pat shrimp dry with paper towel. Season with salt and pepper.
2. Remove snow peas to plate with slotted spoon, leaving fat in pan. Add shrimp and garlic to skillet; sauté, tossing, until shrimp just turn pink, about 3 minutes. Add wine; reduce by one-third, about 2 minutes. Add reserved snow peas, lemon zest, parsley; toss to heat through. Wine should now be somewhat syrupy. Add sesame oil and lemon juice to taste. Correct seasoning. Serve hot. If served as a main course, accompany with rice.

ANDRÉ SOLTNER'S NAVARIN OF LOBSTER IN PERNOD CREAM SAUCE

With this dish, Chef Soltner of Lutèce restaurant demonstrates that great cooking is nothing short of magical. Each ingredient in this briny "stew" emerges clearly and impeccably tender in a delicately seasoned sauce. Serves 6 (one-half lobster per serving)

3 live lobsters (each about 1 ¼ pounds)
¼ cup oil
12 Tablespoons (1 ½ sticks) unsalted butter
½ cup Pernod
1 ½ cups heavy cream
1 ripe tomato, cored, peeled, seeded, finely chopped
1 teaspoon coarse (kosher) salt
¼ teaspoon freshly ground black pepper

½ pound scallops
1 cup julienne of carrot (¹⁄₁₆ × ¹⁄₁₆ × 2)
1 cup julienne of celery (¹⁄₁₆ × ¹⁄₁₆ × 2)
1 cup julienne of leeks, white part only (¹⁄₁₆ × ¹⁄₁₆ × 2)
1 Tablespoon finely chopped fresh parsley
1 Tablespoon finely chopped chives

1. Place lobster, stomach down, on cutting board. Cut tail from body. Repeat with two other lobsters. Cut each tail crosswise into four sections. Twist and pull off two claws from each lobster. Break each claw into two pieces at joint. Cut each lobster body in half lengthwise. Remove and discard stomach and yellow sac on each side.

2. Heat oil in large sauté pan over medium-high heat until sizzling. Add lobster pieces; sauté, turning once or twice, until shells begin to turn red, 2 to 3 minutes. Add 2 Tablespoons of the butter; sauté until all shells are red, 1 to 2 minutes. Add Pernod. Carefully ignite with long kitchen match. When flame subsides, add cream, tomato, and salt and pepper. Cook 4 minutes. Add scallops; cook 2 minutes.

3. Meanwhile, heat 2 Tablespoons of the butter in a saucepan over medium-low heat. When foam subsides, add julienne of carrot, celery, and leek. Sauté, slowly, about 5 minutes.

4. Remove lobster and scallops with slotted spoon to warmed serving platter.

5. Add parsley and chives to sauté pan. Divide remaining 8 Tablespoons

of butter into 8 pieces. Remove sauté pan from heat. Whisk in butter one tablespoon at a time; wait until each piece is just incorporated into sauce before adding next piece. Correct seasonings. Strain sauce over lobster. Scatter vegetable julienne over each portion. Serve immediately.

POULTRY SAUTÉS

Different cuts of chicken—breasts on and off the bone, leg-thigh portions, and cut-up whole birds—can be substituted for specific cuts called for in the following selection of poultry sauté recipes. Adjust the cooking times accordingly, remembering that a boneless breast will cook the fastest. Chicken breast meat, boneless or not, is done when firmly springy to the touch—do not overcook the meat, or boil it once liquids are added, or the flesh will emerge dry and tough. Get in the habit of enjoying chicken less expensively by boning breasts and cutting up chickens yourself. You can also approximate costly veal scaloppine with chicken or turkey breasts by laying a halved boneless breast on a flat surface and slicing ¼-inch horizontal slices (as you would split an English muffin or bagel). Flatten the pieces gently with the side of a broad-bladed knife or cleaver. Sauté these pieces a mere 30 seconds per side.

CHICKEN BREASTS WITH MUSHROOMS AND WHITE WINE

A basic sauté with a chicken breast on the bone, sauced with a rich, brown pan reduction of wine, stock, herbs, and mushrooms. Calf's liver is also delicious treated this way.
Serves 2 to 4

2 whole chicken breasts (12 to 16 ounces each), with skin and bone, halved, excess skin and fat trimmed
Salt
Freshly ground black pepper
2 Tablespoons unsalted butter
1 Tablespoon vegetable oil
3 Tablespoons chopped onion
2 cups thickly sliced fresh mushrooms (about 6 ounces)

Large pinch fresh or dried tarragon
Large pinch fresh or dried thyme
½ cup dry white wine
½ cup Chicken Broth (page 6) or Mixed Meat and Poultry Broth (page 8)
2 Tablespoons cold unsalted butter, cut into small pieces
2 Tablespoons chopped fresh parsley

1. Pat chicken dry with paper towels. Season lightly with salt and pepper.
2. Heat butter and oil in large heavy skillet over medium-high heat. When foam subsides, arrange breasts in skillet skin side down, meaty portion close to center of pan. Sauté, shaking pan occasionally to prevent sticking, until golden brown, about 8 minutes, or less for smaller breasts. Turn breasts over. Lower heat; sauté, shaking pan occasionally, until just tender, about 7 minutes. During last 2 minutes, cover skillet with lid or aluminum foil to steam interior of meat. Meat should be just firm to the touch, but not tough. Remove chicken to platter. Keep warm, covered with foil, or in low oven.
3. Pour off all but 2 Tablespoons excess fat from skillet. Add onion to skillet; toss over medium-high heat about 30 seconds. Add mushrooms and herbs; spread evenly over bottom of skillet. Let sit 30 seconds. Toss until mushrooms are lightly golden, 1 to 2 minutes. Add wine; reduce over high heat, scraping up any browned bits from bottom and sides of skillet, until reduced by one-half, 3 to 5 minutes. Add broth and any juices exuded by chicken. Reduce by one-half, 4 to 5 minutes. Mush-

rooms will give off liquid while mixture reduces. Remove skillet from heat. Swirl in cold butter and parsley, just until butter has been incorporated in sauce. Correct seasonings. Pour sauce over chicken. Serve immediately.

CHICKEN BREASTS WITH MUSTARD AND CREAM

This is the basic technique for a sauté of boneless breast of chicken, with a light pan reduction.
Serves 2 to 4

2 whole chicken breasts (12 to 16 ounces each), boned, skinned, halved, excess fat trimmed
Salt
Freshly ground black pepper
2 Tablespoons unsalted butter
1 Tablespoon vegetable oil
1 to 2 Tablespoons chopped shallot or scallion
1 cup thickly sliced mushrooms (about 3 ounces)

⅓ cup dry white wine
½ cup heavy cream, or more as needed
1 Tablespoon Pommery mustard, or more to taste
1 to 2 teaspoons Dijon mustard
2 Tablespoons chopped fresh parsley

1. Pat chicken breasts dry with paper towels. Season lightly with salt and pepper.
2. Heat butter and oil in large heavy skillet over medium heat. When foam subsides, add chicken breasts. Sauté, shaking pan occasionally to prevent sticking, until lightly golden, about 6 to 8 minutes, or less depending on size. Turn breasts over. Lower heat. Sauté, shaking pan occasionally, until chicken is just tender, 6 to 8 minutes. Steam, covered, during last 2 minutes, if any pink spots remain. Meat should be just firm to the touch. Remove chicken to platter; keep warm.

3. Pour off all but 2 Tablespoons excess fat from skillet. Add chopped shallot; toss over medium-high heat about 30 seconds. Add mushrooms. Spread evenly over bottom of skillet; let sit about 30 seconds. Toss until mushrooms are lightly golden, about 1 minute. Add wine; reduce over high heat, scraping up any browned bits from bottom and sides of skillet, until syrupy, 3 to 4 minutes. Add cream and any juices exuded by chicken. Reduce until lightly thickened, about 3 minutes. Stir in mustards; correct seasonings. Add parsley. Pour sauce over chicken. Serve immediately.

CHICKEN BREASTS WITH VEGETABLE JULIENNE AND CREAM

A delicate version of the poultry sauté, perfect for a light meal on a warm evening. Accompany with a special bottle of a chilled Alsatian Riesling.
Serves 2 to 4

2 whole chicken breasts (12 to 16 ounces each), skinned, boned, halved, excess fat trimmed	inches long)
	1 Tablespoon julienne of leek, white part only (2 inches long)
Salt	2 Tablespoons julienne of mushroom (2 inches long)
Freshly ground black pepper	
2 Tablespoons unsalted butter	¾ cup heavy cream
2 Tablespoons chopped shallot or scallion	1 ½ Tablespoons chopped fresh parsley
2 to 3 Tablespoons dry white wine	1 ½ Tablespoons snipped fresh chives (or more parsley or another fresh herb)
2 Tablespoons julienne of carrot (2	

1. Pat chicken breasts dry with paper towels. Season lightly with salt and pepper.
2. Heat butter in large skillet over medium heat. When foam subsides, add chicken breasts. Sauté, shaking pan occasionally to prevent sticking, until lightly golden, 6 to 8 minutes, or less depending on size. Turn

breasts over. Lower heat; sauté, shaking pan occasionally, until chicken is just tender, 6 to 8 minutes. Steam, covered, during last 2 minutes if any pink spots remain. Meat should be just firm to the touch. Remove chicken to platter; keep warm.

3. Pour off all but 2 Tablespoons excess fat from skillet. Add chopped shallot; toss over medium heat 30 seconds. Add wine, scraping up any browned bits from bottom and sides of skillet. Add julienne of carrot and leek. Steam, covered, 3 to 4 minutes. Add julienne of mushroom, heavy cream, and any juices exuded by chicken. Reduce over high heat until thickened, about 3 minutes. Correct seasonings. Add herbs. Pour vegetable julienne and sauce over chicken. Serve immediately.

CHICKEN BREASTS WITH WINE VINEGAR AND WILD MUSHROOMS

A good wine vinegar is one of the best deglazing agents. If you have a special vinegar such as a vintage sherry or raspberry, use it in this simple tasty treatment.

Serves 2 to 4

½ cup dried mushrooms, such as porcini, cèpes, or morels* (½ ounce)
Warm water
2 whole chicken breasts (12 to 16 ounces each), skinned, boned, halved, excess fat trimmed
Salt

Freshly ground black pepper
2 Tablespoons unsalted butter
1 Tablespoon chopped shallot or scallion
⅓ cup good red wine vinegar
⅓ cup heavy cream
1 to 2 Tablespoons chopped fresh parsley

1. Soak dried mushrooms in warm water to cover until soft, about 20 minutes.
2. Pat chicken breasts dry with paper towels. Season lightly with salt and pepper.

*Mail-order source: H. Roth and Son, 1577 First Avenue, New York, N.Y. 10028 (212-734-1110)

3. Heat butter in large heavy skillet over medium heat. When foam subsides, add chicken breasts. Sauté, shaking pan occasionally to prevent sticking, until breasts are lightly golden, 6 to 8 minutes or less depending on size of breast. Turn breasts over. Lower heat; sauté, shaking pan occasionally, until chicken is just tender, 6 to 8 minutes. Steam, covered, during last 2 minutes if any pink spots remain. Meat should be just firm to the touch. Remove chicken to platter; keep warm.

4. While chicken is cooking, drain mushrooms over small bowl; rinse. Strain liquid through sieve lined with dampened paper towel or coffee filter; reserve ½ cup soaking liquid. Pat mushrooms dry with paper towels. Trim tough stems from mushrooms. Coarsely chop mushrooms.

5. Pour off all but 1 Tablespoon excess fat from skillet. Add chopped shallot; toss 30 seconds over medium heat. Add mushrooms; toss 2 minutes. Add vinegar, scraping up any browned bits from bottom and sides of skillet. Reduce over high heat by one-half, about 4 minutes. Add reserved mushroom liquid and any juices exuded by chicken. Add cream; reduce until thickened, 3 to 4 minutes. Correct seasonings. Add parsley. Pour sauce over chicken. Serve immediately.

CHICKEN WITH PEPPERS AND ARTICHOKES

This robust Italian-style dish, actually a quick braise, calls for plenty of bread to soak up the last of the peppery juices.
Cooking Tip: Leftover sauce is excellent on pasta.
Serves 3 or 4

1 chicken (about 3 pounds), cut into 8 pieces, excess skin, fat, wing tips trimmed	1 package (9 ounces) frozen artichoke hearts, thawed, wiped dry
¾ cup flour	3 or 4 cloves garlic, minced
1 ½ teaspoons salt	½ cup dry white wine
¼ teaspoon freshly ground black pepper, plus more as needed	⅔ cup Chicken Broth (page 6), or more as needed
¼ teaspoon dried thyme, crumbled	18 to 24 oil-cured black olives, halved, pitted
2 Tablespoons olive oil	
3 small red peppers, cored, seeded, cut into 1-inch dice	3 Tablespoons chopped fresh parsley
1 to 3 Tablespoons finely chopped seeded hot green peppers	2 Tablespoons chopped fresh basil, or ½ teaspoon dried, crumbled

1. Pat chicken dry with paper towels. Combine flour, 1 teaspoon of the salt, ¼ teaspoon pepper, and thyme in shallow dish. Toss chicken pieces in seasoned flour to coat, shaking off excess.

2. Select pan large enough to hold chicken in one layer. Heat oil in skillet to rippling over medium heat. Add chicken pieces; sauté, shaking pan occasionally, until pieces are deep brown, about 12 minutes. Turn pieces over; sauté, shaking pan occasionally, another 12 minutes, or until meat is nearly firm. Steam, covered, 3 minutes. Remove pieces to paper-towel-lined plate to drain.

3. Discard all but 3 Tablespoons of the excess fat. Add red and green peppers to pan; sauté, tossing, until slightly softened, about 5 minutes. Add artichoke hearts and garlic; toss until lightly golden, another 4 minutes. Add wine, scraping up any browned bits from bottom and sides of skillet. Reduce by one-half, 3 to 4 minutes. Add broth and the ½ teaspoon salt. Reduce slightly. Arrange chicken pieces in pan, breasts, skin sides up, on top. Add more broth if necessary, so level comes halfway up chicken. Simmer, covered, until dark meat is tender when poked with a knife, about 10 minutes.

4. Add black olives; baste chicken. Simmer, covered, until heated through. Add plenty of black pepper, parsley, and basil. Spoon juices over chicken. Correct seasonings. Serve hot. This dish reheats well.

CHICKEN THIGHS WITH GINGER AND SNOW PEAS

Covering the pan during the cooking process ensures that the dark meat will cook through.

Cooking Tip: Sugar-snap peas, blanched for 1 minute, can be substituted for snow peas.

Serves 3 or 4

6 chicken leg and thigh portions, excess skin and fat trimmed
Salt
Freshly ground black pepper
2 Tablespoons peanut or vegetable oil
6 to 8 ounces snow peas, strings and stem ends removed
1 heaping Tablespoon minced peeled fresh ginger

3 cloves garlic, minced
⅓ cup dry sherry
3 Tablespoons rice wine vinegar or white wine vinegar, plus more as needed
¾ cup Chicken Broth (page 6)
Pinch dried red pepper flakes (optional)
2 Tablespoons sliced scallions, thinly cut on the bias

1. Pat chicken dry with paper towels. Season lightly with salt and pepper.
2. Heat oil in large skillet over medium-high heat until rippling. Add chicken pieces; sauté, shaking pan occasionally, until crisp and golden, about 15 minutes, depending on size of pieces. Turn pieces over; sauté, shaking, until meat is nearly tender, about 12 minutes. Steam, covered, to moist-cook interior of meat, about 5 minutes. Remove chicken pieces with slotted spoon to paper-towel-lined plate to drain; keep warm.
3. Add snow peas to skillet; sauté, tossing, until crisp-tender, about 4 minutes. Remove with slotted spoon; reserve with chicken.
4. Discard all but 1 Tablespoon of the excess fat. Add ginger and garlic; sauté 2 minutes. Add sherry; reduce liquid by one-half, scraping up any browned bits from bottom and sides of skillet, about 3 minutes. Add vinegar and chicken broth; reduce by one-third to one-half, until slightly syrupy, about 4 minutes. Add optional red pepper flakes. Correct seasonings; add more vinegar if necessary.
5. Arrange chicken pieces and peas on heated platter. Pour sauce over. Serve immediately, with rice.

CHICKEN LIVERS WITH MARSALA AND SAGE

A quick and easy variation of veal scaloppine, substituting chicken livers for the veal.
Serves 3 to 4

*1 pound chicken livers, connective
  tissue removed, trimmed, halved*
⅔ cup flour
*1 teaspoon salt, and more as
  needed*
*½ teaspoon freshly ground black
  pepper, plus more as needed*
*½ teaspoon imported Hungarian
  paprika*
*4 Tablespoons unsalted butter, plus
  more as needed*

1 Tablespoon olive oil
¼ cup chopped shallot or scallion
*2 cups quartered or halved
  mushrooms (about 6 ounces)*
¾ cup dry Marsala wine
*Large pinch dried sage leaves, or 2
  Tablespoons chopped fresh sage*
*1 to 2 Tablespoons cold unsalted
  butter, cut into bits (optional)*
*3 Tablespoons chopped fresh
  parsley*

1. Pat chicken livers dry with paper towels. Combine flour, 1 teaspoon salt, ½ teaspoon pepper, and paprika in shallow dish.
2. Heat 2 Tablespoons of the butter and the oil in skillet over medium heat. Toss livers a few at a time in the seasoned flour to coat. Shake off excess, keeping one hand dry. When foam subsides in skillet, gently add livers to skillet. Do not crowd pan; work in two batches if necessary. Let livers sit in fat a few seconds before tossing. Sauté, tossing, until browned on all sides, 3 to 5 minutes. Remove livers with slotted spoon to drain in sieve. Repeat with any remaining livers. Add fat as needed.
3. Add 2 Tablespoons of the butter to the skillet. When foam subsides, add chopped shallot to pan. Toss 1 minute. Add mushrooms; toss until lightly golden, 3 to 4 minutes. Add Marsala and sage, scraping up any browned bits from bottom and sides of pan. Reduce liquid until just slightly syrupy. Swirl in optional butter, off heat, piece by piece. Correct seasonings with salt and pepper. Add parsley.
4. Transfer livers to warm platter. Pour mushrooms and sauce over livers. Serve immediately, with rice.

MEAT SAUTÉS

These are some of the best dishes for a delicious supper after a busy day. If you have a small amount of leftover gravy from a stew or pot roast, use it here for deglazing. The long-simmered juices will lend body to these quick sautés. Remember not to boil the meat once the liquid is added.

STEAK AU POIVRE VERT

A good pepper steak, which most of us consider an expensive restaurant dish, is simple to prepare quickly at home. Green peppercorns are used here, but coarsely ground black and white peppercorns are fine, too. Serves 2

2 sirloin steaks (each about 8 to 10 ounces)	1 Tablespoon unsalted butter
Salt	1 Tablespoon vegetable oil
3 to 4 Tablespoons green peppercorns, drained, crushed slightly, or a mixture of coarsely crushed black and white peppercorns	1 Tablespoon chopped shallot or scallion
	3 Tablespoons Cognac or whiskey
	½ cup heavy cream
	½ teaspoon Dijon mustard, or to taste (optional)

1. Pat steak dry with paper towels. Salt meat lightly. Press peppercorns into both sides of steak.
2. Heat butter and oil in large skillet over medium-high heat. When foam subsides, add meat. Sauté, shaking pan occasionally to prevent sticking, until brown, 5 minutes. Turn steaks over; sauté until brown, 3 to 5 minutes. Remove to plate. Keep warm.
3. Pour off all excess fat. Add shallots; sauté briefly. Carefully add Cognac, scraping up any browned bits from bottom and sides of skillet. Let Cognac simmer briefly to burn off alcohol. Add cream and any juices exuded by meat; reduce until thickened, about 3 minutes. Stir in optional mustard. Correct seasonings. Strain if desired. Pour sauce around and/or over steaks. Serve immediately.

Variation

Hamburgers au Poivre: Press peppercorns into sides of 6-ounce hamburgers. Sauté over medium heat about 5 to 7 minutes per side for medium rare. Then proceed as above.

SLICED STEAK WITH HUNGARIAN PAPRIKA AND SOUR CREAM

Unfortunately, too many floury, overcooked versions of beef stroganoff have given this dish a bad name. This quick version makes superb eating. If you have leftover trimmings from a fillet, you'll have an even more tender dish. Be careful not to boil the sauce once the sour cream is added; this flourless sauce can curdle. And keep the meat rare.
Serves 4

¾ cup dried mushrooms (about ¾ ounce), such as porcini, cèpes, or morels*

1 cup warm water

1 ½ pounds boneless sirloin steak, fat trimmed, cut into strips (2 × 1 × ¼ inches)

Salt

Freshly ground black pepper

2 Tablespoons unsalted butter, and more as needed

2 Tablespoons vegetable oil

1 ½ cups sliced mushrooms (about 5 ounces)

¼ cup chopped onion

2 teaspoons medium-hot imported Hungarian paprika, or 1 teaspoon hot*

3 Tablespoons red wine vinegar

½ cup heavy cream

¼ cup sour cream, plus additional for garnish

2 Tablespoons chopped fresh parsley, plus additional for garnish

*Mail-order source: H. Roth and Son, 1577 First Avenue, New York, N.Y. 10028 (212-734-1110)

1. Soak dried mushrooms in warm water until soft, 20 to 30 minutes.
2. Pat strips of meat dry in paper towels. Season lightly with salt and pepper. Heat half the butter and half the oil in large skillet over medium-high heat. When foam subsides, add half the meat. Sauté, tossing, until browned but still rare, 1 to 2 minutes. Drain in a sieve. Repeat with remaining oil, butter, and meat. Reserve meat.
3. Drain dried mushrooms over small bowl. Strain soaking liquid through sieve lined with dampened paper towel or coffee filter. Reserve. Rinse dried mushrooms in sieve under cold water. Remove tough stems. Dry mushrooms in paper towels. Chop coarsely. Sauté dried and fresh mushrooms in skillet, adding more fat if necessary, over medium heat, tossing, until lightly browned, 2 to 3 minutes. Reserve with meat.
4. Add onion to skillet with more fat if necessary. Sauté, tossing, until wilted, about 2 minutes. Add paprika; toss 30 seconds. Do not burn paprika. Add vinegar, scraping up browned bits from bottom and sides of skillet. Add reserved mushroom soaking liquid; reduce by one-half, about 3 minutes. Add heavy cream; reduce until thickened, about 3 minutes.
5. Return reserved meat, mushrooms, and all exuded juices from meat and mushrooms to skillet. Combine until everything is heated through. Add the ¼ cup sour cream and parsley; heat through without boiling. Correct seasonings. Serve with noodles, topping each portion with a spoonful of sour cream and a sprinkling of chopped parsley.

LAMBURGERS WITH PINE NUTS AND GARLIC

Ground lamb, which we serve too infrequently, can be juicy and full of flavor. Keep the meat rare or medium rare to avoid dryness.
Serves 4

1 ½ pounds ground lamb shoulder
Salt
Freshly ground black pepper
2 cloves garlic, minced
¼ cup pine nuts, toasted, or
  coarsely chopped walnuts

3 Tablespoons chopped fresh
  parsley
2 Tablespoons olive oil
⅓ cup dry wine, either red or
  white

1. Mix meat lightly with salt, pepper, garlic, pine nuts, and parsley. Form mixture into 4 burgers, each 6 ounces. Set aside.
2. Heat oil in large skillet over medium heat until rippling. Add burgers; for medium rare, sauté 5 to 7 minutes per side. Remove burgers to serving plate; keep warm.
3. Pour off excess fat from skillet. Add wine, scraping up browned bits from bottom and sides of skillet. Reduce wine slightly; spoon over burgers. Serve immediately.

BURGERS WITH BASQUE VEGETABLES

The vegetable garnish can be done well in advance, and the meat can be either chopped steak or, for unusually fine flavor, the seasoned lamburgers above.
Serves 4

5 Tablespoons olive oil

BASQUAISE:

1 ½ large onions, coarsely chopped
2 red peppers, cored, seeded, diced
1 green pepper, cored, seeded, diced
4 ounces smoked ham, diced
5 cloves garlic, minced
2 Tablespoons brandy
2 pounds tomatoes, fresh or
    canned, peeled, seeded, chopped

1 teaspoon mixed dried herbs such as thyme, oregano, basil, or rosemary, crumbled
8 Tablespoons dry white wine
1 teaspoon salt
3 Tablespoons chopped fresh parsley, plus additional for garnish
Freshly ground black pepper

4 hamburgers or lamburgers (see recipe above) (each 6 ounces)

1. Heat 3 Tablespoons of the oil in large skillet over medium heat until rippling. Add onions; sauté until soft, about 5 minutes. Add peppers; toss to coat with oil. Cook, covered, 5 minutes. Uncover; sauté, tossing, about 4 minutes. Add ham and garlic; sauté 2 minutes. Add brandy, scraping up any browned bits from bottom and sides of skillet. Cook

1 minute. Add tomatoes, 1 teaspoon herbs, 3 Tablespoons of the wine, and salt. Increase heat; cook, stirring, until peppers are tender and tomatoes have thickened, 10 to 15 minutes. Add parsley and pepper; correct for salt. Keep warm.

2. Preheat oven to 425°. Heat the remaining 2 Tablespoons oil in large skillet over medium-high heat until rippling. Add burgers; sear, about 3 minutes per side. Arrange vegetable mixture in shallow baking dish. Tuck burgers into mixture.

3. Pour off excess fat from skillet. Add the remaining 5 Tablespoons of wine, scraping up any browned bits from bottom and sides of skillet. Reduce slightly. Spoon over burgers.

4. Bake until vegetables are bubbly and meat is medium rare, springy but tender, about 10 minutes. Arrange Basque vegetables and burgers on warm serving platter. Sprinkle burgers with parsley. Serve with rice.

LAMB "RAGOUT" WITH SWEET GARLIC CLOVES AND VEGETABLE GARNITURE

Frequently in the *nouvelle cuisine,* new dishes are playfully called by old names. A quick sauté of seafood may be dubbed a *navarin* or a *blanquette,* both terms for traditional long-simmered meat stews. Here the term *ragoût,* generally used to mean a long-cooking stew of meat, vegetables, and broth, is applied to a quick sauté of lamb and vegetables with a light pan sauce.

This dish, worthy of a dinner party for special friends, is based on a lamb dish cooked by Michel Guérard for a luncheon in the Napa Valley. A warm, spirited personality, Guérard is one of the major shapers of modern French cuisine.

Serve the lamb with a fine California Cabernet Sauvignon (such as that of Robert Mondavi), or a mature Bordeaux.

Serves 4

4 shoulder or loin lamb chops (8 to 10 ounces each)

OPTIONAL MARINADE:

About 3 Tablespoons olive oil

½ teaspoon dried rosemary, crumbled

Freshly ground black pepper

16 to 20 cloves garlic, outer skin removed, but left unpeeled

Salt

Freshly ground black pepper

4 Tablespoons unsalted butter

1 Tablespoon olive oil

6 ounces green beans, trimmed, cut into 2-inch lengths

2 or 3 carrots, trimmed, peeled, cut into batons (2 × ¼ × ¼ inches)

½ cup dry wine, red or white

1 cup Chicken Broth (page 6), Mixed Meat and Poultry Broth (page 8), or lamb broth

1. Pat lamb chops dry with paper towels. To marinate lamb for tenderness and flavor, combine optional marinade ingredients: olive oil, rosemary, and black pepper in shallow dish. Rub marinade over lamb; place lamb in dish. Let stand 1 hour at room temperature, or refrigerate overnight.

2. Boil garlic cloves in water in small saucepan until garlic is tender, about 20 minutes. Remove cloves with slotted spoon; drain. Reserve. Leave pan of water on stove.

3. Remove chops from marinade. Wipe off rosemary. Salt chops lightly. If marinade has not been used, sprinkle chops with salt and pepper. Heat 2 Tablespoons of the butter and the 1 Tablespoon oil in large skillet over medium-high heat. When foam subsides, add chops. Sauté until brown, about 3 minutes per side. Remove to four warm plates; keep warm.

4. While cooking meat, add salt to boiling water in saucepan. Add green beans. Boil, uncovered, about 3 minutes. Add carrots; boil until crisp-tender, 3 to 4 minutes. Drain. Arrange vegetables to one side of lamb on each of the four plates. Keep warm.

5. Add wine to skillet, scraping up any browned bits from bottom and sides of pan. Reduce by one-half, about 3 minutes. Add broth and reserved garlic; reduce until syrupy, about 4 minutes. Remove pan from heat; swirl in remaining 2 Tablespoons butter. Scatter garlic over chops, dividing evenly. Pour sauce around meat and vegetables. Serve immediately.

PORK CHOPS CHARCUTIÈRE

These pork chops are prepared "butcher's wife's style"—aromatic with mustard and sliced gherkins, and kept moist with gentle cooking. Serve with noodles or potatoes and with cool beer or a spicy white wine, such as a Gewürztraminer.
Serves 4

4 shoulder or loin pork chops (each about 7 ounces)
Salt
Freshly ground black pepper
2 Tablespoons unsalted butter
1 Tablespoon vegetable oil
⅓ cup chopped onion
⅓ cup dry white wine
2 Tablespoons vinegar
⅔ cup Chicken Broth (page 6) or

Mixed Meat and Poultry Broth (page 8)
Pinch dried thyme
2 teaspoons Dijon or Pommery mustard
2 Tablespoons thinly sliced cornichons or other sour gherkins
1 to 2 Tablespoons chopped fresh parsley

1. Pat pork chops dry with paper towels. Season lightly with salt and pepper.
2. Heat butter and oil in skillet over medium-high heat. When foam subsides, add chops. Sauté, gradually lowering heat to medium. Turn once, sautéing chops until browned on both sides, 12 to 14 minutes in all. Remove chops to warm platter; keep warm.
3. Pour off all but 2 Tablespoons excess fat from skillet. Add chopped onion. Sauté until slightly soft, 2 to 3 minutes. Add wine and vinegar, scraping up any browned bits from bottom and sides of skillet. Reduce 1 minute. Add broth and thyme; reduce until slightly concentrated, about 3 minutes. Stir in mustard, cornichons, parsley, and any juices exuded from the meat. Correct seasonings with salt, pepper, and vinegar; sauce should be slightly sharp. Pour sauce over and around chops. Serve immediately.

WEISSWURST WITH CIDER, APPLES, AND ONIONS

An easy treatment for weisswurst (white veal sausage) or other mild sausage, reminiscent of *choucroute garnie.*
Cooking Tip: Tuck a pound or so of small boiled potatoes into the skillet for the last 10 minutes of simmering.
Serves 4

6 to 8 *weisswurst (1 ¼ to 1 ½ pounds), depending on size of links*
2 Tablespoons unsalted butter
2 slices bacon, preferably thick, cut into cubes (optional)
4 to 5 cups sliced onions (about 1 ½ pounds)
1 or 2 cloves garlic, minced
1 teaspoon mixed dried herbs, such as thyme or basil, crumbled

2 or 3 *juniper berries, slightly bruised*
½ cup dry white wine
½ cup apple cider or juice
2 firm tart apples, such as Granny Smith or Greening, peeled, quartered, cored, thickly sliced
Salt
Freshly ground black pepper
Chopped fresh parsley

1. Prick sausages with fork. Heat butter in large skillet over medium-high heat. When foam subsides, add sausages. Sauté, turning, until brown on all sides, 8 to 10 minutes. Remove to a paper-towel-lined plate.
2. Add optional bacon to skillet; lower heat slightly. Sauté until fat is rendered and bacon just beginning to brown, 5 to 6 minutes. Add onions (and a little oil if bacon not used). Sauté just until onions begin to wilt, 6 to 8 minutes. Add garlic, herbs, and juniper berries; sauté 2 more minutes. Add the wine, scraping up any browned bits from bottom and sides of skillet. Reduce by one-half, 3 to 4 minutes. Add cider. Correct seasonings. Return sausages to skillet. Simmer, covered, 15 minutes. Add apples to skillet. Simmer, covered, until everything is tender, 5 to 10 minutes. Add salt and pepper; sprinkle with parsley. Serve hot with boiled potatoes.

SAUSAGES WITH PEPPERS, TOMATOES, AND BASIL

A lightened version of an old Italian favorite.
Cooking Tip: Use all sweet sausage for a balance of sausage and the peppery sauce. Or if you prefer, use a combination of sweet and hot. Use leftover sauce on pasta, pizza, or in Pastitsio (page 200).
Serves 6

2 pounds Italian sweet sausage (or half sweet, half hot, or any combination)

3 Tablespoons olive oil

2 medium onions, coarsely chopped

3 red peppers (1 to 1 ¼ pounds), cored, seeded, cut into long slivers that are 1 inch wide at thickest point

2 green peppers (about ¾ pound), cored, seeded, cut into long slivers that are 1 inch wide at thickest point

5 or more cloves garlic, minced

⅓ cup dry red wine

4 or 5 ripe tomatoes (about 1 ¾ pounds), peeled, seeded, coarsely chopped, or 1 can (2 pounds, 3 ounces) imported peeled plum tomatoes, drained, liquid reserved, seeded, coarsely chopped

1 ½ teaspoons salt

½ cup finely shredded fresh basil leaves, or ¾ teaspoon dried, crumbled

1 ½ cups sliced mushrooms (about 5 ounces) (optional)

3 Tablespoons chopped fresh parsley

Freshly ground black pepper

1. Prick sausages with fork or tip of sharp knife. Place in large skillet in single layer. Pour in cold water to depth of ¼ inch. Cook over medium heat, turning once, until water evaporates, about 6 to 8 minutes. Increase heat if necessary. Continue to cook, shaking pan and turning occasionally, until sausages are browned on all sides, another 6 minutes. If skillet becomes too dry at any point, add a little of the olive oil. Remove sausages to paper-towel-lined plate.

2. Add enough olive oil to skillet so there are about 3 Tablespoons fat in skillet. Add chopped onion; sauté, increasing heat slightly, until onion just begins to wilt, about 4 minutes. Add peppers and garlic. Sauté, tossing, 2 minutes. Cover pan; steam until peppers begin to soften slightly, 5 to 7 minutes.

3. Uncover skillet. Add wine, scraping up any browned bits from bottom and sides of skillet. Cook until reduced by one-half, 2 to 3 minutes.
4. Add tomatoes and salt. Cook over medium-high heat, stirring constantly, until mixture begins to thicken, 8 to 10 minutes. Stir in 3 Tablespoons of the fresh basil, or all the dried basil. Lower heat. Tuck sausages into tomato mixture. Spoon juices over sausages. Simmer, partially covered, stirring occasionally, about 20 minutes. Check sauce. If medium thick, continue to simmer, partially covered, until thick, about 10 minutes. If sauce is too thin, continue to simmer, uncovered, increasing heat very slightly, stirring, until quite thick, 5 to 10 minutes. If sauce becomes too thick at any point, add reserved tomato liquid or water; continue to simmer. Total simmering time should be about 30 minutes. If dish is to be served later and reheated, do not allow sauce to thicken completely at this point.
5. Stir in optional mushrooms. Simmer another 5 minutes. Add parsley, remaining fresh basil, and plenty of pepper; correct for salt. Serve with plenty of Italian or French bread.

VEGETABLE SAUTÉS

Many people forget vegetables when they think of sautés. These serve very well as light, meatless main dishes, or as hearty accompaniments to plain meat and fish dishes.

Included are two Chinese dishes that illustrate how the basic sauté technique can be varied to produce different textures and flavors. These have been developed by Barbara Tropp, an old friend whose imaginative work with the authentic cuisines of China can be sampled in *The Modern Art of Chinese Cooking* (Morrow).

SAUTÉ OF SPRING VEGETABLES

A combination of bright colors and crisp textures bathed in a light butter sauce flecked with fresh herbs. This sauté illustrates adding ingredients in order of their cooking times.
Serves 6

GREMOLATA (OPTIONAL):

1 or 2 cloves garlic, minced
Grated zest of 1 lemon and/or 1 orange
2 teaspoons chopped fresh parsley

Salt
4 ounces snow peas, strings removed, halved crosswise if long
4 or 5 medium carrots, trimmed, peeled, sliced on sharp diagonal ⅛ inch thick
6 Tablespoons unsalted butter
2 Tablespoons diagonally sliced scallion
1 medium red pepper, cored, seeded, sliced into long slivers ¼ inch wide

6 ounces tender asparagus spears, peeled if necessary, diagonally sliced into 1½- to 2-inch lengths
2 small zucchini (about 4 ounces), trimmed, halved crosswise, halved lengthwise, then sliced, cut side down, into long strips ¼ inch thick
¾ teaspoon salt
2 Tablespoons cold water
Juice of ½ lemon, or more as needed
2 Tablespoons chopped fresh herbs such as chives, tarragon, basil, or dill
Freshly ground black pepper

1. Combine optional gremolata ingredients in small bowl: garlic, citrus zest, and chopped parsley. Reserve.
2. Heat a large pot of water to boiling over medium heat. Lightly salt. Drop in snow peas. Boil, uncovered, 45 seconds. Add carrots; boil 1 minute. Drain; refresh under cold running water until cool. Drain; reserve.
3. Heat 2 Tablespoons of the butter in large skillet over medium heat. When foam subsides, add sliced scallion. Sauté 30 seconds. Add drained snow peas and carrots, and the slivers of red pepper. Sauté, tossing, 2

minutes. Add asparagus; toss to coat. Sauté 1 to 2 minutes. Add zucchini; toss to coat for less than 1 minute. Add salt and cold water. Cover pan; steam until everything is just tender, 4 to 5 minutes. Push vegetables onto warmed serving platter, leaving juices in pan; keep vegetables warm. Add water if less than 2 Tablespoons liquid in pan. Add lemon juice. Bring to boil. Remove from heat. Swirl in the remaining 4 Tablespoons butter a little at a time. Each time a chunk is nearly liquefied, add a bit more.

4. Add 2 Tablespoons chopped herbs. Correct seasonings with salt and pepper and lemon juice. Drizzle butter sauce over vegetables. Sprinkle some of the gremolata over all; pass remaining gremolata separately.

BARBARA TROPP'S HOT AND SOUR HUNAN-STYLE VEGETABLES

Barbara Tropp explains that the cooking of Hunan—the Chinese province just west of Szechwan—is characterized by fire plus flavor, a lively conspiracy of hot, sweet, and tart condiments that never overshadows the main ingredients.

Two special techniques are used in this dish. One, the brief stir-frying is followed by steam-cooking under a lid, giving the vegetables time to cook to doneness and exchange flavors with the sauce. Two, the hardest vegetables are either cut thinner or stir-fried longer once in the pot, enabling all components of the dish to emerge with a nearly uniform crispness. This method of stir-frying in stages is one of the hallmarks of real Chinese cooking.

You can cut the vegetables and combine the seasonings a day in advance, provided everything is refrigerated airtight and the vegetables are packed in water-misted plastic bags.

Ms. Tropp suggests serving these vegetables with grilled or roasted meats or poultry, or simply cooked fish. A Zinfandel accompanies the vegetables well. See page 179 for Barbara Tropp's notes on ingredients. Serves 4 to 6

AROMATICS:

1 Tablespoon finely minced pared fresh ginger (see Note)

1 Tablespoon finely minced garlic

2 Tablespoons Chinese salted black beans (see Note), coarsely chopped

¾ teaspoon dried red pepper flakes (see Note)

SAUCE INGREDIENTS:

½ cup unsalted rich chicken broth

2½ Tablespoons thin (regular) soy sauce (see Note)

2 Tablespoons unseasoned Chinese or Japanese rice vinegar or white vinegar

¼ teaspoon sugar

¼ cup corn or peanut oil

¾ pound cauliflower flowerets, cut into small walnut-size pieces

½ pound trimmed, peeled, sweet carrots, cut diagonally into ⅛-inch thick coins

1 pound small, slender, firm zucchini, cut into ¼-inch thick rounds

1 Tablespoon cornstarch dissolved in 1½ Tablespoons cold stock or water

1. Combine aromatics in small dish.
2. Combine sauce ingredients in small bowl; stir to dissolve sugar.
3. Have all ingredients within easy reach of stovetop. Heat wok or large heavy skillet over high heat until bead of water evaporates on contact. Add the ¼ cup oil; swirl to glaze pan. Heat oil until piece of ginger when added sizzles. Add aromatics to pan. Adjust heat to maintain sizzle without scorching red pepper flakes. Stir-fry until fully fragrant, 15 to 20 seconds. Add cauliflower; toss briskly to glaze flowerets and start them cooking, about 45 seconds. Add carrots; toss until carrots are hot and glazed and edges are slightly curled, about 1 minute. Dribble in a bit more oil from side of pan if necessary to prevent sticking. When everything is combined and hot, add zucchini. Toss well to glaze and start cooking, about 30 seconds. Stir sauce ingredients; add to pan. Toss to combine; shake pan to distribute ingredients evenly. Increase heat to bring liquids to boil. Adjust heat to maintain steady simmer; cover pot. After 1 minute, test zucchini for doneness. If zucchini needs further cooking, stir ingredients; replace cover for another 30 seconds. Zucchini should be just crisp-tender. Stir cornstarch mixture; add to pan. Stir until sauce thickens slightly and becomes glossy, 10 to 20 seconds.
4. Remove contents of skillet to heated serving vessel. Serve immediately with noodles, rice, or a crusty hunk of garlic or French bread.

BARBARA TROPP'S DRY-FRIED SZECHWAN EGGPLANT

Ms. Tropp points out that this dish is first cousin to the well-known restaurant dish "Dry-Fried Stringbeans," which similarly involves deep-frying a vegetable, then saucing it speedily over high heat, so as to evaporate the liquids and create a "dry" sauce that penetrates and clings to the vegetable.

Deep-frying the eggplant prior to stir-frying gives it a dual texture: brittle on the outside and creamy smooth within. Soaking the eggplant briefly in cold water makes it resistant to the oil and encourages a crispy skin.

The eggplant can be cut and the seasonings combined a day in advance; refrigerate airtight.

Serve hot, tepid, or chilled overnight and returned to room temperature. Barbara Tropp suggests serving the eggplant as an accompaniment to simply cooked fish or pasta dressed with butter and fresh herbs. Serves 4 to 6

PORK MARINADE:

2 teaspoons thin (regular) soy
sauce (see Note)
2 teaspoons Chinese rice wine or
pale dry sherry
1 teaspoon cornstarch

4 ounces ground pork butt

AROMATICS:

1 Tablespoon minced garlic
1 Tablespoon minced pared fresh
ginger (see Note)
4 Tablespoons chopped scallion,
green and white parts
2 to 2 ½ teaspoons Chinese chili
sauce (see Note), or ½ to ¾
teaspoon dried red pepper flakes
(see Note)

SAUCE INGREDIENTS:

1 Tablespoon thin (regular) soy
sauce
1 to 1 ½ Tablespoons brown sugar
¼ teaspoon coarse (kosher) salt
1 ½ Tablespoons unsalted chicken
broth or water
2 to 3 teaspoons Chinese rice
vinegar (see Note), or well-aged
black or Balsamic vinegar

2 pounds firm, young eggplant (see
Note), cut into large walnut-size
hunks, skin left on
4 cups corn or peanut oil for
deep-frying plus 3 Tablespoons

GARNISH:

*1 scant teaspoon Chinese or
Japanese sesame oil*

*Chopped scallion or whole
coriander leaves*

1. Mix marinade ingredients in small bowl. Combine with pork, stirring in one direction. Seal airtight until ready to use. Refrigerate overnight, if you wish.
2. Combine the aromatics in small dish.
3. Mix sauce ingredients; stir to dissolve sugar and salt.
4. Soak eggplant in cold water to cover, 5 to 10 minutes. Drain eggplant; pat dry with paper towels. Place eggplant, a tray lined with 4 layers of paper towels, and a large Chinese mesh spoon or strainer within easy reach of stovetop.
5. In large wok or heavy pot, heat 4 cups oil until smoking, 400° on deep-fry thermometer. Allow 2 inches of space on top for bubbling. Gently slip eggplant into hot oil; with large lid protect yourself from spattering. Do not overcrowd pan; work in batches if necessary. Deep-fry eggplant, turning pieces, until golden, about 2 minutes. Remove eggplant with mesh spoon or strainer to paper-towel-lined tray to drain.
6. Arrange fried eggplant, pork, aromatics, sauce ingredients, and sesame oil within easy reach of stovetop.
7. Heat wok or large heavy skillet over high heat until bead of water sizzles on contact. Add 3 Tablespoons corn or peanut oil; swirl to coat pan. When oil is hot enough to sizzle piece of garlic, add aromatics. Adjust heat to maintain sizzle without burning chili sauce. Stir-fry until mixture is fully fragrant, 10 to 20 seconds. Add pork; toss, breaking pork into bits; dribble in more oil from side of pan to prevent sticking if necessary. When most of the meat has lost its raw look, add sauce. Stir; increase heat to bring liquid to full simmer. Add eggplant to pan. Toss gently to combine, 1 to 2 minutes, until sauce is nearly evaporated. Remove pan from heat. Correct seasonings with sugar, salt, or vinegar. Drizzle with sesame oil. Remove to serving platter. Garnish with scallion or coriander. Serve hot, tepid, or at room temperature.

Note: Barbara Tropp offers the following helpful information about ingredients:

- *Fresh ginger:* Best when rock-hard and smooth-skinned.
- *Soft black beans preserved in salt:* Available in Chinese markets and typically bagged in plastic. Do not buy beans preserved in five-spice powder, a Cantonese spice inappropriate here. Do not wash beans prior to cooking; allow for saltiness of beans when seasoning.
- *Dried red pepper flakes:* Best bought in ethnic markets. Should be cherry-red in color and finely cut as opposed to ragged.
- *Thin (regular) soy sauce:* Kikkoman soy sauce is a good middle ground between sweeter Japanese soys and saltier Chinese soys. If using a saltier Chinese soy, use less.
- *Chinese chili sauce:* A fruity, spicy hot sauce different in character from hot bean sauce. Use Szechwan brand, which comes in a small can with a black label. Very fresh dried red chili flakes can be substituted.
- *Well-aged Chinese black vinegars:* Use Narcissus brand, or substitute a Balsamic vinegar or a California Barengo vinegar.
- *Chinese and Japanese eggplants:* Long and tender with amethyst to purple-black skins and few seeds. Substitute small firm eggplant with smooth, unblemished skin.

❖ 6 ❖

ONE-DISH MEALS

BRAISED POULTRY AND MEAT DISHES

BRAISED CHICKEN WITH LEEKS AND CREAM
BRAISED CHICKEN WITH HUNGARIAN PAPRIKA AND SOUR CREAM
BRAISED DUCK WITH SOUR FRUIT
BRAISED WHOLE GAME HENS WITH MUCH GARLIC
BRAISED GAME HENS BASQUAISE
BRAISED LAMB SHANKS

TRADITIONAL HEARTY MEAT DISHES

CARBONNADES
A SIMPLIFIED CHOUCROUTE GARNIE
CHICKEN CURRY
PASTITSIO
MEAT LOAF/PATÉ WITH SPINACH AND PINE NUTS

HEARTY PIES

BASIC CONSIDERATIONS FOR HEARTY PIES
CHICKEN POT PIE
SOUR CREAM FLAKY PASTRY
BEEF POT PIE
TEX-MEX BEEF CASSEROLE WITH CORNMEAL BISCUIT TOPPING
PIZZA RUSTICA
SAUSAGE-APPLE-CHEDDAR PIE
PIZZA

*I*n a book of easy-to-accomplish dishes for people with busy lives, a long chapter of rather substantial dishes might seem a bit out of place, but these dishes are meals in themselves, so one night's cooking can provide good eating for two or three days.

Moreover, these hearty dishes utilize and combine all the simple techniques of the previous five chapters. By concentrating on the many small details of technique in each recipe, you can ensure that every ingredient in the finished dish emerges clearly, perfectly cooked, while at the same time playing its part in a larger whole.

When I prepare these dishes, I aim for light, simple treatments with clearly perceptible elements, but ones that are still robust enough—full-bodied and flavorful—to create strong sense impressions. In many cases in this chapter, this has meant new or streamlined versions of traditional recipes: simplified cooking procedures, readily available ingredients, shorter cooking times, flourless thickeners, and lighter, crisper textures.

The following are some guidelines on how to create a variety of sense impressions through your cooking; gradually you should feel your own personality emerge in your finished dishes.

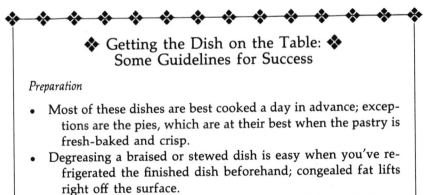

❖ Getting the Dish on the Table: ❖ Some Guidelines for Success

Preparation

- Most of these dishes are best cooked a day in advance; exceptions are the pies, which are at their best when the pastry is fresh-baked and crisp.
- Degreasing a braised or stewed dish is easy when you've refrigerated the finished dish beforehand; congealed fat lifts right off the surface.
- If you are going to freeze part of a dish (or leftovers), freeze without garnishes. Garnish and correct all seasonings only after thawed, reheated, and ready to serve.
- Set out all your ingredients before you being cooking. This putting things in place, the chef's *mise en place,* will ease the cooking process once it begins.

Ingredients: Maximizing Textural and Visual Appeal

- Cut such ingredients as meat, vegetables, and fish in large, even chunks or slices so they are clearly perceptible in the finished dish. No stew or braised dish should be cooked to a mush.
- When you are preparing multiple ingredients for one dish, such as several vegetables for a stew or pot pie, cooking each one separately or adding them to the pot in decreasing order of cooking time required will ensure that each is perfectly cooked in the finished product.
- Generally, when precooking vegetables, undercook them slightly. They will emerge crisp-tender during the final baking or simmering.
- Adjust ingredients where necessary. If you can't get good tomatoes, chunks of red pepper can provide color. You may also prefer a sauce more generously flecked with parsley or herbs than my quantities provide.

Finishing Touches

- Use all your senses while cooking: listen for a rapid boil warning you that a delicate simmer has gotten out of hand, or the sizzling in the oven signaling an overflow that needs to be caught by a sheet of aluminum foil under a casserole.
- Learn to adjust liquid consistencies: if in a finished stew or braised dish the liquid "gravy" is too thin, lift out the solids, reduce the liquid by vigorous boiling, and reassemble the ingredients to heat through. If the liquid has become too thick, simply thin with water, broth, or other appropriate liquid.
- No matter what any recipe says, season to your taste. Be sure these hearty dishes are fairly assertive, but don't allow one flavor to predominate. And always reseason foods after freezing and thawing.
- With leftovers, reheat only as much as you're going to serve, garnishing each serving at the last minute. Remaining portions will not be overcooked.
- Take a moment to arrange a casserole attractively for serving. Take advantage of the beautifully designed oven-to-table serving dishes now available.

BRAISED POULTRY AND MEAT DISHES

❖ Braising ❖

The braising process—long, slow simmering in a small amount of liquid—while providing excellent results with fish and vegetables, is most advantageously suited to the tougher, less expensive cuts of meat. The process involves a few simple steps:

- The meat is first *browned* in fat to seal in juices.
- *Seasoning vegetables* and *aromatics* are cooked briefly in fat, and the meat is arranged on top of this aromatic bed—*fonds de braise* —in a deep heavy pot.
- The *pot* should be just large enough to hold the meat and liquid without crowding.
- *Liquid* is first used to deglaze any pans used for sautéing and is then added with a little wine, broth, water, leftover meat gravy, tomatoes, or other flavorful liquid to the pot to moisten the meat.
- *Simmering* may be done on top of the stove or in the all-around heat of the oven.
- The sauce or juices are thoroughly *degreased* and *reseasoned* before serving.

BRAISED CHICKEN WITH LEEKS AND CREAM

Chicken marries well with a remarkable range of flavors. Here the meat is combined with the mellow flavor of leeks in a dish light enough for a summer supper.
Serves 4 to 6

4 pounds chicken pieces, cut up
  (thighs, legs, and breasts)
Flour for dredging
Salt for dredging plus ½ teaspoon
2 to 3 Tablespoons chicken fat, or
  butter and vegetable oil
10 to 12 leeks, cleaned, trimmed,
  and sliced into 1-inch lengths
Pinch dried thyme
18 to 20 baby carrots, or 1 ½
  cups 1 ½-inch lengths of carrot
2 cloves garlic, minced

1 cup dry Madeira or dry
  Marsala wine
2 to 2 ½ cups Chicken Broth (page
  6) or Mixed Meat and Poultry
  Broth (page 8)
½ cup heavy cream, or more as
  needed
2 Tablespoons unsalted butter
1 cup thickly sliced mushrooms
Chopped fresh parsley
Freshly ground black pepper
Few drops fresh lemon juice

1. Remove excess skin and fat from chicken pieces. Wipe chicken dry with paper towels. Dredge in flour mixed with a little salt.
2. Heat fat in large skillet over medium heat until rippling. Add chicken, working in batches; sauté until lightly golden. Remove to platter lined with paper towels.
3. Add leeks to skillet; toss. Cook over low heat, about 3 minutes. Add thyme and the ½ teaspoon salt. Increase heat to medium; cook until leeks begin to soften, about 5 minutes. Add carrots and garlic; toss. Cook another 3 minutes. Remove and reserve vegetables. Drain off excess fat. Add wine, scraping any browned bits from bottom and sides of skillet. Boil hard 3 minutes. Add 1½ cups broth; boil hard 3 minutes.
4. Preheat oven to 375°.
5. Select a casserole large enough to hold chicken pieces in two layers. Arrange most of the vegetable and wine mixture in bottom of casserole. Arrange chicken legs and thighs in single layer over vegetables. Arrange breasts, skin side up, in single layer over thighs and legs. Add enough broth to come to bottom of breasts. Add remaining vegetables. Bring to boil on top of stove. Cover top of casserole with sheet of aluminum foil;

cover with lid. Place in oven. Bake until chicken is tender, 25 to 30 minutes. Adjust heat if necessary to maintain bare simmer. Remove chicken and vegetables from casserole with slotted spoon and arrange on heated platter; keep warm.

6. Transfer sauce to a saucepan and bring to boil. Push pan to one side of heat. Boil steadily until slightly thickened, 15 to 20 minutes. Remove and discard fat and foam that collects at side of pan away from heat. Add ½ cup cream, or more to taste. Return pan to center of heat. Lower heat; simmer until slightly thickened, about 3 minutes.

7. Meanwhile, melt butter in skillet over medium heat. When foam subsides, add mushrooms; sauté until slightly colored, about 3 minutes. Add to sauce. Add parsley, pepper, and lemon juice; correct seasonings.

8. Nap chicken with sauce. Serve hot with rice or noodles.

BRAISED CHICKEN WITH HUNGARIAN PAPRIKA AND SOUR CREAM

This is a lightened version of a traditional Hungarian recipe; the sauce is thickened only with a purée of the cooking vegetables.

Cooking Tips: If you plan to serve this dish on more than one occasion, add the mushrooms and the sour cream in step 6 only to the amount being served. Use leftover sauce to nap a sautéed chicken breast. Or treat yourself to the Hungarian favorite *Hortobági Palacsinták* (crêpes Hungarian style): roll some crêpes around leftover chopped braised veal or beef, or a cut-up leftover piece of this chicken, or any stewlike mixture; nap with the paprika sauce; bake in a greased gratin dish until heated through; and serve with more sour cream. Use as a first course, or as a delicious supper or lunch on its own.

Serves 6

4 to 4 ½ pounds chicken pieces
(breast halves, thighs, legs)
Salt
¼ cup lard, bacon fat, or vegetable
oil
8 ounces mushrooms
4 ½ cups chopped onion (4 to 5
medium onions)
4 carrots, trimmed, peeled, halved
lengthwise, cut into ½-inch
slices
3 ribs celery, thickly sliced
2 red peppers, cored, seeded, cut
into coarse dice
1 green pepper, cored, seeded, cut
into coarse dice

4 cloves garlic, minced
⅓ cup medium-hot Hungarian
paprika, or ¼ cup sweet
paprika plus 2 Tablespoons hot
paprika *
1 can (14 ounces) imported whole
plum tomatoes, drained, chopped
½ teaspoon dried marjoram,
crumbled
1 ¾ cups Chicken Broth (page 6)
Freshly ground black pepper
1 to 1 ⅓ cups sour cream
2 to 3 Tablespoons chopped fresh
parsley

1. Remove excess fat from chicken. Pat pieces dry on paper towels. Lightly salt. Sauté in fat in large skillet over medium heat, working in batches, until lightly golden, about 8 to 10 minutes for each batch. Drain on paper-towel-lined plates. If more than thin film of fat remains in skillet, drain off excess.

2. Meanwhile, trim mushroom stems flush with caps. Coarsely chop stems; reserve. Reserve caps.

3. Add onion; sauté over medium heat until onion begins to wilt, 4 to 5 minutes. Add carrot, celery, and peppers. Toss to coat with fat; sauté until vegetables begin to soften, about 5 minutes. Add garlic and chopped mushroom stems. Toss; sauté 2 minutes. Add paprika; toss to coat, about 2 minutes. Add tomatoes and marjoram; toss until mixture is lightly thickened, about 2 minutes. Add chicken broth; scrape up any browned bits from bottom and sides of skillet. Stir to combine.

4. Select a casserole large enough to hold chicken pieces in two layers. Arrange one-third of vegetable mixture in bottom of casserole. Arrange legs and thighs in one layer on top. Spread second third of vegetable mixture over chicken; top with breasts, skin side up. Scatter remaining vegetable mixture, with liquid, over top. Liquid should come up to bottom of breasts; add broth or water if necessary. Cover; bring to boil over medium heat. Lower heat; simmer, covered, until chicken is tender, 20 to 30 minutes. Degrease.

*Mail-order source: H. Roth and Son, 1577 First Avenue, New York, N.Y. 10028 (212-734-1110)

5. Remove from heat. Remove 1½ to 2 cups vegetables with slotted spoon. Purée in food processor or blender; stir purée back into stew. If sauce is not thick enough, repeat puréeing with more vegetables.

6. Cut reserved mushroom caps into ¼-inch slices. Add to casserole; simmer 5 minutes. Stir in about ⅔ cup sour cream. Sauce should be rosy salmon color; if too dark, add another spoonful or two more of sour cream. Correct seasonings, adding salt and pepper as needed. Bring stew to simmer, but do not boil.

7. Stir remaining sour cream in small bowl. Serve each piece of chicken napped with chunky sauce. Top with dollop of sour cream and sprinkle of chopped parsley. Accompany with wide noodles or spaetzle.

BRAISED DUCK WITH SOUR FRUIT

Vary this robust dish from southwest France by substituting dried apricots or small ripe plums, halved and pitted, for the prunes.

Cooking Tip: Sauté the duck slowly and carefully, pricking the skin to release all possible fat; pour off fat and reserve for sautéed poultry, potatoes, rice, and soups. Degrease the dish thoroughly at serving time.
Serves 4

8 to 10 ounces pitted prunes (about 1 ½ cups)	Salt
¾ cup dry red wine	2 Tablespoons brandy
2 to 3 Tablespoons unsalted butter and oil, or duck fat	1 small rib celery
1 medium onion, chopped	2 or 3 parsley sprigs
1 carrot, trimmed, peeled, quartered lengthwise, cut into 1-inch lengths	1 bay leaf
2 cloves garlic, chopped	½ teaspoon dried thyme
1 duck (4 to 5 pounds), back removed and reserved, quartered, fat and excess skin trimmed, neck and wings cut off and reserved	1 leek, trimmed, halved
	2 cups Chicken Broth (page 6), Mixed Meat and Poultry Broth (page 8), or duck broth
	Freshly ground black pepper
	Chopped fresh parsley

1. Soak prunes in wine while preparing rest of recipe.

2. Heat butter and oil in large skillet over medium heat. When foam subsides, add onion and carrot. Sauté until lightly golden, tossing occasionally, 10 to 12 minutes. Add garlic; sauté another 2 to 3 minutes. Scrape mixture into strainer over small bowl. Reserve vegetable mixture; return strained fat to skillet.

3. Wipe pieces of duck dry with paper towels. Prick skin all over with fork. Sprinkle pieces lightly with salt. Sauté pieces, including neck, wings, and back, over medium heat in skillet with reserved fat, turning occasionally. Drain off fat as necessary; reserve for other uses. Sauté slowly; pieces should become a rich brown color, which will lend color to the sauce.

4. When all pieces are browned, drain off excess fat. Add brandy, scraping up any browned bits from bottom and sides of skillet. Reserve skillet.

5. Drain prunes over small bowl; reserve wine and prunes separately. Tie celery, parsley sprigs, bay leaf, and thyme between leek halves; reserve bouquet garni.

6. Arrange neck, wings, and any other duck trimmings with sautéed vegetables in bottom of a casserole, then arrange duck pieces in one layer. Tuck in the bouquet garni. Add the brandy-deglazing juices from skillet, the broth, wine drained from the prunes, and enough water to nearly cover the duck pieces. Bring to boil over medium heat. Skim. Reduce heat; simmer, covered, until duck is tender, 45 to 55 minutes. Adjust heat as necessary to maintain simmer.

7. Scatter reserved prunes over duck. Simmer, uncovered, until everything is tender, 10 to 12 minutes.

8. Transfer duck pieces, vegetables, and prunes with slotted spoon to warm platter. Cover with foil and keep warm. Remove and discard bouquet garni and duck trimmings. Bring sauce to boil; move casserole to side of heat. Carefully spoon off fat and foam as it collects at side of casserole away from heat. When sauce is reduced by half, add pepper, and salt if needed.

9. Return duck pieces, vegetables, and prunes to casserole. Baste duck pieces over low heat, about 5 minutes. Sprinkle with chopped parsley. Serve hot, with a purée of potatoes and turnips or celery root.

BRAISED WHOLE GAME HENS WITH MUCH GARLIC

The name of this variation of the Provençale dish chicken with forty cloves of garlic may alarm many people—at least until they taste the sweet, mild flavor of the slowly cooked garlic cloves. This is an easy dish, for everything is literally thrown in the pot and simmered.
Cooking Tip: One-inch lengths of carrot and halved new potatoes can be cooked along with the hens as a vegetable garnish.
Serves 4 (1 hen per serving)

4 fresh Cornish game hens (1 to
    1 ¼ pounds each)
Salt
Freshly ground black pepper
1 lemon, quartered
½ cup fruity olive oil
30 to 40 cloves garlic, outer
    papery peel removed, thin skin
    left on

1 teaspoon dried thyme, crumbled
½ teaspoon dried rosemary,
    crumbled
½ teaspoon dried marjoram or
    oregano, crumbled
1 bay leaf
Chopped fresh parsley

1. Rinse hens; wipe dry with paper towels. Season cavities with salt and pepper. Place lemon quarter in each cavity. Truss. Season outside with salt and pepper.
2. Preheat oven to 350°.
3. Place oil, garlic, thyme, rosemary, and marjoram in casserole large enough to hold hens comfortably. Toss mixture together. Add hens; turn hens over in oil mixture to coat. Arrange breast side up. Lay a piece of aluminum foil over top of casserole; cover with lid. Heat over moderate heat until oil begins to sizzle. Transfer to oven. Bake until juices run clear when thigh is pierced, about 1 hour and 10 minutes.
4. Remove hens from casserole to warm platter. Remove trussing strings and lemon quarters. Serve each bird whole or halved with garlic and herbed oil and juices spooned over. Sprinkle with parsley. Squeeze softened garlic onto the hen or pieces of French bread.

BRAISED GAME HENS BASQUAISE

This dish makes use of a "Basquaise"—the tomato-pepper-garlic-ham mixture characteristic of the sheepherding tribes along the Spanish-French border. Serve with rice to soak up the juices.

Cooking Tips: Use the Basquaise mixture as a topping for pizza (page 215) or in a fish gratin (page 140).

Serves 4

4 fresh Cornish game hens (1 to 1 ¼ pounds each)
3 Tablespoons olive oil, plus more for basting
Salt

BASQUAISE:

1 can (2 pounds, 3 ounces) imported whole plum tomatoes
2 medium onions, chopped
3 or 4 cloves garlic, minced
2 medium peppers, red or green or both, cored, seeded, cut into 1-inch dice

3 to 4 ounces prosciutto or smoked ham, thickly sliced, cut into 1-inch dice
¼ cup dry white wine
2 Tablespoons brandy
¼ teaspoon dried thyme, crumbled
¼ teaspoon dried basil, crumbled
1 bay leaf
Freshly ground black pepper
2 Tablespoons chopped fresh parsley

1. Rinse hens; wipe dry with paper towels. Truss hens. Heat oil in large skillet over medium heat until rippling. Add hens; lightly salt. Lower heat slightly. Sauté slowly until lightly browned on all sides, 20 to 25 minutes. Adjust heat to maintain a slow sauté. Brown breast side last; breast should be golden brown. Be careful not to rip the skin.

2. Meanwhile, drain tomatoes in sieve over a bowl, reserving liquid.

3. Preheat oven to 350°.

4. Remove hens to a plate. Drain off all but 3 tablespoons fat. Add onions to the skillet. Toss to coat; sauté until just beginning to wilt, 3 to 4 minutes. Add garlic, pepper, and ham; toss 2 to 3 minutes. Add wine and brandy. Raise heat slightly. Cook, scraping up any browned bits from the bottom and sides of skillet, until the liquid is nearly all evaporated, 4 to 5 minutes. Add the drained tomato pulp; toss. The mixture should be chunky but moist. If soupy, reduce for a few more minutes.

If too dry, add a little reserved drained tomato liquid. Add thyme, basil, and bay leaf, and salt if necessary.

5. Transfer vegetable mixture to shallow casserole. Tuck hens into mixture, breast side up. Cover. Bake until hens are tender and juices run clear when thigh joint is pierced, about 45 minutes. Uncover casserole during last 10 minutes of cooking; increase oven to 400°. Baste hens with olive oil.

6. Remove hens to warm platter; remove trussing strings. If vegetable mixture has become thin from juices from hens, reduce over medium heat, stirring until very thick, 3 to 4 minutes. Remove bay leaf; correct seasonings. Add pepper. Spoon vegetable mixture around the hens. Sprinkle with parsley. Serve with rice.

BRAISED LAMB SHANKS

If you've never cooked lamb shanks, you'll be delighted by the succulence of this inexpensive, gelatinous cut. Some people like to have their butchers saw the shanks crosswise, but I prefer to serve a whole shank to each person.

Cooking Tip: If you have difficulty finding enough shanks to prepare this dish, buy them as you see them, then freeze until you have collected enough.

Serves 4

OPTIONAL MARINADE:

1 ½ cups dry, full-bodied red wine

3 or 4 cloves garlic, sliced

½ teaspoon dried rosemary leaves, crumbled

4 lamb shanks, knob ends of knuckle sawed off by butcher, excess fat trimmed

2 Tablespoons olive oil, or more as needed

1 teaspoon salt

1 onion, coarsely chopped

1 leek, trimmed, cleaned, thickly sliced

1 carrot, trimmed, peeled, thickly sliced

4 cloves garlic

2 Tablespoons Cognac or brandy

2 or 3 ripe tomatoes, peeled, seeded, coarsely chopped, or 1 cup drained, canned, chopped tomatoes

½ teaspoon dried thyme, crumbled

¼ teaspoon dried marjoram or oregano, crumbled

Pinch of rosemary (if not used in marinade)

¼ teaspoon dried savory, crumbled (optional)

¼ teaspoon dried basil, crumbled, or 2 Tablespoons chopped fresh basil

1 bay leaf

1 strip (2 inches) orange peel, stuck with 1 clove

1 cup dry red wine (or 1 cup of the marinade, strained)

1 ½ cups Mixed Meat and Poultry Broth (page 8), or meat broth, or as needed

Freshly ground black pepper

3 Tablespoons chopped fresh parsley, or chopped fresh parsley and basil

1. If using marinade, combine the 1½ cups wine, garlic, and rosemary in shallow dish that will hold the shanks. Add shanks; turn to coat with marinade. Marinate 1 to 2 hours at room temperature, or overnight, covered, in refrigerator. Turn occasionally. Remove shanks from marinade; wipe off garlic and rosemary. Wipe shanks dry with paper towels. Strain and reserve the marinade.

2. Heat olive oil in large skillet over medium-high heat until rippling. Add shanks; sprinkle with salt. Brown shanks well on all sides, about 15 minutes. Remove shanks to plate. Pour off all but 2 Tablespoons of fat from skillet. Add onion, leek, and carrot; sauté until slightly wilted, 5 to 6 minutes. Add 4 cloves whole garlic; sauté, tossing about 2 minutes. Add Cognac, scraping up any browned bits from bottom and sides of skillet. Add tomatoes, all the remaining herbs, and the orange peel. Raise heat slightly; cook until slightly thickened, 5 to 6 minutes. Add wine; reduce about 2 minutes.

3. Transfer mixture to heavy casserole; tuck in shanks. Add enough broth so that shanks are one-half to two-thirds covered, adding water if necessary. Bring to boil; lower to simmer. Cover top of casserole with sheet of aluminum foil; cover with lid. Simmer on top of stove or in preheated 375° oven, turning shanks occasionally. Adjust heat if necessary to maintain bare simmer. Cook until shanks are tender, about 2 hours. Begin to check after 1 hour, 20 minutes.

4. Transfer shanks with slotted spoon to warm platter; keep warm. Strain remaining contents of casserole into small saucepan. Discard bay leaf and orange peel. Arrange vegetables around shanks; keep warm.

5. Bring sauce to boil; reduce 5 minutes. Move saucepan to side of heat. Gently boil until very slightly syrupy, 20 to 25 minutes. Discard fat and foam as it collects at the side of saucepan away from heat. Do not overreduce.

6. Nap shanks with sauce. Sprinkle with chopped parsley. Serve with noodles, rice, or potatoes.

TRADITIONAL HEARTY MEAT DISHES

Many of these are streamlined versions of familiar favorites from several cuisines. Most are ideal for a crowd, and can be prepared in advance. But don't wait for a party: all of these dishes make fine everyday eating, with delicious effort-free leftovers.

CARBONNADES

This aromatic Flemish beef stew with beer got its name from the centuries-old cooking method in which the meat is cooked in direct contact with the coals. Serve with boiled potatoes or noodles, and more of the dark beer used in the stew.
Serves 6

6 ounces mushrooms	3 cloves garlic, minced
2 or 3 sprigs parsley	2 ¼ to 2 ½ pounds bottom round
1 sprig fresh thyme, or pinch dried	beef, cut into ¾-inch cubes
thyme	Salt
1 bay leaf	2 bottles (12 ounces each) dark
1 leek, trimmed, halved, cleaned	beer
4 Tablespoons unsalted butter, or	1 cup Mixed Meat and Poultry
as needed	Broth (page 8), or water
1 Tablespoon vegetable oil, or as	1 small ripe tomato, peeled, seeded,
needed	chopped, or ⅓ cup drained
7 or 8 medium onions, thickly	canned tomatoes, sieved
sliced	2 Tablespoons red wine vinegar
3 or 4 carrots, trimmed, peeled,	Freshly ground black pepper
quartered lengthwise, cut into	Chopped fresh parsley
1 ½-inch lengths	

1. Trim mushroom stems flush with caps. Coarsely chop stems; quarter caps. Reserve separately. Tie parsley sprigs, thyme, and bay leaf between leek halves; reserve bouquet garni.
2. Heat 2 Tablespoons of the butter and oil in large skillet over medium heat. When foam subsides, add onions and carrots. Sauté, tossing frequently, until vegetables are quite soft and beginning to turn light gold, about 20 minutes. Add garlic and reserved chopped mushroom stems; sauté another 2 minutes. Remove to large strainer to drain.
3. In same skillet, brown the meat, sprinkling with salt, and adding fat as necessary, over medium heat until rich, deep brown, 10 to 15 minutes. Do not crowd skillet; work in batches if necessary. Remove meat to platter, reserving all juices.
4. Pour off any excess fat from skillet. Slowly add some of the beer,

scraping up any browned bits from bottom and sides of skillet. Remove from heat. Arrange half of the strained vegetables in bottom of large casserole. Add meat and exuded juices, beer and bits from deglazed skillet, and top with remaining vegetables. Add remaining beer and enough stock or water to barely cover. Add tomato and the reserved bouquet garni; stir. Bring to boil. Lower heat; simmer, partially covered, until meat is tender but not mushy, about 1¾ hours. Begin to check meat after 1¼ hours. Adjust heat as necessary to maintain simmer. Skim fat and foam occasionally.

5. Degrease. Remove and discard bouquet garni. Remove about 1½ cups of onion and carrot with slotted spoon to food processor or blender; purée. Stir purée back into casserole; sauce should be medium thick. If too thin, repeat with more onion and carrot until desired consistency is reached. Recipe can be prepared a day ahead up to this point.

6. Heat the remaining 2 Tablespoons of butter in a large skillet over high heat. When foam subsides, add reserved quartered mushroom caps. Sauté until light golden. Add vinegar; boil 1 to 2 minutes. Add contents of skillet to casserole. Simmer to combine flavors, about 10 minutes. Add pepper. Correct seasonings. Sprinkle with chopped parsley.

A SIMPLIFIED CHOUCROUTE GARNIE

In this scaled-down version of the Alsatian classic, ideal for a hungry crowd, the best pre-prepared sauerkraut you can find is simmered with juniper berries, wine, and apples and then combined with only two or three meat ingredients (some traditional versions call for ten or more). Serves 4 to 6

3 Tablespoons lard or vegetable oil
½ pound bacon, thickly sliced, cut into 1-inch squares
2 medium onions, halved, sliced crosswise
2 cloves garlic, minced
2 pounds prepared sauerkraut, rinsed (vacuum-packed preferred)
2 small to medium apples, peeled, cored, grated
1 potato, peeled, grated
1 cup dry white wine
½ cup apple cider or juice
½ cup Chicken Broth (page 6) or water

½ teaspoon dried thyme, crumbled
1 bay leaf
8 juniper berries, bruised, or 1 tablespoon gin
3 cloves
Salt
4 to 6 knockwurst (about 1 to 1 ½ pounds) or good-quality frankfurters
4 to 6 weisswurst (white veal sausage) (about ¾ to 1 ¼ pounds)

1. Heat lard in large casserole over medium heat. Add bacon; sauté until browned, about 8 minutes. Remove bacon; reserve.
2. Add onion to casserole; add more lard if necessary. Lower heat. Sauté until onions are soft but not browned, 5 to 7 minutes. Add garlic; toss until fragrant. Add sauerkraut, apple, and potato; toss 2 minutes. Add wine, apple cider, broth, thyme, bay leaf, juniper berries or gin, cloves, and salt to taste. Simmer, covered, 30 to 35 minutes.
3. Prick sausages all over with fork. Tuck sausages into sauerkraut. Add reserved bacon. Simmer, covered, until sausages are heated through, about 30 minutes. Correct seasonings. Serve with an assortment of mustards, pickles, boiled potatoes if you like, dark bread, and beer or light white wine, and follow with a salad.

CHICKEN CURRY

The trick for this untraditional curry is to mix your own spices; grind them yourself if at all possible. Adjust the balance of the sweet, hot, and sour elements of the vegetable-thickened sauce to your own taste. Serve with rice or a rice pilaf and cold beer.

Cooking Tip: Any leftover sauce can be used to top cooked cauliflower, poached or boiled eggs, or a layered chicken and rice pilaf.

Serves 6 to 8

2 Tablespoons unsalted butter
1 Tablespoon vegetable oil
3 medium onions, quartered, thinly sliced
1 rib celery, diagonally sliced
2 carrots, trimmed, peeled, diagonally sliced
2 or 3 cloves garlic, minced
2 teaspoons minced peeled fresh ginger
1 ½ Tablespoons curry powder
1 teaspoon ground coriander
1 teaspoon ground cinnamon
½ teaspoon mustard seeds
½ teaspoon ground allspice
½ teaspoon ground turmeric
½ teaspoon ground mace or nutmeg
½ teaspoon ground cardamom
1 teaspoon salt
1 ½ apples, peeled, cored, diced
1 ripe banana, halved lengthwise, sliced

2 ½ cups Chicken Broth (page 6)
½ cup plus 2 Tablespoons plain yogurt
¼ cup Coco López or other canned sweetened coconut cream, or to taste
3 cups cooked chicken meat, preferably breast, cut into 1-inch dice (about 2 pounds)
½ cup dried apricots, cut into strips
¼ cup raisins
Grated zest of 1 orange

GARNISH:

1 banana, sliced
½ apple, peeled, cored, diced
Cayenne pepper (optional)

1. Heat butter and oil in large sauté pan over medium heat. Add onions; sauté until wilted, about 6 minutes. Add celery and carrots; sauté 3 to 4 minutes. Add garlic and ginger; toss 2 minutes. Add all the remaining spices and salt; sauté 2 to 3 minutes, tossing, until very fragrant. Add

the apples and banana; toss to coat. Add broth; bring to boil. Lower heat; simmer, covered, until everything is tender but still intact, 15 to 20 minutes. Remove pan from heat.

2. Remove about 1½ cups of solids with slotted spoon. Purée in food processor or blender. Return purée to sauce. Stir in yogurt and Coco López. Add chicken, apricots, raisins, orange zest, and the cut-up banana and apple for garnish. Fold everything together. Bring to boil; lower heat. Simmer, covered, to blend flavors, 7 to 10 minutes. Correct seasonings; add cayenne, if you wish.

PASTITSIO

This layered Greek casserole of macaroni, seasoned meat, tomatoes, and a creamy custard topping can be prepared in advance and gently reheated; it's perfect for a large party or a late supper.

Cooking Tip: If you do not have the zucchini ragout on hand, increase the quantities in the meat filling as follows: onions to 3, garlic to 5 cloves, wine to ⅔ cup, and tomatoes to 3 cans. Proceed with the recipe, increasing the spices to taste. Eliminate the zucchini ragout layering in the assembly.

Serves 12 to 16

MEAT FILLING:

2 Tablespoons olive oil

2 medium onions, chopped

3 cloves garlic, minced

1 ½ pounds ground lamb shoulder,
or 2 to 3 cups diced leftover
lamb, or a mixture of lamb and
beef

2 teaspoons salt

⅓ cup dry red wine

1 can (1 pound, 12 ounces)
imported whole plum tomatoes,
drained

1 teaspoon ground cinnamon, or
more to taste

Pinch dried marjoram or oregano

Pinch ground cumin (optional)

½ cup chopped fresh parsley

TOPPING:

4 Tablespoons unsalted butter

¼ cup flour

2 ½ cups cold milk

1 ¼ cups ricotta cheese

4 eggs, separated

1 teaspoon salt

½ teaspoon ground nutmeg

ASSEMBLY:

2 Tablespoons unsalted butter

3 cups small dried elbow macaroni
(about 12 ounces)

4 cups (approximately) Zucchini
Ragout (page 91; see Cooking
Tip above)

1 to 1 ¼ cups freshly grated
Parmesan cheese

Pinch cayenne pepper

1. *Meat Filling:* Heat olive oil in large skillet over medium heat until rippling. Add onion; sauté until wilted, 5 to 6 minutes. Add garlic; sauté 2 minutes. Add meat and 2 teaspoons salt, crumbling meat in skillet with wooden spoon. Cook, stirring, until most of the meat has lost its pink, raw look. (If using leftover meat, simply toss over medium heat for 3 minutes.) Place lid on skillet; carefully drain off excess fat. Return skillet, uncovered, to heat.

2. Add wine to skillet. Bring to boil; boil 1 to 2 minutes. Add tomatoes, cinnamon, marjoram, and optional cumin. Simmer, breaking up tomatoes, until just slightly thickened. Transfer to bowl; add parsley. Correct seasonings to taste, if necessary; mixture should be assertively seasoned.

3. *Topping:* Heat the 4 Tablespoons butter in heavy saucepan over medium heat. Stir in flour; cook, stirring, 3 minutes, until opaque and smooth. Add milk all at once; bring to boil, whisking. Simmer 10 minutes, whisking occasionally. Remove from heat. Whisk in ricotta, 4 egg yolks (reserve whites), salt, and nutmeg until well blended. Place sheet of waxed paper on surface of sauce until needed.

4. *Assembly:* Preheat oven to 400°. Use 1 Tablespoon of the butter to grease 14 × 10 × 2½-inch baking pan. Bring large pot of salted water to boil.

5. Add pasta to boiling water; boil until almost *al dente,* about 6 minutes. Drain; rinse under cold water; drain again. Set out all ingredients within convenient reach.

6. Dribble a few Tablespoons of zucchini ragout or meat filling in buttered pan. Arrange one-third of pasta in even layer in bottom of pan. Top with half the meat mixture; sprinkle lightly with some of the Parmesan cheese. Top with half the zucchini ragout; sprinkle lightly with Parmesan. Repeat layering with one-third of the pasta, the remaining half of the meat mixture, sprinkling of Parmesan, remaining half of zucchini ragout, and sprinkling of Parmesan. Layer remaining third of pasta evenly over top.

7. Stir about 3 Tablespoons of Parmesan cheese into the topping. Correct seasonings. Whip the 4 egg whites until stiff but not dry. Whisk a large spoonful of the whites into the topping; fold in remainder quickly. Pour over pasta. Sprinkle with more Parmesan. Dot with remaining 1 Tablespoon butter. Sprinkle very lightly with cayenne.

8. Bake until top begins to brown, 20 to 25 minutes. Lower heat to 350°. Continue to bake until top is golden brown, slightly puffed, and set, about 45 to 55 minutes in all. Let rest 5 to 10 minutes before cutting into squares. Serve with a green salad and good bread.

MEAT LOAF/PÂTÉ WITH SPINACH AND PINE NUTS

This coarse version of a *pâté de campagne,* Italian in spirit and lightened with bread crumbs, is fine for a picnic or buffet table. Serve hot or cool; if cool, let it mellow a day or so before serving, and serve at cool room temperature, not chilled. Cornichons (tiny sour gherkins) nicely offset the richness of the meat.

Makes two 8 × 4-inch loaves

1 ½ pounds fresh spinach,
  stemmed, washed, or two
  10-ounce packages frozen
  spinach, thawed, drained
1 ½ Tablespoons olive oil, plus
  more for tops of loaves
1 Tablespoon unsalted butter
2 medium onions, chopped
3 cloves garlic, minced
1 ½ pounds ground round
1 ½ pounds ground veal shoulder
¾ to 1 pound sweet Italian
  sausage, casings removed
4 eggs, lightly beaten
¼ cup tomato juice

¼ cup dry red wine
1 ⅔ cups fresh bread crumbs
¾ cup freshly grated Parmesan
  cheese
½ to ¾ cup pine nuts (optional)
  (about 4 ounces)
2 Tablespoons chopped scallion
  greens or fresh parsley
1 ½ teaspoons dried basil,
  crumbled
½ teaspoon ground nutmeg
1 teaspoon salt
1 teaspoon freshly ground black
  pepper
¼ teaspoon cayenne pepper

1. If using fresh spinach, place spinach in large pot with just the water that clings to the leaves from washing. Steam, covered, over medium heat, stirring occasionally, until just wilted, about 5 minutes. Drain; rinse under cold water to stop cooking. Set aside and drain. (If using frozen spinach, omit this step.)

2. In same pot, heat oil and butter over medium heat. When foam subsides, add onion. Sauté until wilted, about 5 minutes. Add garlic; sauté another 2 minutes.

3. Meanwhile, squeeze spinach dry, fresh or frozen; coarsely chop. Add to pot; toss over medium-high heat until excess moisture has evaporated, about 4 minutes. Remove from heat.

4. In large bowl, mix together lightly with hands, without squeezing or pressing, the beef, veal, and sausage. Add the spinach-onion mixture, eggs, tomato juice, wine, bread crumbs, Parmesan, optional pine nuts, scallion, basil, nutmeg, salt and pepper, and cayenne. Mix lightly but thoroughly.

5. Preheat oven to 300°.

6. Transfer meat mixture to two 8 × 4-inch loaf pans. Tap pans on hard surface to remove air bubbles. Moisten palms with cold water; smooth top of meat in each pan into dome shape, high in center and low along sides. Brush with olive oil. Place in oven on sheet of aluminum foil to catch drippings. Bake until juices run clear when top is lightly pressed, about 1½ hours. Serve hot, warm, or at cool room temperature.

HEARTY PIES

Cuisines all over the world top savory ingredients with crusts made of pastry, bread, or biscuit doughs, corn, potatoes, kasha, and so forth. British cooking is rich with such examples as shepherd's pie, Cornish pasties, and a Welsh oddity called Tiddy Oggy, a pastry turnover sometimes made with meat at one end and jam at the other, providing local miners with lunch and dessert in one tidy package.

This selection of hearty pies ranges from a crisp flat-crust pizza to a savory sausage-apple-cheddar pie.

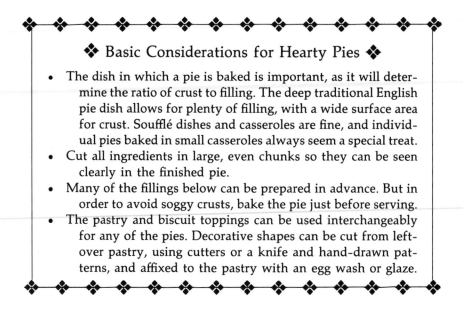

❖ Basic Considerations for Hearty Pies ❖

- The dish in which a pie is baked is important, as it will determine the ratio of crust to filling. The deep traditional English pie dish allows for plenty of filling, with a wide surface area for crust. Soufflé dishes and casseroles are fine, and individual pies baked in small casseroles always seem a special treat.
- Cut all ingredients in large, even chunks so they can be seen clearly in the finished pie.
- Many of the fillings below can be prepared in advance. But in order to avoid soggy crusts, bake the pie just before serving.
- The pastry and biscuit toppings can be used interchangeably for any of the pies. Decorative shapes can be cut from leftover pastry, using cutters or a knife and hand-drawn patterns, and affixed to the pastry with an egg wash or glaze.

CHICKEN POT PIE

This all-American version is now most frequently found, sadly, in a pasty, bland frozen version. Prepared well, this plain traditional dish is anything but humdrum. If you have poached a chicken in making broth, this is a good use for the meat.
Serves 6

8 Tablespoons (1 stick) unsalted
  butter
2 ½ to 3 pounds chicken breasts,
  with bones, or 3 to 4 cups
  leftover cooked chicken meat, cut
  into large dice
2 cups Chicken Broth (page 6)
3 carrots, trimmed, peeled, thickly
  sliced
¾ cup frozen peas, or fresh shelled
  peas
2 ribs celery, cut into large dice
1 red pepper, cored, seeded, cut into
  large dice
2 cups quartered mushrooms (about
  6 ounces)
2 cups diced onions (1 to 2
  medium onions)

2 cloves garlic, minced
6 Tablespoons flour
Pinch dried thyme
Pinch ground allspice or nutmeg
⅓ cup heavy cream
1 teaspoon salt, or more as needed
Freshly ground white or black
  pepper
Pinch cayenne pepper
½ cup chopped fresh parsley
1 recipe Sour Cream Flaky Pastry
  (page 206)

EGG WASH:

1 egg yolk mixed with 1 teaspoon
  milk or heavy cream

1. Grease deep 2-quart pie dish, casserole, or soufflé dish with 1 Tablespoon of the butter. Set aside.
2. In a heavy saucepan large enough to hold the chicken breasts, overlapping, if using, heat broth to boiling. Cut breasts in half; arrange in
broth. Adjust heat to maintain bare simmer; poach, covered, until
breasts are just cooked through, 10 to 15 minutes. Remove chicken with
slotted spoon to platter, draining briefly over pan.
3. Add carrots and peas to broth; return to boil, covered. Boil 2 minutes.
Add celery and red pepper; cook 2 minutes. Drain vegetables in sieve
over a bowl, reserving broth. Set vegetables aside in large bowl. Measure
the broth in measuring cup; add any juices exuded by chicken on platter.
If necessary, add water so broth measures at least 1¾ cups. Reserve.
4. Heat 2 Tablespoons of the butter in large skillet over medium high
heat. When foam subsides, add mushrooms. Sauté until lightly
browned, about 3 minutes. Add mushrooms to vegetables. Heat 2 Tablespoons of the butter over medium heat in same skillet. When foam
subsides, add onions. Sauté until wilted, about 6 minutes. Add garlic;
sauté 2 minutes. Add remaining 3 Tablespoons butter; stir until melted.
Sprinkle on the flour. Cook, stirring, 3 minutes, until mixture is light
and opaque. Add reserved broth, thyme, and allspice; whisk until boil-

ing. Boil gently, whisking, until thickened and smooth, 5 to 10 minutes. Add cream; boil gently until quite thick, about 5 minutes. Add pepper and cayenne. Reserve sauce.

5. While sauce is cooking, remove skin and bones from chicken. Cut flesh into large even dice. Add to vegetables in bowl. Add reserved sauce and parsley; fold together gently. Mixture should be quite thick. Correct seasonings with salt and pepper to taste. Scrape into the buttered dish. Reserve.

6. Roll out pastry on lightly floured surface to fit top of dish; it should be about ¼-inch thick and overhang dish edges by 1 inch. Chill rolled-out pastry briefly.

7. Preheat oven to 450°.

8. Brush rolled-out pastry with egg wash. Moisten outer rim of dish with cold water. Lay pastry over top of dish, egg-wash-side down. Trim edges of pastry; press pastry to rim and sides of dish. Brush any excess flour from pastry; brush top of pastry with egg wash. Arrange decorative cutouts from pastry trimmings on top, if you like; brush cutouts with egg wash. Cut steam vents in pastry. Chill briefly.

9. Glaze pastry again with egg wash. Place pie in oven. Immediately lower heat to 400°. Bake until pastry begins to brown, 20 to 25 minutes. Lower heat to 350°; continue to bake until pastry is crisp and golden brown, 40 to 45 minutes in all. Let pie sit 5 to 10 minutes before serving a portion of crust and juicy filling to each person.

SOUR CREAM FLAKY PASTRY

Cooking Tip: To make this pastry in a food processor, combine dry ingredients with butter and solid shortening in processor, pulsing briefly until crumbly. Do not overmix. Transfer mixture to a mixing bowl and proceed to add sour cream and liquid by hand, as in step 2 below. Makes one 8- to 10-inch pie shell or pot pie topping

1 ½ cups flour
1 teaspoon salt
Pinch sugar
6 Tablespoons (¾ stick) unsalted
*   butter, cut up, chilled*

¼ cup solid vegetable shortening,
*   cut up, chilled*
2 Tablespoons sour cream
2 Tablespoons cold water, or more
*   as needed*

1. Sift dry ingredients into large bowl. Add cut up butter and shortening, tossing to coat. Cut with two knives or crumble with fingers until the mixture forms coarse crumbs.

2. Beat sour cream with 2 Tablespoons water in a small cup; add to flour mixture, stirring gently with a fork. Add enough water to gather dough together, without letting it become too moist.

3. Roll the dough immediately on floured board into approximately 10 × 5-inch rectangle. Fold in thirds like a business letter, starting with top third. Turn pastry so folded side is on left. Repeat rolling and folding. Wrap dough; chill at least 1 hour before rolling out.

BEEF POT PIE

The dark mahogany sauce for this pie uses no stock, and is nicely offset by the sour cream pastry.
Serves 6

3 Tablespoons unsalted butter

4 Tablespoons vegetable oil

2 or 3 onions, chopped

3 carrots, trimmed, peeled, quartered lengthwise, cut into 1-inch lengths

1 ½ to 2 pounds beef chuck, with bone, fat trimmed

1 teaspoon salt

¼ cup flour

1 ½ cups dry red wine

1 small ripe tomato, peeled, seeded, chopped, or ⅓ cup drained canned tomatoes, sieved

¼ teaspoon dried thyme, crumbled

1 bay leaf

1 medium red pepper, cored, seeded, cut into ¾-inch dice

18 to 24 tiny onions (optional), peeled (blanch 2 minutes in water for easier peeling)

24 small mushrooms, stems trimmed flush with caps

2 Tablespoons chopped fresh parsley

1 recipe Sour Cream Flaky Pastry (page 206)

EGG WASH:

1 egg yolk mixed with 1 teaspoon milk or heavy cream

1. Heat 1 Tablespoon butter and 1 Tablespoon oil in large skillet over low heat. When foam subsides, add onions and carrots. Sauté slowly, stirring occasionally, until lightly golden, about 20 to 30 minutes.

2. Meanwhile, remove bone from chuck; reserve. Cut meat into ¾-inch cubes.

3. Transfer sautéed vegetables to platter. Add 1 Tablespoon butter and 1 Tablespoon oil to skillet. Raise heat to medium. Add half the meat; sauté, turning often, until very brown, 10 to 12 minutes. Lightly salt after 5 minutes. Add meat to vegetables. Sauté remaining half of meat.

4. Return all meat and vegetables to skillet. Sprinkle flour over all, blending in well. Stir continually until thick roux-like coating browns slightly, 4 to 5 minutes. Add wine; stir, scraping up any browned residue from bottom and sides of skillet. Add tomatoes, and cold water if necessary to cover ingredients generously. Stir in thyme and bay leaf. Tuck in reserved bone. Simmer, partially covered, adjusting heat as necessary, until meat is nearly, but not quite, tender, 1 to 1¼ hours. Stir occasionally.

5. Blanch diced red pepper in boiling salted water until just crisp-tender, 2 to 3 minutes. Drain; add to meat mixture.

6. Heat 1 Tablespoon butter in clean skillet over medium-low heat. When foam subsides, add optional tiny onions. Sauté, shaking pan frequently, until onions are lightly golden and almost tender, 12 to 15 minutes. Add to meat mixture.

7. Add 1 Tablespoon oil to skillet. Increase heat to medium high. Add mushrooms; quickly sauté until brown, 4 to 5 minutes. Add to meat mixture.

8. Remove meat mixture from heat; meat should be tender. Remove and discard bay leaf and bone. Add parsley, and salt if necessary. Cool slightly; skim off excess fat.

9. Preheat oven to 450°. Butter 6- or 7- cup baking dish, such as a deep pie dish or soufflé dish.

10. Roll out pastry on lightly floured surface to fit top of dish; pastry should be about ¼ inch thick and overhang dish edges by 1 inch. If there is excess pastry, use some for decorative cutouts for top of pie, and refrigerate the rest for another use. Chill rolled-out pastry briefly.

11. Fill dish with beef stew. Brush rolled-out pastry with egg wash. Moisten outer rim of dish with cold water. Lay pastry over top of dish, egg-wash-side down. Trim edges to allow for border around edge of dish. Press pastry to rim and sides of dish. Brush any excess flour from pastry; brush top of pastry with egg wash. Arrange decorative cutouts on top, if you like; brush cutouts with wash. Cut steam vents in top. Chill briefly.

12. Glaze pastry again with egg wash. Place pie in oven. Immediately lower heat to 400°. Bake until pastry begins to brown, 20 to 25 minutes. Lower heat to 350°; continue to bake until pastry is crisp and golden brown, 40 to 45 minutes in all. Let pie sit 5 to 10 minutes before serving a portion of crust and juicy filling to each person.

TEX-MEX BEEF CASSEROLE WITH TOASTED WALNUTS AND CORNMEAL BISCUIT TOPPING

The ground toasted walnuts in this pungently seasoned casserole lend thickening as well as an elusive flavor. Try the cornmeal biscuits baked on their own, or as an accompaniment to soups such as the Chili-Bean (page 22). Serve with plenty of chilled beer.
Serves 6 to 8

4 Tablespoons vegetable oil, or more as needed
2 ¼ pounds bottom round, cut into ¾-inch cubes
3 medium onions, chopped
2 green peppers, cored, seeded, cut into 1-inch dice
2 red peppers, cored, seeded, cut into 1-inch dice
2 cloves garlic, minced
1 to 2 cups tomato juice, or as needed
2 to 3 teaspoons ground coriander
2 teaspoons ground cumin
1 ½ teaspoons ground cinnamon

1 bay leaf
Salt
1 cup walnuts
¾ teaspoon crushed red pepper flakes
½ teaspoon cayenne pepper
Freshly ground black pepper
2 Tablespoons chopped fresh coriander or parsley leaves
1 recipe unbaked Cornmeal Biscuits (page 210)
1 ½ Tablespoons unsalted butter, melted
¼ cup coarsely shredded sharp Cheddar cheese

1. Heat 2 Tablespoons of the oil in a wide shallow casserole over medium heat until rippling. Add meat. Don't crowd pan; work in batches if necessary. Sauté meat until dark brown, about 20 minutes. Remove meat with slotted spoon to platter. Pour off excess fat.

2. Add remaining 2 Tablespoons oil to casserole. Add onion; sauté until soft but not brown, 5 to 10 minutes. Add peppers; sauté until slightly softened, about 5 minutes. Add garlic; toss 2 minutes. Add a little tomato juice to casserole, scraping up any browned bits from bottom and sides of casserole. Return meat to casserole.

3. Stir in enough tomato juice to barely cover ingredients. Add coriander, cumin, cinnamon, bay leaf, and salt; stir to combine ingredients. Simmer, partially covered, stirring occasionally, until meat is nearly but not quite tender, about 1¼ hours. Remove bay leaf.

4. Meanwhile, heat oven to 375°.

5. Place walnuts in cake pan. Toast, shaking pan occasionally, until lightly browned, 8 to 10 minutes. Cool slightly. Grind coarsely in food processor or blender. Reserve. Increase oven to 450°.

6. When meat is almost tender, add crushed red pepper flakes, cayenne, and black pepper. Stir in reserved ground walnuts and chopped coriander or parsley. Correct seasonings. Arrange unbaked biscuits on top of casserole. Brush biscuits with melted butter; scatter cheese over top.

7. Bake casserole, uncovered, until biscuits are puffed and golden and cheese is bubbly, 12 to 15 minutes. Serve some of the biscuit topping and meat filling to each person.

CORNMEAL BISCUITS

Makes about twelve 2½-inch biscuits

1 ½ cups unsifted flour
½ cup yellow cornmeal (coarsely ground)
1 Tablespoon baking powder
¾ teaspoon baking soda
½ teaspoon salt
5 Tablespoons chilled unsalted butter, cut into small bits

½ cup milk, or more if needed
¼ cup sour cream
¼ cup chopped scallion greens (optional)
2 to 3 Tablespoons chopped roasted peppers, patted dry (optional)

1. *With food processor:* Place flour, cornmeal, baking powder, baking soda, and salt in food processor. Process to sift together ingredients, about 3 seconds. Add bits of butter. Process until mixture is coarse crumbs, about five on/off pulses. Add milk and sour cream, and optional scallion greens and chopped peppers. Process until mixture just gathers together, about 10 seconds. If mixture is too dry, add more milk.

2. *By hand:* Sift flour, cornmeal, baking powder, baking soda, and salt into bowl. Cut in butter with fingertips, pastry blender, or two knives until mixture is coarse crumbs. Add remaining ingredients; stir to combine. Knead once or twice in bowl.

3. Turn dough out onto lightly floured surface. Roll out to ½-inch thickness. Cut out 2½-inch rounds with cutter or a glass. Re-roll leftover dough; cut out additional biscuits.

4. Arrange on ungreased baking sheet; brush biscuits lightly with melted butter. Bake in preheated 450° oven until puffed and golden, 12 to 15 minutes.

PIZZA RUSTICA

This luscious two-crust Italian pie is a re-creation, after many attempts, of a pie vaguely described to me by an Italian friend whose grandmother prepared it decades ago. Try the same technique with other fillings, and other shapes, such as a horseshoe for a special occasion. Also serves well as an hors d'oeuvre in thin slices, just slightly warm.
Serves 12 as a main course

10 to 12 ounces fresh spinach, stemmed, washed, or one package (10 ounces) frozen spinach, thawed, squeezed dry
2 egg yolks
1 egg
1 container (15 ounces) ricotta cheese
¾ cup freshly grated Parmesan cheese
3 Tablespoons unsalted butter
1 medium onion, chopped
2 cloves garlic, minced
½ teaspoon salt
½ teaspoon freshly ground black pepper
¼ teaspoon ground nutmeg
1 Tablespoon olive oil

1 to 1 ¼ cups thickly sliced mushrooms (about 4 ounces)
½ pound sweet Italian sausage, meat removed from casings
3 to 4 ounces prosciutto, cut in small squares
¼ cup chopped fresh parsley
1 teaspoon dried basil, crumbled, or ¼ cup chopped fresh basil
Pinch cayenne pepper
Double recipe Sour Cream Flaky Pastry (page 206)

EGG WASH:

1 egg yolk beaten with 1 teaspoon milk or heavy cream

1. If using fresh spinach, blanch briefly in large pot of boiling salted water until wilted, 1 to 2 minutes. Drain; rinse under cold water to stop cooking. Squeeze dry thoroughly. Coarsely chop fresh or frozen spinach. Reserve.
2. Beat egg yolks and egg together in bowl. Sieve in ricotta; stir to combine. Stir in Parmesan.
3. Heat 2 Tablespoons of the butter in large skillet over medium heat. When foam subsides, add onion. Sauté until wilted, about 5 minutes. Add garlic; sauté 2 minutes. Add chopped spinach, salt, pepper, and

nutmeg. Raise heat; dry out spinach, tossing, about 4 minutes. Add to ricotta mixture.

4. Heat remaining 1 Tablespoon butter and olive oil in skillet. When foam subsides, add mushrooms. Sauté until lightly golden, 3 to 4 minutes. Add to ricotta mixture. Crumble sausage meat into skillet; sauté until meat loses raw look, about 4 minutes. Drain excess fat; add sausage to bowl. Add ham, parsley, basil, and cayenne to bowl; toss to combine. Chill. Correct seasonings.

5. Preheat oven to 425°.

6. Roll out slightly more than one-third of the pastry on a lightly floured surface into ⅛-inch-thick rectangle or circle. Transfer pastry to baking sheet. Brush lightly with egg wash. Arrange filling on pastry, leaving 1- to 1½-inch border all around. Mound filling in center, building up sides.

7. Roll out remaining pastry into rectangle or circle to match bottom. Lay pastry loosely over filling. Press edges of top piece of pastry together with bottom piece of pastry. Trim pastry, leaving 1-to-1½-inch border. Brush top piece of pastry with egg wash. Roll up pastry border all around; press against top piece of pastry. Press edge with fork; brush border with egg wash. Cut two or three steam vents in top. Chill.

8. Brush pastry again with egg wash. Form decorations with pastry trimmings, if you like. Affix to top; brush with egg wash. Bake until pastry begins to brown, about 10 minutes. Lower heat to 400°. Bake another 10 minutes. If browning too fast, lower oven heat to 350°. Bake until golden, about 45 minutes in all. Let pizza sit about 10 minutes. Cut pie in half lengthwise with long serrated knife; then cut in thin crosswise slices. Serve hot or warm.

SAUSAGE-APPLE-CHEDDAR PIE

Ground pork as a savory pie filling is a favorite in many cuisines, from the formally arranged *pâtés en croûte* of the French *charcutier* to the home-baked *tourtière* of Quebec, and the English raised pies made with lard pastry. This version, spiked with sharp Cheddar cheese, is best made with tart, firm apples.

Serves 6 to 8

1 dish (9 × 1-inch pie) lined with
   ½ recipe Basic Pastry for
   Quiches and Tarts (page 94)
1 pound sweet Italian sausage
¼ cup plus ⅓ cup dry white wine
4 Tablespoons unsalted butter
3 tart apples, such as Granny
   Smith or Greening, peeled,
   quartered, cored, sliced, and
   tossed in bowl with a little fresh
   lemon juice
2 teaspoons brown sugar
¼ teaspoon ground cinnamon

Pinch allspice
Pinch mace (optional)
2 medium onions, coarsely chopped
2 cloves garlic, minced
1 egg, lightly beaten
2 Tablespoons chopped fresh
   parsley
1½ cups grated sharp Cheddar
   cheese (4 ounces)
1 teaspoon fresh lemon juice
Salt
Freshly ground black pepper
Cayenne pepper

1. Preheat oven to 400°.
2. Line pastry with aluminum foil; weight with dried beans or rice. Bake crust 10 minutes. Remove weights and foil. Prick pastry lightly with fork. Bake until very lightly golden brown, about 10 minutes. Remove to wire rack.
3. Prick sausage casings with fork. Place sausages in single layer in large skillet. Add the ¼ cup wine and enough water to come to depth of ¼ inch. Cook over medium-high heat, turning sausages once, until liquid evaporates, about 8 minutes. Continue to cook until sausages begin to render their fat, 2 to 3 minutes. Remove sausages to plate lined with paper towels. Wipe out skillet with other paper towels.
4. Heat 2 Tablespoons of the butter in the skillet over medium-high heat. When foam subsides, add apples, sugar, cinnamon, allspice, and optional mace. Toss until apples just begin to soften, about 4 minutes. Transfer to large bowl.

5. Heat remaining 2 Tablespoons butter in skillet over medium heat. When foam subsides, add onion. Sauté, tossing often, until onion begins to brown, about 10 minutes. Add garlic; cook 1 to 2 minutes. Add the ⅓ cup wine, scraping up any browned bits from the bottom and sides of the skillet. Reduce wine slightly, 1 to 2 minutes. Transfer to bowl with apples.

6. Remove sausage meat from casings and crumble into bowl. Add egg, parsley, cheese (reserving about ¼ cup), lemon juice, and salt and black pepper to taste. Pile mixture into crust, mounding slightly in center. Sprinkle remaining cheese over top; sprinkle small amount of cayenne over all.

7. Bake pie on baking sheet in middle level of oven until surface begins to brown, 10 to 15 minutes. Lower heat to 375°; bake until browned, about 30 minutes in all. Let sit about 10 minutes before serving in wedges.

PIZZA

This is little more than a quick suggestion. If you are making bread dough, tear off a piece to be rolled for a home-baked pizza. Or make the quick dough in the recipe. Toppings are unlimited: tomato sauce and grated mozzarella cheese, stewed onions with tomato sauce or oil-cured black olives and anchovies, or a Basquaise mixture topped with cheese. Serves 4 to 6

DOUGH:

2 teaspoons dry yeast (about ⅔ envelope)

¾ cup lukewarm water

2 teaspoons olive oil

2 cups flour, or more if needed

1 teaspoon salt

2 teaspoons cornmeal (optional)

TOPPING:

2 to 2½ cups Basic Chunky Tomato Sauce (page 61)

or

1½ to 2 cups leftover Zucchini Ragout (page 91)

or

1½ to 2 cups Basquaise (page 192)

or

1 recipe onions for Onion Tart (page 97), mixed with ½ to ¾ cup Basic Chunky Tomato Sauce (page 61)

12 ounces grated mozzarella cheese

1. *Dough:* In a small bowl, combine yeast and water. Let sit until foamy, 10 to 15 minutes. Add oil. In food processor, blend flour and salt with a few on/off pulses. With motor running gradually add yeast mixture; process 30 seconds.

2. Turn dough out onto floured surface. Knead until smooth, about 2 minutes. If dough is sticky, knead in a bit more flour. Place dough in lightly oiled bowl; turn to coat dough. Cover with clean cloth. Let rise until doubled in volume, about 30 minutes.

3. Preheat oven to 500° for at least 15 minutes.

4. Punch dough down. Turn out onto floured board. Roll out as thinly as possible into 10 × 14-inch rectangle (or into a large circle). Place dough on heavy baking pan sprinkled with cornmeal or 1 teaspoon flour. Quickly spread topping evenly over top of dough. Sprinkle cheese over all.

5. Place pizza in oven. Spray water into oven or throw 1 to 2 Tablespoons water on oven floor, avoiding pizza, pilot light, and heating elements. Repeat process after 5 minutes; again after 15 minutes. Bake until edges are brown and topping is bubbly, 15 to 20 minutes. Eat immediately.

DESSERTS

Being, as I freely admit, very greedy,
I have always had enough to eat before dessert.
After the joint I eat from sheer politeness.
But then, I am very polite.
　　　　　—ALIN CAUBREAUX, *The Happy Glutton*

A DESSERT SAUCE SAMPLER

CRÈME ANGLAISE
SABAYON
   WHIPPED-CREAM-LIGHTENED SABAYON
   FRUIT GRATIN WITH LIGHTENED SABAYON
RASPBERRY COULIS
CANNOLI CREAM

FROZEN DESSERTS

MELON ICE
GRANITA DI CAFFE CON PANNA (COFFEE ICE WITH CREAM)

BAKED FRUIT DESSERTS

PEACH COBBLER
PLUM CRUMBLE
FRESH CHERRY CLAFOUTI
   FRESH PLUM CLAFOUTI

CAKES, TARTS, PIES, AND COOKIES

CURRANT POUND CAKE
CHOCOLATE SOUFFLÉ CAKE
SOUR CREAM BANANA CAKE
WALNUT-CASSIS TORTE
LEMON MOUSSE CAKE ROLL
A PASTRY PRIMER
TARTE AU CITRON (FRESH LEMON TART)
   FRESH ORANGE TART
SWEET TART PASTRY
DEEP-DISH PUMPKIN PIE WITH BOURBON
ALMOND BRITTLE COOKIES
COOKIE CRUST
LACY HAZELNUT WAFERS
OLD-FASHIONED HAZELNUT DROPS

CUSTARDS, PUDDINGS, AND MOUSSES

CARAMEL POTS DE CRÈME
   VANILLA POTS DE CRÈME
   CHOCOLATE POTS DE CRÈME
   COFFEE POTS DE CRÈME
   MOCHA POTS DE CRÈME
COACH HOUSE BREAD AND BUTTER PUDDING
   POUND CAKE PUDDING
MOLDED RICE PUDDING WITH CARAMEL SAUCE
HOMEMADE DOUBLE CHOCOLATE PUDDING
LEMON MOUSSE
RASPBERRY CHARLOTTE

F or some reason, many people look on desserts as frivolous. Not me, however. The technical mastery of a first-rate *pâtissier,* or pastry chef, indisputably rivals that of a great chef. My first exposure to "cooking" was as a small child at a friend's family bakery. The bakers would clear off a far corner for us, give us each a plain cupcake, and watch as we crowded our tiny cakes with a mess of buttercream roses and stars.

More to the point: in a perfectly planned meal, the impressions are as carefully paced as the movements of a symphony. And the dessert, often a climactic moment, should be as carefully thought out as the rest.

This chapter is a repertoire, admittedly very selective, of fine dessert recipes. To finish a dinner, you need not overwhelm your guests with the baroque: a lemon tart or a granita provide intensity of flavor in a light form. A dessert with tart flavor, such as a raspberry charlotte, can accent the sweetness of a Sauternes, California late-harvest Riesling, or other sweet wine.

Some of the cakes and pies in this chapter can be too substantial to follow any but the lightest dinner. Enjoy these baked desserts on their own, with good coffee or tea.

A homemade dessert is always a much-appreciated contribution to a dinner party. I've never known anyone not delighted to receive a home-baked tart from an arriving dinner guest. And a coffee and dessert buffet —five or six desserts served attractively with plenty of rich strong coffee —is not only an unusual form of entertaining but one that will have your guests raving long after they have finished off the last remaining crumbs.

A DESSERT SAUCE SAMPLER

When a homemade dessert is too much bother, a simple one can be improvised by using one of the following sauces to top fresh fruit, a plain cake, or ice cream.

CRÈME ANGLAISE

This is the basic pouring custard, delicious as a cool vanilla sauce, or as the basis for a Bavarian cream or ice cream. Use to accompany fresh berries or peaches, toasted Currant Pound Cake (page 228), Chocolate Soufflé Cake (page 230), or a hot or cold soufflé. Vary the flavor with melted chocolate, dissolved instant coffee, preferably instant espresso, grated citrus zest, or Cognac or a liqueur.

Cooking Tip: When preparing this custard, stir constantly over low heat; do not let the sauce boil, or the yolks will curdle. A double boiler may be used as a precaution.

Makes about 2½ cups.

2 cups milk	*6 egg yolks*
½ vanilla bean, split lengthwise,	*½ cup sugar*
or 1 ½ teaspoons pure vanilla	*Pinch salt*
extract	

1. Heat milk with vanilla bean in heavy saucepan over medium heat until bubbles appear around edges.
2. Meanwhile, whisk yolks, sugar, and salt briefly in bowl until blended.
3. Gradually whisk scalded milk into yolk mixture; return to pan. Stir constantly with wooden spoon over medium heat until thickened, about 7 minutes. Do not boil. Strain into clean bowl. Stir in vanilla extract if using instead of bean. Cool.

SABAYON

Sabayon, a frothy custard and cousin to the Italian *zabaglione,* whether in its simplest form or lightened with whipped cream, is a luxurious topping for ripe berries or other fruits. Or for a remarkable dessert, many French chefs have been glazing sabayon-topped fruit under a broiler for a fruit gratin.

Serves 4 (about 2 to 2½ cups)

1 egg	¼ cup sugar
3 egg yolks	1 ½ Tablespoons Cointreau, or
2 Tablespoons cold water	other liqueur

1. Select a double boiler or a medium metal bowl that fits snugly into a medium saucepan. Pour water into the saucepan to a depth of about 1 inch. Water should not touch the bottom of bowl. Heat water to simmering.

2. Meanwhile, combine egg, egg yolks, water, and sugar in the bowl. Whisk vigorously until combined and foamy, about 1 minute. Place bowl in pan over simmering water. Adjust heat to maintain bare simmer. Whisk vigorously, without stopping, until mixture is tripled in volume, and very pale, frothy, and thick, 8 to 10 minutes. Sabayon should hold soft mounds when dropped from the whisk. Remove bowl from pan.

3. Continue to whisk until sabayon is lukewarm. Gradually add Cointreau.

Variations

Whipped-Cream-Lightened Sabayon: Whip ½ cup heavy cream until nearly stiff. Gently fold into lukewarm sabayon. Leftovers can be frozen for a delicious frozen custard.

Fruit Gratin with Lightened Sabayon: While some versions use a flour-thickened pastry cream, you'll appreciate the lightness of this gratin made with a sabayon. The play of textures and temperatures makes this a spectacular summer dessert.

Serves 4

Preheat broiler. Arrange 2 cups soft fruits such as raspberries, strawberries, sliced peaches, nectarines, and/or plums in a buttered gratin or other shallow heatproof dish. Top with whipped-cream-lightened sabayon. Briefly glaze under broiler 4 to 5 inches from flame, until just golden brown. Serve immediately.

RASPBERRY COULIS

This is an excellent use for frozen raspberries, which are available year-round. Accent the flavor of this purée with sugar, lemon juice, and a liqueur such as framboise, kirsch, or Cognac. Use to top fresh whole berries, such as a combination of strawberries and blueberries, or fruit sorbet, to surround a slice of plain cake, or as the basis for a raspberry charlotte (page 253). A small amount of the purée can also be stirred into a *crème anglaise* for a fruit-flavored custard sauce.
Makes about 1 cup

Generous half-pint fresh raspberries, or 2 packages (10 ounces each) frozen raspberries, thawed, drained, liquid reserved

Sugar, as needed
Few drops fresh lemon juice
Framboise, kirsch, or Cognac

1. Purée berries in food processor or blender. Pass through sieve to eliminate seeds.
2. Sweeten with sugar as necessary. If using frozen berries, thin purée, as needed, with some of reserved strained liquid. Add lemon juice and liqueur to taste. Combine thoroughly. Chill before using.

CANNOLI CREAM

Not to be confused with canneloni, a cannoli is a deep-fried Italian pastry with a cream filling. This sauce, developed by Johanne Killeen, a Rhode Island photographer and restaurateur, is a light version of that Italian cream filling. Spooned over berries or other fresh fruits it makes a knockout dessert. It takes seconds to prepare, and can be refrigerated for two or three days. Serve bowls of this and the Raspberry *Coulis* above on a buffet table with berries or other fresh fruit, and let guests dip as they please.
Makes about 2 cups

1 container (15 ounces) ricotta
cheese
½ cup orange marmalade, or to
taste
2 Tablespoons Cointreau, or other
orange liqueur

½ teaspoon pure vanilla extract
1 ½ Tablespoons semisweet
chocolate bits

1. In a food processor, blend ricotta with on-off motion until smooth. Or whisk by hand. *Do not use* a blender.
2. Add marmalade, liqueur, and vanilla to ricotta; process very briefly, just until blended. Add chocolate bits. Process briefly with on-off motion until most of the bits are chopped, but a few are left whole. Or chop bits with a knife, then fold into mixture without processing.
3. Chill for an hour or so before serving.

FROZEN DESSERTS

None of these simple frozen desserts requires any special equipment. They are a refreshing conclusion to warm-weather meals.

MELON ICE

A food processor makes easy work of this light ice, and it can be made with any sort of ripe melon.
Serves 6

¾ cup sugar
2 cups water
2 ripe medium cantaloupes

Juice of 2 lemons or limes
Orange-flavored liqueur (optional)

1. Combine sugar and water in heavy saucepan. Heat to boiling over medium heat; boil for 5 minutes. Cool completely.
2. Cut melons in half; remove seeds. Scoop out flesh. Purée flesh in processor or blender with the lemon or lime juice until smooth. Transfer to bowl.

3. Stir cooled syrup into the purée. Add optional liqueur.

4. Pour the mixture into bowl or shallow metal tray. Place in freezer. As soon as the mixture begins to freeze around the edges, beat crystals into mixture with wooden spoon or whisk. Continue same process every 30 to 45 minutes, until the mixture is uniformly crystallized. Fewer stirrings will produce a coarser-textured ice.

GRANITA DI CAFFE CON PANNA (COFFEE ICE WITH CREAM)

Italian espresso, broken up into coarse crystals as it freezes, then served in tall glasses with barely whipped cream—a leisurely way to linger over coffee and dessert, all in one.
Serves 4 to 6

3 cups very strong coffee, preferably espresso, hot
½ to ⅔ cup sugar, or to taste

½ to ¾ cup heavy cream, cold
Sambuca or anisette to taste

1. Brew the coffee; add sugar while hot. Cool; chill thoroughly in the refrigerator.

2. Pour coffee into shallow pan such as a pie plate or ice cube trays without dividers. Carefully place in freezer about 2½ hours before serving.

3. When mixture is firm around edges, about 45 minutes, use 2 knives to combine firm and liquid portions, cutting mixture into coarse crystals. Return to freezer.

4. Repeat blending and cutting one or two more times. The last time, mixture should be quite firm throughout. Cut into large, even crystals; spoon into wine glasses. Whip cream until just fluffy but not too stiff (soft peaks). Top each serving with some of the cream. Serve immediately. Flavor cream with a little anisette or Sambuca, if you like.

BAKED FRUIT DESSERTS

PEACH COBBLER

Topping fresh fruit with biscuit dough is one of our oldest American dessert traditions. This version calls for summer's freshest ripe peaches, or it can be done equally well with plums, nectarines, cherries, pears, or apples. Try combining this peach filling with a crumble topping (page 226).
Serves 6 to 8

1 ½ Tablespoons unsalted butter
2 ½ to 3 pounds ripe peaches
  (about 9 medium)
2 teaspoons fresh lemon juice
⅔ cup brown sugar
¼ cup flour
½ teaspoon ground cinnamon
Pinch salt

BUTTERMILK BISCUIT TOPPING:

1 cup plus 2 Tablespoons flour
1 Tablespoon granulated sugar
1 teaspoon baking powder

½ teaspoon baking soda
Pinch salt
3 Tablespoons chilled unsalted
  butter, cut into bits
⅓ cup buttermilk, or ¼ cup
  yogurt plus 1 Tablespoon milk,
  or more as needed

EGG WASH:

1 egg yolk beaten with 1 teaspoon
  water or milk

Granulated sugar

1. Preheat oven to 425°. Butter 9½ × 1½-inch pie dish with ½ Tablespoon of the butter.
2. Blanch peaches for 30 seconds in boiling water. Drain. Rinse under cold water to stop cooking. Place lemon juice in large bowl. Peel, halve, stone, and thickly slice peaches. There should be about 5 cups of slices. Drop slices into bowl with lemon juice; toss to coat to prevent discoloration.
3. In another bowl, combine sugar, flour, cinnamon, and salt. Drain off any juices exuded by peach slices. Add slices to flour mixture. Toss

gently to combine. Scrape mixture into prepared dish. Top with remaining 1 Tablespoon butter, cut into bits.

4. *Buttermilk Biscuit Topping:* Sift together into large bowl the flour, sugar, baking powder, baking soda, and salt. Cut in butter with fingers or two knives, until mixture is crumbly. Add buttermilk or yogurt mixture, stirring with a fork until the mixture coheres. Dough should be soft but not sticky. If dough is too dry, dribble in a bit more liquid. Knead gently two or three times in bowl. Turn dough out onto floured board. Roll into circle ½ inch thick. Cut into large diamond shapes with crisscrossing diagonal cuts, or into rounds with a cutter. Arrange cutouts attractively over fruit, leaving a little space between.

5. Brush biscuits with egg wash. Sprinkle granulated sugar over all. Bake. If biscuits are golden after 20 minutes, lower heat to 350°. Bake 30 minutes in all, or until biscuits have risen and are light golden. Serve warm with heavy cream or vanilla ice cream.

PLUM CRUMBLE

Crumbles are a favored dessert in England, where they are concocted with rhubarb, apples, currants, gooseberries, and other fruits from the garden. This rich, shortbread-like topping, based on a recipe of English cook Tina Walker, contrasts nicely with the tart plums below. Or substitute an equal weight of another soft fruit.
Serves 6 to 8

*1 ¾ pounds plums, stoned, thickly
  sliced (about 4 cups)*
*½ cup granulated sugar, or more
  depending on tartness of fruit*
3 Tablespoons flour
½ teaspoon ground cinnamon
*Unsalted butter, softened, for pie
  dish*

TOPPING:

1 cup brown sugar, lightly packed
¾ cup oatmeal
¾ cup flour
*1 stick (4 ounces) chilled unsalted
  butter, cut up*

1. Preheat oven to 375°.
2. Combine plum slices, granulated sugar, flour, and cinnamon in bowl; toss gently to combine.
3. Butter 10-inch pie dish.
4. *Topping:* Rub sugar, oatmeal, flour, and butter together with fingers in a bowl or process in food processor until crumbly. Arrange mixture evenly over plums.
5. Lay sheet of aluminum foil under dish in oven to catch drips. Bake until golden brown, about 45 minutes.
6. Serve warm or at room temperature with heavy cream or vanilla ice cream.

FRESH CHERRY CLAFOUTI

This traditional French farm dessert resembles a huge, puffy pancake baked in a shallow dish. It is a specialty of the Limousin region in central France. Remind guests to be wary of pits. When cherries or plums are not available, substitute prunes soaked in Cognac.
Serves 6 to 8

1 ¼ *pounds fresh sour cherries,*
   stems removed, pits left in
1 ½ *Tablespoons unsalted butter,*
   softened, for pie dish

BATTER:

½ *cup plus 3 Tablespoons flour*
⅓ *cup sugar*

Pinch salt
3 *Tablespoons sour cream or yogurt*
2 *eggs*
5 *ounces milk*
1 ½ *teaspoons Cognac or brandy*
¾ *teaspoon pure vanilla extract*

Confectioner's sugar

1. Preheat oven to 375°.
2. Rinse cherries; pat dry with paper towels. Butter 10 × 1-inch pie dish; set aside.
3. In mixing bowl, sift together flour, sugar, and salt. Whisk in sour cream and eggs until blended and smooth. Add milk, Cognac, and

vanilla; whisk briefly. Stir in cherries. Pour batter into prepared dish. 4. Bake until toothpick inserted in center emerges clean and top is golden brown, 35 to 45 minutes. Place on wire rack. Sieve confectioner's sugar over top. Cool just until warm. Sieve more confectioner's sugar over top. Serve warm with heavy cream, sour cream, or vanilla ice cream. If clafouti becomes too cool, texture will become dense.

Variation

Fresh Plum Clafouti: Toss 1½ pounds quartered, pitted small fresh plums, Italian blue plums if possible, with 2½ Tablespoons sugar in bowl. If plums are very juicy, toss with 1½ Tablespoons flour. Add plums to batter in step 3 above.

CAKES, TARTS, PIES, AND COOKIES

Baking was my first exposure to the adventure of cooking; and I once had a job producing nothing but cookies, petits fours, and breads. Watching a master baker is fascinating: the speed, precision, and grace of the movements are awe-inspiring. And every baker I've known well has been kind-spirited and generous.

CURRANT POUND CAKE

This recipe, which I make every Christmas, is one to hold on to. It is a moist, buttery cake, delicious with coffee or tea. Try it toasted; dress it up with ice cream, fresh fruit, or a sauce; or use it as a basis for a pound cake pudding (page 248).
Cooking Tip: Bake this cake in foil loaf pans; wrap in plastic wrap, then with ribbon for holiday gifts.
Makes 2 cakes (each about 7½ × 4½ × 2½ inches)

¾ to 1 cup currants or raisins (4
  to 5 ounces)
½ cup brandy, bourbon, or rum
Unsalted butter and flour for cake
  pans
2 ½ sticks (10 ounces) unsalted
  butter, softened
Grated zest of 1 orange
1 ⅓ cups sugar

2 ¼ cups flour, lightly spooned into
  measuring cups
½ teaspoon salt
½ teaspoon baking powder
5 eggs
¼ cup milk
2 teaspoons pure vanilla extract
Confectioner's sugar

1. At least 1 hour before baking, soak currants or raisins in brandy, stirring occasionally.

2. Preheat oven to 325°. Butter and flour cake pans; shake out excess flour.

3. With an electric mixer, cream butter with orange zest at medium speed until light. Gradually add sugar, beating until mixture is very fluffy, about 6 minutes.

4. Meanwhile, sift flour, salt, and baking powder onto large sheet of waxed paper. Lower mixer speed; add flour mixture gradually, reserving ½ cup. Scrape down sides of bowl with rubber spatula as necessary.

5. Increase mixer speed to medium. Add eggs, one at a time. Add milk and vanilla.

6. Drain currants. Toss currants with reserved ½ cup flour; stir into batter just until currants are evenly distributed.

7. Pour batter into pans. Bake until golden and toothpick inserted in center emerges clean, about 1 hour and 15 minutes. Time can vary; do not overbake.

8. Cool cakes in pans on wire rack a few minutes. Sieve confectioner's sugar over cakes while still warm. Remove cakes from pans; reserve pans. Cool cakes completely. Sieve confectioner's sugar again over tops of cakes. Return cakes to pans. Wrap in plastic wrap. Allow to ripen at least 24 hours before serving. Cakes keep well 3 days, tightly wrapped. Cakes can also be refrigerated. Sprinkle cake with confectioner's sugar just before serving.

CHOCOLATE SOUFFLÉ CAKE

Actually a fallen soufflé, this rich but light cake pleases even the most determined chocolate addicts. You might like to arrange a decorative pattern on the finished cake by·first sifting cocoa onto the surface, then laying on strips or cutouts of foil, and then dusting with confectioner's sugar. When you lift the foil away, the pattern will show clearly. Serves 10 to 12

Unsalted butter and flour for the cake pan

8 ounces best-quality semisweet chocolate, cut up coarsely

¼ cup hazelnuts or walnuts

6 egg yolks

1 teaspoon grated orange zest

⅔ cup sugar

3 Tablespoons strong coffee, or 2 Tablespoons instant espresso powder mixed with 1 Tablespoon hot water

1 ½ Tablespoons Armagnac or brandy

8 egg whites

Cocoa and/or confectioner's sugar

Vanilla-flavored whipped cream

1. Preheat oven to 350°. Arrange oven rack in lower third of oven. Butter and flour a 9- or 10-inch tube or angel-food cake pan and set aside. Melt chocolate over hot water, stirring until smooth. Set aside. Toast nuts in small pan in the oven for 10 minutes, then set aside to cool.

2. With a whisk or electric mixer, beat egg yolks with orange zest until light; gradually beat in sugar, reserving about 2 tablespoons of sugar. Whip until mixture is pale, fluffy, and forms a ribbon, about 5 minutes. Meanwhile, grind the nuts fine in a food processor or blender.

3. Gradually add to the egg yolk mixture the nuts, chocolate, coffee, and Armagnac or brandy. Set aside.

4. Beat egg whites until soft peaks form; gradually beat in reserved sugar until mixture is stiff but not dry.

5. Stir about a quarter of the whites into chocolate mixture, beating vigorously. Add this mixture to the whites; fold quickly but gently until the mixture is nearly homogeneous. Gently scrape the mixture into prepared cake pan and place in oven. Bake until cake has puffed, is dry

on top, and a toothpick inserted into it emerges not quite clean, about 35 to 40 minutes. Cool the cake, in its pan, on a rack for about an hour.

6. Invert cake onto a plate. To serve, sift cocoa and/or confectioner's sugar over the cake, and offer whipped cream separately. (If you like, whipped cream can be piped into the center and around the cake.)

SOUR CREAM BANANA CAKE

Well into her seventies, my paternal grandmother cooked huge, delicious feasts every Sunday for our extended family. In summer, she packed her specialties in coolers and we'd drive into the country for lakeside picnics. These family events are infrequent now that we are grown and she is gone, but all the cousins remember her by baking Grandma's banana cake.

Cooking Tips: Originally this cake was frosted with a fluffy chocolate icing, then topped with large walnut halves. These days I find that a little powdered sugar is enough, but the flavors of chocolate and banana do combine well, if you'd like to use a favorite frosting recipe.

This recipe will also make two small loaves. Reduce the baking time to about 45 minutes, or until cakes test done.

Serves 8 to 10 (makes one 10-inch cake)

Unsalted butter and flour for cake pan
¾ cup (1 ½ sticks) unsalted butter, softened
1 ½ cups sugar
2 ¼ cups cake flour, spooned lightly into measuring cups
1 ½ teaspoons baking powder
1 ½ teaspoons baking soda
¼ teaspoon salt
3 eggs
¾ cup (generous) mashed bananas (about 2 very ripe bananas)
¼ cup plus 2 Tablespoons sour cream
2 teaspoons pure vanilla extract
Confectioner's sugar

1. Preheat oven to 350°. Place rack in middle level of oven.
2. Generously butter 10-inch tube or Bundt pan. Flour pan, shaking out excess. Set aside.

3. With electric mixer, cream butter until very fluffy. Gradually beat in sugar, beating until very light.
4. Sift flour with baking powder, baking soda, and salt onto large sheet of waxed paper.
5. Beat eggs one at a time into butter mixture.
6. Lower mixer speed to very slow. Beat in half the flour mixture alternately in batches with the mashed bananas. Add the remaining half of the flour mixture alternately in batches with the sour cream. Add vanilla. Pour batter into prepared cake pan. Bake until toothpick inserted in center of cake emerges clean, about 50 to 55 minutes. Do not overbake.
7. Cool cake briefly on wire rack. Remove cake from pan. Dust with confectioner's sugar. Cool thoroughly on wire rack. Dust again. The cake keeps well tightly wrapped and covered at room temperature.

WALNUT-CASSIS TORTE

This light elegant cake can be made in several flavor combinations. Serves 8 (makes one 8- or 9-inch torte)

¾ cup walnuts (about 3 ounces), or a mixture of hazelnuts and walnuts
Unsalted butter and flour for cake pan
3 eggs, at room temperature
⅓ cup sugar
⅓ cup flour
½ teaspoon baking powder
Pinch salt
1 teaspoon pure vanilla extract
2 ½ Tablespoons unsalted butter, melted, cooled slightly

GARNISH:

3 Tablespoons (about) crème de cassis
⅓ to ½ cup black currant preserves
1 cup heavy cream, cold
1 teaspoon pure vanilla extract (optional)
Chopped nuts (optional)
Confectioner's sugar
8 walnut halves (optional)

1. Preheat oven to 350°.

2. Place nuts in baking pan with sides. Toast in oven, tossing occasionally, until lightly golden, about 10 minutes. Place nuts in jar of blender or bowl of food processor. Cool slightly. Leave oven at 350°.

3. Line bottom of 8- or 9-inch cake pan, such as a layer cake or génoise cake pan, with round of waxed paper. Butter paper and sides of pan. Flour; shake out excess. Set pan aside.

4. With an electric mixer, beat together eggs and the ⅓ cup less 2 Tablespoons sugar at medium speed until very light, frothy, and nearly tripled in volume, 5 to 7 minutes.

5. Meanwhile, add reserved 2 Tablespoons sugar, flour, baking powder, and salt to nuts. Grind, using on/off motion, until finely chopped but not oily. Reserve.

6. Add vanilla to egg mixture; beat another minute. Pour melted butter onto beaten eggs. Quickly fold in butter with large rubber spatula, until almost but not quite incorporated. Add one-third of the nut mixture. Fold until nearly but not quite homogeneous. Add another third of the nuts; repeat folding. Add remaining nuts; fold gently until mixed. Scrape batter into prepared pan.

7. Bake cake until center is springy to the touch and sides begin to pull away from pan, 30 to 35 minutes. Cool cake in pan on wire rack about 10 minutes. Sprinkle surface of cake lightly with granulated sugar to prevent sticking. Invert cake onto rack. Peel off paper. Cool cake thoroughly. Cake can now be wrapped or frozen.

8. Cut cake horizontally into two layers with serrated knife. Sprinkle cut surface of each cake with crème de cassis. Spread cut surface of one layer with black currant preserves; place layer, cut side up, on serving plate. Whip cream until just stiff; add vanilla or a little crème de cassis, and chopped nuts, if you wish. Spread cream, reserving some for garnishing the top, over top of jam-covered layer. Lightly press top layer, cut side down, on top of bottom layer. Sieve confectioner's sugar over top. For a simple but elegant garnish, pipe 8 whipped-cream rosettes on top of cake. Lightly press a nut into each rosette.

9. Refrigerate decorated cake at least 1 hour before serving, to allow flavors to blend.

Variations

For the black-currant preserves and crème de cassis, substitute apricot jam and Cognac or Amaretto, orange marmalade and Grand Marnier, or raspberry jam and framboise or kirsch. Also try a rolled variation of this cake, using the ingredients above and following instructions for Sponge Cake Roll below.

LEMON MOUSSE CAKE ROLL

This light, lemony roll is one of the most popular desserts from my catering days.

Cooking Tip: Be sure to spread the mousse when almost, but not quite, set for smooth results.

Serves 8

SPONGE CAKE ROLL:

3 Tablespoons unsalted butter

5 egg yolks

½ cup sugar plus 1 Tablespoon, plus more as needed

1 teaspoon pure vanilla extract

⅔ cup flour

4 egg whites

1 recipe Lemon Mousse (page 252)

GARNISH:

Confectioner's sugar

½ cup heavy cream, cold

½ lemon (cut lengthwise)

1. Preheat oven to 400°.
2. *The Cake:* Melt 2 Tablespoons and 1 teaspoon of the butter in small saucepan over low heat. Set aside to cool. Use some of the remaining butter to grease edges of 15½ × 10½-inch jelly roll pan. Line pan with parchment or waxed paper. Use remaining butter to grease paper. Set aside.
3. With a whisk or an electric mixer, vigorously whisk egg yolks and ½ cup sugar in medium bowl until thick and light, 3 to 4 minutes. Add the vanilla.
4. Sift in flour, stirring gently until combined. Stir in melted butter.
5. Beat egg whites until they form soft peaks. Add the 1 Tablespoon sugar. Beat until stiff. Stir large spoonful whites into yolk mixture to

lighten; fold in remaining whites. Gently scrape batter into prepared pan, smoothing batter evenly. Bake until just beginning to turn pale gold, about 9 minutes.

6. Lay sheet of waxed paper on towel on flat surface. Sprinkle lightly with sugar. Invert pan onto waxed paper. Carefully remove pan from cake. Cover cake with damp towel for a few minutes. Remove towel; peel paper from top of cake, and replace towel. Let cake cool.

7. Prepare the Lemon Mousse. Place in refrigerator, but do not allow to set completely.

8. Grab ends of towels and flip cake over. Remove top towel and paper. Trim uneven edges from cake with serrated knife. Give mousse a quick fold or two every couple of minutes to encourage even setting. When the mousse is beginning to set, thickening without becoming firm, spread evenly over surface of cake, leaving a wide border all around. Some mousse will be left over. Roll cake up, beginning with a long side. Smooth off any excess filling. Smooth ends of cake, adding mousse if necessary to fill in empty spots. Reserve leftover mousse at room temperature.

9. Chill cake thoroughly. Add more mousse to ends of cake if needed.

10. At serving time, sieve confectioner's sugar over cake. Whip cream. Pipe whipped cream rosettes down center of roll. Cut lemon half into thin crosswise slices. Insert slice at an angle in each rosette.

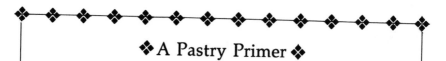

❖ A Pastry Primer ❖

Nothing in the kitchen frightens people so much as making perfect pastry; yet with just a little hands-on practice, pastry-making can be one of the simplest and most satisfying aspects of cooking. For detailed discussions of different types of pastry, both sweet and savory, have a look at *Lenôtre's Book of Desserts and Pastries* (Barron's) and Bernard Clayton, Jr.'s *The Complete Book of Pastry* (Simon and Schuster); and keep the following guidelines in mind (see Basic Pastry for Quiches and Tarts, page 94, and Sour Cream Flaky Pastry, page 206).

To Make Pastry Dough:

- Combine the fat and flour with a light touch, working quickly with fingers, two knives, a pastry blender, or a food processor. Lift the ingredients with your fingers as you work. As soon as you achieve a crumbly, mealy texture, stop; a few unblended pieces of fat will add flakiness.
- A food processor makes quick work of combining fat with flour. When the mixture is crumbly, I prefer to transfer it to a mixing bowl, then stir in the liquid with a fork. The processor can homogenize the ingredients to the point where the butter is too finely crumbled to form a tender, flaky pastry.
- For a light, crisp pastry, add just enough liquid to hold the dough together.
- Wrap the dough in flattened pieces large enough for one tart or pie. Let dough rest in the refrigerator for at least one hour before rolling to relax the gluten and firm up the dough.
- Make more dough than you need, and freeze the rest for those unexpected moments when a dessert is needed.

To Line a Tart Pan:

- Roll out the dough, lightly flouring the board and the rolling pin. Roll evenly, always from the center out, avoiding back and forth strokes. Pick up the dough occasionally to prevent sticking.

When the rolled-out dough is about ⅛ inch thick and slightly larger than the pan to be lined, fold it in half over your hand, or in quarters for large pans, and transfer it gently and quickly to the pan. Unfold the dough and gently press it into place against the bottom and sides. Do not stretch the dough; leave a bit of slack.

- Cut off excess dough. Build up an even edge all around, forming a decorative border if you like. Chill before baking, if you have time.

To Partially Bake a Shell:

- When a moist filling, such as a custard, might make the crust soggy, partial prebaking helps ensure crispness.
- Line the raw dough in the pan with a sheet of aluminum foil. Fill the shell with raw rice or beans (keep these in a jar to be reused for this purpose); this will keep the dough in place as it bakes. Place the tart shell on a heavy sheet pan and bake in preheated 400° oven until the sides have set, about 10 minutes.
- Carefully remove the foil and beans; prick the shell gently with a fork without going all the way through the dough, and replace the pan, on its sheet, in the oven. Bake until very light gold, about 10 to 12 minutes, pricking any air bubbles as they rise during the baking. Remove from the oven, fill, and continue to bake as directed.

To Fully Bake a Pastry Shell "Blind":

- This refers to a crust fully baked without a filling, to be used with a filling cooked separately or with uncooked fillings such as fresh berries.
- Proceed as you would in partially baking a shell, but in the last stage, fully bake the crust until crisp and golden, about 15 to 20 minutes from the time the foil and weights are removed.

TARTE AU CITRON (FRESH LEMON TART)

This tart, intense with the flavor of fresh lemons, is one of my favorite dinner desserts. I tasted lemon tarts all over Paris until I found this one at a superb Left Bank pâtisserie called *Nézard.* After weeks of asking, the owner finally gave me this recipe—with the stipulation that I never bake it in Paris.

Serves 8 (makes one 8- or 9-inch tart)

1 recipe Sweet Tart Pastry (page 239)	10 Tablespoons chilled unsalted butter, cut up
Grated zest of 3 lemons; juice of 2 lemons	3 Tablespoons orange marmalade or apricot preserves
6 eggs	1 paper-thin slice lemon
1 cup (scant) sugar	

1. Roll out well-chilled dough on lightly floured surface into large circle; crust for this tart should be very thin. Line 9- or 10-inch quiche pan with removable bottom with pastry; trim off excess dough. Form a decorative edge if you wish. Chill.

2. Preheat oven to 400°.

3. Line dough with aluminum foil; fill with dried beans or rice. Place on heavy sheet pan. Bake until edges are set, 8 to 10 minutes. Remove foil and beans. Prick dough very lightly with fork. Bake until pastry is very pale gold, about 8 minutes longer. Cool slightly. Leave oven at 400°.

4. Select double boiler or medium bowl that fits snugly into top of a saucepan. Pour water in saucepan to depth of about 1 inch. Bottom of bowl should not touch water when set in pan. Heat water to simmering.

6. Set lemon zest aside. In bowl, whisk together lemon juice, eggs, and sugar until blended. Add butter. Place bowl over simmering water in saucepan. Whisk mixture until thick and smooth, about 8 minutes. Do not boil mixture; be sure to scrape bottom of bowl as you whisk. Remove bowl from pan. Strain mixture; whisk in reserved zest. If filling is not used immediately, lay sheet of waxed paper directly on surface of custard.

7. Pour custard into tart shell. Bake until set and lightly golden, about 30 minutes. Cool briefly on wire rack.

8. Strain a thin layer of preserves directly over surface of tart (if you are using a stiff marmalade, it may need to be heated before straining). Gently brush over surface, glazing evenly. Lay a thin slice of lemon in center of tart; glaze lemon. Remove tart from pan rim and serve at room temperature.

Variation

Fresh Orange Tart: For lemon zest and juice, substitute zest of 1 orange and 1 lemon, and ¼ cup freshly squeezed orange juice and juice of ½ lemon.

SWEET TART PASTRY

Cooking Tip: To make this pastry in a food processor, combine dry ingredients and butter in processor, pulsing briefly until crumbly. Do not overmix. Transfer mixture to a mixing bowl and proceed to add liquid by hand.
Makes one 8- to 10-inch shell

1 ½ cups flour
2 Tablespoons sugar
Pinch salt
1 stick (4 ounces) chilled unsalted
butter, cut up

3 Tablespoons water or orange
juice, or as needed

1. If making dough by hand, sift together flour, sugar, and salt into large bowl. Cut in butter with two knives or fingers until mixture has texture of crumbly meal.
2. Sprinkle 3 Tablespoons of the liquid over flour mixture, tossing with a fork all the while until the pastry just comes together. Add more liquid if necessary; do not make dough too wet. Gather pastry together in ball. Wrap; chill at least 1 hour before rolling out.

DEEP-DISH PUMPKIN PIE WITH BOURBON

Make the pumpkin purée for this pie filling in quantity and store in freezer for future pies.

Cooking Tip: For soufflé-like texture, separate eggs. Beat the whites until stiff but not dry; fold gently into the filling in step 4.

Serves 8 (makes one 9½ × 1½-inch pie)

½ recipe Basic Pastry for Quiches and Tarts (page 94)

2 cups pumpkin purée (page 36)

⅔ cup brown sugar, lightly packed

⅓ cup granulated sugar

1 Tablespoon flour

½ teaspoon salt

1 ½ teaspoons ground cinnamon

½ teaspoon freshly grated nutmeg, or more to taste

¼ teaspoon ground ginger

¼ teaspoon ground allspice (optional)

¼ teaspoon ground coriander (optional)

Tiny pinch freshly ground black pepper (optional)

1 ⅓ cups heavy cream

2 eggs, lighten beaten

3 Tablespoons bourbon, whisky, rum, or brandy

1 teaspoon pure vanilla extract

Whipped cream flavored with bourbon or vanilla

1. Roll out dough on lightly floured surface into circle about 3 inches larger than 9½ × 1½-inch pie dish. Line dish with dough; trim off excess. Form a fluted edge, if you wish.

2. Preheat oven to 400°.

3. Line dough with aluminum foil; fill with dried beans or rice. Place on heavy sheet pan. Bake until edges are set, 8 to 10 minutes. Remove foil and beans. Prick dough very lightly with fork. Bake until pastry is very pale gold, about 8 minutes longer. Cool slightly. Leave oven at 400°.

4. Meanwhile, in large bowl whisk together pumpkin purée, brown and granulated sugars, flour, salt, and spices until blended. Add cream, eggs, bourbon or other spirits, and vanilla; whisk until smooth. Pour filling into pie shell.

5. Place pie dish on heavy baking sheet. Bake in middle or lower third of oven until filling is set in the center, 45 to 50 minutes. Cool pie on wire rack to room temperature.

6. Serve with whipped cream flavored with bourbon or vanilla to taste.

ALMOND BRITTLE COOKIES

I used to bake quantities of these in the early mornings, high above Wall Street, for an executive dining room. Because these addictive cookies are easy to do in quantity—a large sheet is cut into one-inch squares—they are ideal for a large party, or to give as gifts.
Makes 60 one-inch cookies.

Unsalted butter for baking pan
1 recipe Cookie Crust (page 242)
½ cup jam, such as raspberry, black currant, or apricot
1 ½ Tablespoons brandy or liqueur (optional)
9 Tablespoons (1 stick plus 1 Tablespoon) unsalted butter
9 Tablespoons (½ cup plus 1 Tablespoon) sugar
¼ teaspoon salt
2 heaping Tablespoons honey
¼ cup heavy cream
1 teaspoon pure vanilla extract
Few drops fresh lemon juice
2 cups sliced blanched almonds (6 ounces)

1. Lightly butter 15½ × 10½ × 1-inch baking pan. Roll out dough slightly larger than pan. Carefully transfer dough to pan, allowing rough edges to hang over sides of pan. Chill for 20 minutes or more.
2. Preheat oven to 400°.
3. Trim edges of dough flush with outside edges of pan. Prick dough all over with fork. Bake until just lightly golden, 16 to 18 minutes, pricking any bubbles with a fork as they rise. Do not overbake as pastry will be baked a second time. Cool pastry slightly.
4. In a small cup or bowl, stir together jam and optional liqueur. Brush or spoon a thin layer of jam over pastry.
5. For the remainder of the topping, melt the 9 Tablespoons butter in heavy saucepan. Add sugar, salt, and honey; cook over low heat, stirring, until sugar dissolves. Increase heat to medium. Add cream; boil, stirring, until mixture is smooth and thickened. Remove from heat; add vanilla, lemon juice, and almonds. Stir. Gently spread a smooth layer over pastry. Bake until bubbly and golden brown, 17 to 20 minutes.
6. Cool thoroughly on wire rack. Cut into 1-inch squares; trim rough edges and save for snacking.

COOKIE CRUST

This recipe belongs to a wonderful Italian baker named Carlo Bussetti.
Makes one 10½ × 15½-inch sheet, or two 10-inch tart shells

2 sticks (8 ounces) unsalted butter
1 cup sugar
Pinch salt
Grated zest of 2 oranges
¼ cup lightly beaten egg (1
  extra-large egg, or 1 large egg
  plus 1 yolk)

2 Tablespoons milk
2 teaspoons pure vanilla extract
2 cups cake flour (6 ounces)
1 ½ cups all-purpose flour (6
  ounces)

Cream butter with electric mixer. Add sugar, salt, and grated orange
zest; beat until fluffy. Beat in egg, milk, and vanilla. Lower mixer speed;
add flours. Stop mixing as soon as flour is mixed in. Do not overmix or
dough will be tough. Dough should be soft, but not sticky. Gather
dough together. Dust with flour; wrap, and chill well. Let dough soften
briefly before rolling out.

LACY HAZELNUT WAFERS

A crisp, not-too-sweet "adult" nut cookie, perfect with a sorbet or a
mousse as a dinner dessert.
Makes 32 to 36 cookies

4 ounces whole hazelnuts (generous
  ¾ cup)
2 ounces whole almonds (generous
  ½ cup)
3 Tablespoons granulated sugar
1 stick (4 ounces) unsalted butter,
  softened, plus additional for
  aluminum foil
½ cup (packed) brown sugar
1 egg
1 teaspoon pure vanilla extract
½ cup currants or raisins
Grated zest of 1 orange
¼ cup flour, sifted before
  measuring
Pinch salt
Pinch baking soda
½ teaspoon ground cinnamon
½ teaspoon ground nutmeg
½ teaspoon ground allspice

1. Preheat oven to 350°.

2. Place nuts in small cake pan. Toast, shaking occasionally, until light gold, about 8 minutes. Remove; cool slightly.

3. Working in batches, chop nuts with 1 Tablespoon of the sugar in food processor with pulsing motion or with a knife, until half the nuts are in small pieces and the remainder are powdery. Set aside.

4. Cream 1 stick butter until light and fluffy. Gradually beat in remaining granulated sugar, and the brown sugar; continue to beat another minute or so. Beat in the egg and vanilla. Add the currants and orange zest.

5. Resift the flour with the salt, baking soda, and spices. Add to creamed butter mixture along with nuts; mix just until blended.

6. Line two baking sheets with aluminum foil. Butter generously. Use 2 teaspoons to arrange balls of batter on aluminum foil at least 2 inches apart.

7. Bake each sheet until batter is spread and golden at the edges, 11 to 13 minutes. Use a spatula to carefully transfer the cookies to a wire rack to cool. If cookies lose crispness, re-crisp in oven for about 2 minutes.

OLD-FASHIONED HAZELNUT DROPS

Based on an old American recipe using pecans, these cookies melt in your mouth.
Makes about 3 dozen

1 cup whole hazelnuts, with skins
1 cup sifted cake flour
6 Tablespoons sugar
1 stick (4 ounces) unsalted butter,
  softened

1 teaspoon pure vanilla extract
Confectioner's sugar

1. Preheat oven to 300°.
2. Place nuts in small cake pan. Toast in oven until light golden, shaking occasionally, about 12 minutes. Cool slightly.
3. Sift together flour and 2 Tablespoons of the sugar. Place in food processor with nuts. Process with on/off motion until finely ground.
4. Cream butter with remaining 4 Tablespoons sugar until fluffy. Add vanilla. Blend nut mixture into creamed butter just until homogeneous. Chill mixture if it is too soft to handle.
5. Roll mixture into ¾-inch balls. Arrange in rows on buttered baking sheet. Chill.
6. Bake cookies until set and very faintly golden, but not dry and crumbly, about 45 minutes. Remove from oven.
7. Place cookies on wire rack over large sheet of waxed paper. Sift confectioner's sugar into a bowl. Very gently roll cookies in sugar to coat while still warm. Arrange cookies on rack and cool completely. When cool, sift another layer of sugar over cookies. Serve soon, or store in airtight tin, protecting layers with waxed paper.

CUSTARDS, PUDDINGS, AND MOUSSES

"Love and hunger, I reflected, meet at a woman's breast."

—SIGMUND FREUD, *The Interpretation of Dreams*

The soft creaminess of rich custards, called nursery foods by Craig Claiborne, is a source of primal comfort for many of us. In their light versions, custards and mousses can be a superb conclusion to a special meal.

Principally composed of eggs and liquid, custards assume a wide variety of forms: stirred custards, baked custards and puddings, Bavarian creams, ice creams, frozen soufflés, and so forth. Eggs provide thickening, with yolks producing a richer, softer texture than whole eggs. Cornstarch, while often called for in mousses and sauces, is unnecessary.

When baking custards, cook just until set near the center; if overcooked, eggs form watery curds. For this reason, custards are often baked in a *bain-marie* (water bath) or with a crust. For mixtures cooked on top of the stove, such as a *crème anglaise* (custard sauce), I prefer not to use a double boiler. Stir constantly, watching carefully so as not to let the mixture curdle (this happens when egg yolks are heated higher than 180°, well below the boiling point).

Gelatin should be used minimally, and usually only for items to be unmolded.

CARAMEL POTS DE CRÈME

A small but intensely flavored dessert with a smooth, silky texture. Easily prepared and chilled in advance, this is an ideal dinner-party dessert. You may wish to buy some small dessert pots to use especially for these rich custards.
Serves 6

CARAMEL:

¾ cup sugar
3 Tablespoons cold water
3 Tablespoons hot water

1 ¾ cups milk
¾ cup heavy cream
1 Tablespoon sugar
8 egg yolks

1 egg
1 teaspoon pure vanilla extract

GARNISH (OPTIONAL):
Lightly whipped cream
Crushed praline or chopped nuts

1. Preheat oven to 325°. Heat a kettle of water to boiling.
2. *Caramel:* In small heavy saucepan combine sugar with cold water. Heat over medium heat, stirring. Occasionally brush down any crystals that cling to sides of pan with a brush dipped in warm water. When sugar is dissolved, increase heat. Boil until medium amber color, 5 to 10 minutes. Remove from heat. Hold pan away from you. Carefully add hot water, avoiding spatters. Stir until smooth; keep warm.
3. While making caramel, heat milk, cream, and 1 Tablespoon sugar in saucepan over medium heat until small bubbles appear around edges. Slowly stir caramel into scalded milk and cream.
4. Whisk together egg yolks and egg in bowl until well blended, about 1 minute. Very gradually whisk caramel mixture into yolk mixture. Add vanilla. Strain into large measuring cup. Carefully spoon off all froth from surface.
5. Place six pots de crème or small ramekins, each about 4 ounces, in large casserole or roasting pan. Divide custard mixture equally among them. Pour simmering water into pan to come nearly halfway up sides of pots. Cover pan with lid, aluminum foil, or baking sheet to prevent formation of crust on custards.

6. Place pan in preheated oven. Bake until just set but still trembling in center, 23 to 26 minutes. Test after 18 minutes, as timing can vary. Do not overcook.

7. Remove pan from oven. Let stand 5 minutes. Remove pots from pan. Cool on wire rack. Chill thoroughly. Garnish with whipped cream and praline or chopped nuts, if you like.

Variations

Vanilla Pots de Crème: Omit caramel. Increase 1 Tablespoon sugar to ½ cup. Increase vanilla to 1½ teaspoons.

Chocolate Pots de Crème: Omit caramel. Melt 3½ ounces semisweet chocolate and add to milk. Increase 1 Tablespoon sugar to ⅓ cup.

Coffee Pots de Crème: Omit caramel. Increase 1 Tablespoon sugar to ⅓ cup. Stir together 2 Tablespoons instant coffee, preferably espresso, with 3 Tablespoons of the scalded milk until smooth. Add to remaining milk mixture.

Mocha Pots de Crème: Omit caramel. Increase 1 Tablespoon sugar to ⅓ cup. Stir together 3 ounces semisweet chocolate, melted, and 2 teaspoons instant coffee, preferably espresso, with 2 Tablespoons of the scalded milk until smooth. Add to remaining milk mixture.

Note: For a deeper flavor, you can combine the caramel with the coffee or mocha flavorings. In that case, keep the sugar at 1 Tablespoon.

COACH HOUSE BREAD AND BUTTER PUDDING

Lingering childhood memories of stodgy bread puddings may have made people forget how good a bread pudding can be. One of the best is a version served by Leon Lianides at the Coach House Restaurant in New York's Greenwich Village. Use leftover bread, and serve as is, or, as Leon does, with a purée of raspberries (page 222).
Serves 10

12 thin slices French bread, day-old	⅛ teaspoon salt
	4 cups milk
3 to 4 Tablespoons unsalted butter	1 cup heavy cream
5 eggs	1 teaspoon pure vanilla extract
4 egg yolks	Confectioner's sugar
1 cup sugar	

1. Preheat oven to 375°.
2. Trim crusts from bread. Butter one side of each slice.
3. In large bowl, beat together eggs, yolks, sugar, and salt until sugar is well blended.
4. Heat milk and cream in heavy saucepan over medium heat until small bubbles appear around edges. Gradually stir scalded milk and cream into yolk mixture. Stir in vanilla.
5. Arrange slices of bread, buttered side up, in 2-quart baking dish. Strain custard mixture over bread. Set baking dish in roasting pan filled with hot water to depth of 1 inch.
6. Bake pudding in preheated oven until knife inserted in center is withdrawn clean, about 45 minutes.
7. Preheat broiler.
8. Generously sieve confectioner's sugar over pudding. Briefly place under broiler until glazed. Serve at cool room temperature or chilled, as is, or with a raspberry purée.

Variation

Pound Cake Pudding: Replace the bread with leftover Currant Pound Cake (page 228) for an even richer pudding.

MOLDED RICE PUDDING
WITH CARAMEL SAUCE

This creamy molded version with a Bavarian cream base is particularly attractive for a special party or buffet when prepared in a kugelhopf mold. Try substituting a berry purée (page 222) for the caramel sauce. Serves 8 to 10

¾ cup currants

3 Tablespoons Cognac or brandy

1 envelope gelatin

⅓ cup cold water

¾ cup long-grain white rice

1 ⅔ cups milk

⅓ cup sugar

Pinch of salt

CRÈME ANGLAISE:

2 cups milk

6 egg yolks

½ cup sugar

2 ½ teaspoons pure vanilla extract

¾ cup heavy cream, cold

Flavorless vegetable oil for mold

CARAMEL SAUCE:

1 cup sugar

¼ cup cold water

½ cup hot water

1. Soak currants in Cognac; reserve. Sprinkle gelatin over cold water; reserve.

2. In large saucepan of boiling water blanch rice for 5 minutes; drain. Rinse.

3. Heat the 1⅔ cups milk and the ⅓ cup sugar in heavy saucepan to simmering. Stir in rice and pinch of salt. Simmer, covered, until rice is quite tender, 35 to 40 minutes. Let rice cool.

4. *Crème Anglaise:* Heat the 2 cups milk in heavy saucepan over medium heat until bubbles appear around edges. Whisk together yolks and the ½ cup sugar in bowl until blended. Gradually whisk hot milk into yolk mixture. Return custard to pan. Stir constantly with wooden spoon over medium heat until thickened, about 7 minutes. Do not boil. Remove from heat and add vanilla and softened gelatin; stir thoroughly. Strain into a bowl. Cool in refrigerator or ice bath, stirring often, without allowing mixture to set. Stir in rice and currants and their soaking liquid; continue to stir, in ice bath or refrigerator, until syrupy.

5. Whip heavy cream in chilled bowl with chilled beaters or whisk to soft peaks. Fold cream into custard until partially blended. Place bowl in refrigerator 5 minutes. Fold cream and custard together quickly, distributing rice and currants. Pour into well-oiled 6- or 7-cup mold, such as a kugelhopf mold. Chill well.

6. *Caramel Sauce:* Stir together the 1 cup sugar and cold water in small heavy saucepan. Heat to boiling, stirring, brushing down any crystals from sides of pan with brush dipped in warm water. Be sure the sugar has dissolved before mixture comes to boil. Boil, without stirring, until mixture turns deep amber, 8 to 10 minutes. Remove from heat. Carefully add hot water, avoiding spatters, stirring. Cool to room temperature.

7. To unmold, run tip of knife blade around edge of pudding; dip mold in hot water for about 3 seconds. Place a round serving plate over mold; invert plate and mold. Carefully lift off mold. Chill again briefly.

8. Drizzle caramel sauce down sides of pudding and around edges. Pass extra sauce.

HOMEMADE DOUBLE CHOCOLATE PUDDING

Nearly everyone has a favorite chocolate mousse recipe, but when was the last time you had a real homemade chocolate pudding?
Serves 4

2 ¼ cups milk	2 egg yolks
½ cup sugar	5 ounces semisweet chocolate,
Pinch salt	preferably imported, cut up
2 Tablespoons cornstarch, sifted	2 Tablespoons unsalted butter
3 Tablespoons Dutch cocoa	1 teaspoon pure vanilla extract
1 egg	Lightly whipped cream

1. Heat 2 cups of the milk, ¼ cup of the sugar, and salt in heavy saucepan over medium heat to boiling.
2. Mix together cornstarch, cocoa, and the remaining ¼ cup of the sugar in a bowl.
3. Whisk the remaining ¼ of the milk into the dry ingredients until smooth and thoroughly blended. Slowly whisk in the hot milk mixture; return to saucepan. Slowly bring to the boil over medium heat, stirring constantly. Gently boil 2 minutes, stirring constantly; the mixture should become fairly thick.
4. Whisk egg and yolks together in small bowl. Slowly whisk in 1 cup of cocoa mixture. Whisk back into cocoa-cornstarch mixture. Cook, whisking constantly, over medium heat, about 2 minutes, until mixture becomes slightly thicker. Do not allow the mixture to boil or overcook. Transfer to clean bowl and lay a sheet of waxed paper directly on surface. Cool slightly on wire rack.
5. Melt semisweet chocolate in top of double boiler over simmering water. Blend in the butter. Cool slightly; chocolate should remain pourable.
6. Whisk chocolate into thickened egg mixture. Stir in vanilla. Cool pudding in bowl on wire rack. Refrigerate.
7. Serve chilled with lightly whipped cream.

LEMON MOUSSE

This quick mousse, airy and tart, is a perfect dinner dessert for any time of year. It uses only fresh lemon juice for liquid, producing a cleaner taste than a milk-based mousse.

Cooking Tip: The small tool called a zester removes citrus zest, the outermost rind without the bitter white pith, quickly and efficiently. Chop the long strands of zest with a knife. Alternatively, use a vegetable peeler to remove the zest; chop with a knife.

Serves 4

1 ¼ teaspoons gelatin	2 egg whites
⅓ cup fresh lemon juice (2 or 3 lemons)	1 to 2 teaspoons Cointreau (optional)
3 egg yolks	1 cup heavy cream, cold
⅓ cup sugar, preferably superfine	A few strands lemon zest for garnish (optional)
1 Tablespoon grated or chopped lemon zest (from about 3 lemons)	

1. In small saucepan, sprinkle gelatin over lemon juice. Let stand until softened.

2. Meanwhile, combine egg yolks, sugar, and lemon zest in medium bowl; whisk briefly until combined and smooth. Heat gelatin mixture, stirring, over low heat, until the gelatin is dissolved. Whisk gelatin mixture into yolk mixture. Chill until syrupy and slightly thickened, whisking every few minutes. Do not allow to set or become too firm.

3. Whisk egg whites until stiff but not dry. Stir large spoonful into lemon mixture, along with Cointreau if using. Fold in remaining whites until partially combined.

4. Whip cream in chilled bowl with chilled beaters or whisk until not quite stiff. Fold into mousse. Transfer to glass serving bowl or individual wine goblets. Chill for at least 1 hour before serving. Garnish with lemon zest, if you wish.

RASPBERRY CHARLOTTE

This summer treat is based on a family recipe of the Charvet brothers of Aix-en-Provence, who own and operate a restaurant there and an *auberge* in the nearby countryside. Its tart flavor is well complemented by a sweet wine such as a Sauternes or a late-harvest California Gewürztraminer.

Cooking Tip: For a more delicate mousse filling, reduce the amount of gelatin to 2 teaspoons. The full envelope is recommended if the charlotte will sit on a buffet table.

Serves 8 to 12

1 ½ pounds fresh raspberries (2 to 2 ½ pints), or 5 packages (10 ounces each) frozen raspberries, thawed, drained, and juice reserved

3 to 4 Tablespoons framboise, kirsch, or Cognac

⅔ cup sugar, plus additional as needed

1 envelope gelatin

¼ cup cold drained raspberry juice or cold water

1 ½ cups milk

½ vanilla bean, split lengthwise, or 1 teaspoon pure vanilla extract

6 egg yolks

Pinch salt

About 2 dozen homemade or store-bought ladyfingers, split

1 cup heavy cream, cold

OPTIONAL GARNISH:

Whipped cream

Several whole raspberries

1. Select about ⅔ cup nice whole berries; reserve, refrigerated. Purée remaining berries; strain to remove seeds. If using frozen berries, thin purée with reserved strained liquid, ⅓ to ½ cup, to a medium consistency. There should be a total of about 2 cups purée. Add framboise or other spirits to taste. Set aside 1 cup at room temperature. Remainder will be used as a sauce. Sweeten, if necessary, with a little sugar; chill.
2. Sprinkle gelatin over ¼ cup raspberry juice or water; set aside to soften. Heat milk with vanilla bean, if using, in heavy saucepan over medium heat until bubbles appear around edges. In mixing bowl, whisk egg yolks, ⅔ cup sugar, and salt until blended. Gradually whisk hot milk into yolk mixture. Return custard mixture to pan. Stir constantly

with wooden spoon over medium heat until lightly thickened, about 7 minutes. Do not boil. Remove from heat; stir softened gelatin into custard until dissolved. Strain mixture into a bowl. Add 1 cup room temperature purée and vanilla extract, if using. Chill custard in refrigerator or ice water bath, stirring often, until thickened but not set.

3. Meanwhile, line bottom of 6-cup charlotte mold or tall soufflé dish with round of waxed paper. Cut ladyfingers to fit bottom, arranging them tightly, curved side down, in a flower or star pattern. Line sides of mold with ladyfingers, curved side out. Cut top edges even with rim of mold. Set aside.

4. Whip cream until it forms soft peaks. Stir large spoonful into custard. Gently fold in remainder with reserved ⅔ cup berries and more framboise to taste. Pour mixture into prepared mold. Chill thoroughly until set.

5. Run thin knife between ladyfingers and mold. Unmold onto round serving platter. Peel off waxed paper. Drizzle remaining chilled purée down sides and around base of charlotte. Garnish, if you like, with whipped-cream rosettes and whole berries. The Charvet brothers arrange a halo of fresh mint leaves around the top surface.

A WORD ABOUT COFFEE

I hated the taste of coffee until I was well into my twenties; only as I began to eat in good restaurants did I realize what I'd been missing. Gradually coffee has become one of the major pleasures of my life.

I'm always amazed, though, at how few Americans insist on drinking really good coffee. There's nothing difficult about it: insist on beans that are freshly roasted and ground, use a simple drip pot, and drink it just after brewing.

Once you get used to fine coffee, you may find yourself agreeing with Prince Talleyrand, who wrote about coffee that it "detracts nothing from your intellect; on the contrary, your stomach is freed by it and no longer distresses your brain; it will not hamper your mind with troubles but give freedom to its working. . . . The organ of thought receives from it a feeling of sympathy; work becomes easier and you will sit down without distress to your principal repast which will restore your body and afford you a calm delicious night [quoted by Claudia Roden in *Coffee*, Penguin, 1981]."

❖ A Few Basic Techniques Explained ❖

Different cooking techniques produce different results; be sure you understand precise distinctions among terms used in the recipes:

Boil: to heat liquid to a point where bubbles break the surface and steam rises. Ranges from a gentle but steady eruption to a violent rolling boil.

Simmer: to cook just below the boiling point on a very low heat. Tiny, steady bubbles just barely break the surface.

Smile: French chef's term for a bare simmer. The surface murmurs and a tiny bubble appears only occasionally.

Blanch: to cook an ingredient quickly in a large quantity of boiling liquid; often a precooking step for firm ingredients.

Sauté: to quickly cook ingredients in a very small amount of fat in a heavy pan or skillet, usually over high heat (see Chapter 5 for more details). Sautéing seals in juices.

Deglaze: to dissolve the flavorful crusty bits left in a sauté pan by adding a liquid; frequently done over heat. These residues add flavor to many dishes, and should never be discarded unless burned.

Sweat: to cook ingredients in a small amount of fat over low heat in a covered pan. Sweating releases natural juices.

Stir-fry: to cook cut-up ingredients by tossing continually in a minimum of fat over high heat over a large surface area, such as a wok or large skillet.

Steam: to cook foods in a covered pan in a steam-filled environment large enough for the steam to surround the food. The food is frequently suspended on a rack over a boiling liquid.

❖ A Few Basic Cuts: Even and Precise ❖

Learn the distinction between the different cuts specified in the recipes. Cutting ingredients evenly is important so that they cook at the same rate. Equally important are aesthetic choices: identical ingredients cut in hair-fine julienne versus large fat chunks will be perceived differently by eyes and mouth. As you begin preparing a dish, try to have a conception, however hazy, of your final result.

Mince: to chop very finely, in pieces no larger than $\frac{1}{16}$ inch. Minced garlic is often called for. Each clove is first bruised with the flat of a knife blade to release its peel, then minced. You can also crush garlic to a pulp with a mortar and pestle or with the flat of a knife. Or many people prefer to use a garlic press; however, this can add a metallic taste, and it's another tool to clean.

Fine chop: to cut in even $\frac{1}{8}$- to $\frac{1}{4}$-inch pieces, usually square-shaped.

Medium chop: to cut in even pieces about $\frac{1}{2}$ inch square.

Coarse chop: to cut in even pieces about $\frac{3}{4}$ to 1 inch square.

Slice: to cut parallel pieces ranging in thickness from $\frac{1}{16}$ to $\frac{1}{2}$ inch.

Dice: to cut in cube shapes, ranging from very small, $\frac{1}{8}$ inch, to large, $\frac{1}{2}$ to 1 inch.

Shred: to cut in long, thin even strands, often done with greens. *Chiffonade* is a fine shred.

Julienne: to cut in long even stick-shapes, usually $1 \times \frac{1}{8} \times \frac{1}{8}$ inch. These range from tiny "matchsticks," $1 \times \frac{1}{16} \times \frac{1}{16}$, to large "batons," $2 \times \frac{1}{4} \times \frac{1}{4}$ inch.

INDEX

ABOUT THE AUTHORS

RICHARD SAX recently spent one and a half years in London as consultant to the new Time-Life series, *The Good Cook.* He was responsible for the step-by-step photography for several volumes in the series. Previously, he was chef-director of the test kitchen at *Food & Wine* magazine, working with many leading chefs in that capacity.

Mr. Sax trained as a chef at schools in New York, and at the Cordon Bleu in Paris, where he also served an apprenticeship at the Hotel Plaza-Athénée. Among his experiences as a working chef, Mr. Sax most enjoyed running a restaurant on Martha's Vineyard with David Ricketts. He has served as consultant to restaurants and several publishing companies, notably Larousse, and has contributed material to *Cuisine, Gourmet, Food & Wine, Bon Appétit, House Beautiful, The Pleasures of Cooking,* and *Family Circle.* His cooking courses have been praised by *The New York Times.*

DAVID RICKETTS is currently assistant editor of *Cuisine* magazine, and a freelance food writer and consultant. Prior to this, he was on the editorial and kitchen staffs at *Food & Wine* magazine. He has managed a restaurant on Martha's Vineyard, and subsequently cooked in restaurants and for caterers in East Hampton and New York City. Mr. Ricketts has been a faculty member in the Culinary Arts Division of the New School in New York, and has conducted cooking classes privately. He has an M.A. and a law degree, and has taught English literature at the college level.